Women in American History

BOOKS IN THE SERIES

Women Doctors in Gilded-Age Washington: Race,
Gender, and Professionalization
Gloria Moldow

Friends and Sisters: Letters between Lucy Stone and
Antoinette Brown Blackwell, 1846-93
edited by Carol Lasser and Marlene Deahl Merrill

Friends and Sisters

Friends and Sisters:

Letters between Lucy Stone and

Antoinette Brown Blackwell, 1846-93

Edited by Carol Lasser and Marlene Deahl Merrill

University of Illinois Press · *Urbana and Chicago*

This book is printed on acid-free paper.

Library of Congress Cataloging-in-Publication Data

Stone, Lucy, 1818-1893,
   Friends and sisters.

   (Women in American history)
   Bibliography: p.
   Includes index.
   1. Stone, Lucy, 1818-1893 — Correspondence.
2. Blackwell, Antoinette Louisa Brown, 1825-1921 —
Correspondence.   3. Feminists — United States —
Correspondence.   4. Women social reformers —
United States — Correspondence.   5. Women's rights —
United States.   I. Blackwell, Antoinette Louisa
Brown, 1825-1921.   II. Lasser, Carol.   III. Merrill,
Marlene.   IV. Title.   V. Series.
HQ1413.S73A4   1987   305.4′2′0922   86-24984
ISBN 0-252-01396-4 (alk. paper)

For Rowena Jelliffe
Oberlin College Class of 1913

Contents

Preface   xi

General Introduction   xv

Editorial Method   xxv

List of Abbreviations   xxix

Part 1:   "Agreeing to Disagree," 1846-50   3

Part 2:   "Actual Contact with the World," 1850-61   85

Part 3:   "Full to Overflowing," 1862-81   161

Part 4:   "Fruitage-Weighted," 1882-93   225

Note on Sources   265

Index   271

Preface

When we began this project, we imagined ourselves embarked upon a clearly delimited, straightforward course in which we would transcribe and annotate the letters that passed between two fascinating nineteenth-century women. Our goal was the production of a definitive textual edition of their correspondence. As we conceptualized it, our transcriptions would improve upon the readability of the handwritten originals, thus providing an important tool for scholars, and our annotations would map the concerns of the writers, making their words comprehensible to general readers. We believed that this project would also necessarily reveal the character and nature of the relationship between Lucy Stone and Antoinette Brown Blackwell, and thus illuminate the texture of one special friendship.

Our initial efforts culminated in the publication of *Soul Mates: The Oberlin Correspondence of Lucy Stone and Antoinette Brown, 1846-1850* (Oberlin, Ohio: Oberlin College, 1983), a commemorative book produced for the sesquicentennial of the alma mater of Stone and Brown Blackwell. Documenting the early years of the relationship, this work was a neat, clearly defined project; it launched us on the work for the present volume.

When we immersed ourselves in the larger project, we found both the transcriptions and the friendship they illuminated to be more complex matters than we had anticipated. In particular, our work revealed the paucity of published information on the lives of these two remarkable women. Our research into published and unpublished primary sources provided a wealth of detail that has enabled us to provide new pictures of the lives of Antoinette Brown Blackwell and Lucy Stone. The biographical narratives informed by this research supply continuity often absent from the extant letters presented in this collection.

We have grouped the letters into four chronological periods, each with an introduction framing the major milestones and issues relevant to the life of each woman during the particular span of years. We supply further details and contextual information, where necessary, in the notes to individual letters. We have, however, intended throughout this volume to maintain a focus primarily on the relationship between Lucy Stone and Antoinette Brown Blackwell.

Each of the editors came to this project with a different background and a different set of skills; we have come away with new knowledge and new concerns learned from each other. We discovered that interpretative differences could be debated with passion and goodwill, and result in enlarged understandings of often complex issues. Documenting the relationship of two nineteenth-century women has enriched the evolving friendship of their two twentieth-century editors.

Although we shared the work throughout, we developed complementary roles. Marlene Merrill had initial responsibility for transcribing and editing the letters; this often included using magnification and contextual clues to transform fragments of nearly illegible manuscript into meaningful documents. We jointly wrote the introduction to the first chronological section. Carol Lasser wrote all other introductory essays, although we shared our thoughts and our editing skills at all stages. We also shared the task of researching and compiling the annotations, the many stages of proofing the documents, and the various administrative aspects of the project.

The assistance of Margo Horn was crucial to our work. Margo originally suggested the project, and actively participated with us in its early stages. She took time from her own busy career to share with us her knowledge of the Blackwell family, her enthusiasm for the subject, and her skill as a historian. At key moments, she contributed to the research and writing of some footnotes; she collaborated in developing editing policy; and she assisted our efforts to understand the later years of the friendship. She has been throughout a valued consultant.

We thank the Blackwell family, especially George Blackwell, for their enthusiasm and support for this volume. In their generosity, the Blackwells have deposited their family papers at the Schlesinger Library, Radcliffe College, Cambridge, Massachusetts, where these manuscripts have been impeccably cared for and cataloged. Both the Blackwell family and the Schlesinger Library made our research not only possible, but also pleasant.

We gratefully acknowledge the support and assistance of others who have aided us, including Cindy Nord, who provided the funding that made our work possible; Oberlin College Director of Libraries William Moffett, who welcomed our work into a well-furnished office and encouraged us at crucial moments; and Jim Lubetkin, who first suggested Oberlin's involvement in this work. We especially thank Oberlin College Archivist Bill Bigglestone and also thank the Oberlin College Library staff, including Mary Cowles, Ray English, Katie Frohmberg, Allison Gould, Margot McClure, Margi Rogal, and Dina Schoonmaker. Eva Moseley and Kathy Kraft at the Schlesinger Library in Cambridge, Massachusetts, cheerfully responded to difficult requests. We also thank our colleagues Jeff Blodgett, Larry Buell, and Sandy Zagarell at Oberlin, and Pat Holland and Ann Gordon at the Stanton and Anthony Papers at the University of Massachusetts, Amherst. Leah Matthews assisted us throughout the project with proofing and research skills, as well as important insights into religious and theological questions. We were fortunate to have the assistance of the following people who worked for us doing research, typing, or photocopying: Charlotte Briggs, Kimberly Brookes, Liz Chose, Karen Merrill, April Paramore, and Bonnie Sheldon. Andrea Kerr used her expert knowledge of Blackwell handwriting to confirm our surmises at the Library of Congress; Christine Marshall similarly aided us in verifying documents at the Schlesinger Library. Other Oberlinians to whom we are grateful include: Ricarda Clark, Gertrude Jacob, Christine Monroe, Anne Pearson, former Oberlin College Acting President James Powell, who made possible our use of college support systems, and the staff of the Irwin Houck Computing Center at Oberlin College. We appreciate useful information received from: Kenneth Brock, archivist, Emma Willard School, Troy, New York; Marie Byrne, Manuscripts Division, University of California, Berkeley; John R. Condon, pastor, First Church, Gardner, Massachusetts; Kenneth C. Cramer, archivist, Dartmouth College Library, Hanover,

New Hampshire; Deborah De Roo, museum coordinator, Avon Charter Township Museum, Rochester, Michigan; Mary M. Huth, Department of Rare Books and Special Collections, University of Rochester Library, Rochester, New York; Janet Ing, Special Collections librarian, Mills College, Oakland, California; Kathleen Major, keeper of manuscripts, American Antiquarian Society, Worcester, Massachusetts; Lois H. Phillips, Barnesville, Ohio; Jane Sullivan, staff geneologist, Connecticut Historical Society, Hartford, Connecticut; Ruth Van Ostrand, Henrietta, New York; Melanie Yollef, manuscripts specialist, New York Public Library.

We appreciate the assistance of those who guided the manuscript through the production process at the University of Illinois Press, especially Carole S. Appel, senior editor; Susan L. Patterson, managing editor of the press's Chicago office, and Carol Saller, assistant editor. We also thank Jim O'Brien for his technical assistance.

We also thank our respective husbands, Gary Kornblith and Dan Merrill, for their patience, their faith in the project and in us, and their support throughout. The birth of Russell Lasser Kornblith did little to speed this project to a conclusion, but his voice has been a welcome one.

General Introduction

"Please think of *every thing* and remind me . . . I mean to tell all there is to tell and not a bit more," wrote Antoinette Brown Blackwell to Lucy Stone in the spring of 1892. As she appealed to her friend and sister to remember the details of the literary and debating society the two founded together during their college years, she looked back with Stone over nearly half a century of their special relationship. As young women studying together, the two established the remarkable relationship that each helped sustain over the years, and that in turn sustained each of them in her public and private lives. When, just one year before her death, Stone looked back to reconstruct the origins of this special sisterhood, she could review the correspondence the two had conducted over the years.

The letters between Lucy Stone and Antoinette Brown Blackwell chronicle the friendship of two highly talented and professionally accomplished nineteenth-century women. Stone, who lectured for woman's rights and black emancipation before the Civil War, subsequently became the leading figure in the American Woman Suffrage Association and the editor of its regular newspaper, the *Woman's Journal.* Brown Blackwell, the first woman ordained into the regular

Protestant ministry, conducted a lifelong feminist exploration of Protestant theology and its relation to social mores and science. The two met while students at the Oberlin Collegiate Institute in 1846 and, in 1856, became sisters-in-law when Antoinette Brown married Samuel C. Blackwell, brother of Henry B. Blackwell, whom Lucy Stone had wed the previous year. The correspondence presented here documents the enduring attachment between Stone and Brown Blackwell, illuminating its multiple facets, including its personal and familial concerns, and the public and political commitments the two pursued jointly and individually.

Well known to their nineteenth-century contemporaries for their boldness and their achievements, Stone and Brown Blackwell have received little attention from twentieth-century scholars in American history and women's studies. Although they left voluminous records of their own, both received at best passing attention in most of the historical accounts of the origins of the woman suffrage movement. Thus, when activist scholars in the first stages of the rebirth of women's history began investigating "foremothers," they generally overlooked Stone and Brown Blackwell. Only now are the two becoming the subjects of the serious study their lives and works deserve.[1] Although notice has been taken of their presence among the female members of the Blackwell clan, which included the pioneer women doctors Elizabeth and Emily Blackwell, the journalist Anna Blackwell, and the author Ellen Blackwell, the special friendship between Stone and Brown Blackwell has not received the sustained, careful analysis it deserves.[2]

This special attachment is the central focus of this volume. As the correspondence demonstrates, Lucy Stone and Antoinette Brown Blackwell looked to each other throughout their lives for support in careers and family life, personal and political decisions, public and private crises. In the process, they established a privileged intimacy that they recognized as a sororal relation. For Lucy Stone and Antoinette Brown Blackwell "sisterhood" encompassed several different aspects. First, their sex established between them the cultural "bonds of womanhood"; this shared gender identity with its dual implications of the burdens and obligations of domesticity on the one hand, and the power of female sympathy on the other, encouraged the development of a deep emotional tie between the two women. Second, drawing upon the political rhetoric of their shared commitments to abolitionism and woman's rights, the two joined the sisterhood of those who labored for equality between the races and the sexes. Finally, the two generated between themselves the relations of kinship, first on a fictive basis and after 1856 as relatives, through their marriages to the Blackwell brothers Samuel and Henry. In a sense, they established their sisterhood emotionally and politically before it became a legal familial relation.[3]

"My own dear Sister" begins the very first letter in this collection, revealing how the two used the language of consanguinity to express their feelings for each other long before they had any expectations they would ever become kinswomen. The close ties of both Lucy Stone and Antoinette Brown to their natal sisters served as models of loving relationships with other female members of the same generation. Particularly after the loss of two sisters in the late 1830s, Lucy Stone's remaining sister, Sarah, became her lifelong confidante and close friend. Sarah Stone demonstrated to Lucy by example how sisters could love and support each other even when they disagreed over politics and personal conduct; Sarah's declarations of affection for her sister transcended her disapproval of women—even her own sister—engaging as public lecturers. Lucy Stone always appreciated her sister's genuine warmth, and reciprocated with assistance and emotional support. Throughout her life, Stone frequently returned to the home her sister's family established in Gardner, Massachusetts, for the unconditional love and solace she found there.

Although Antoinette Brown lost three of her sisters when they were quite young, she still counted three living sisters when she began her years at Oberlin. The two youngest, Augusta and Ella Florella, later followed her to the institute, and served as touchstones during those difficult years. In the letters collected here, Brown reveals the emotional intensity of her ties to her sisters, her enjoyment of their family visits, her involvement in their mental and physical well-being, and her bereavement at Augusta's death. For Antoinette Brown, sisters formed an important support system and an intimate network, offering security and a sense of self. Like Lucy and Sarah Stone, the Brown sisters shared their thoughts, their hopes, their fears, their studies, their picnics, their travels, their rooms, and probably even their beds.

For young women like Lucy Stone and Antoinette Brown accustomed to communicating their most intimate feelings with their sisters, fervent friendships enabled them to extend familiar relationships outside the familial circle, or, in a sense, to incorporate their female friends into their families. Both Stone and Brown early sought to integrate each other into the kinship networks in which they had been raised. In their early letters references to the whereabouts of siblings, the health of parents, the plans of cousins abound. As young women, the two arranged to visit each other's homes and relatives, and at one point Stone even suggested that Brown's brother take a ministerial post close to her own brother's pulpit in order to bring their families closer together.

The sense of sisterhood Stone and Brown established while students at Oberlin matured even when their postgraduate careers drew them apart. The texture of their mutual affection changed as the two integrated professional vocations, marriage, and family into their lives, but the reciprocity of their commitment remained. Blood ties between their households added a new dimension that reconfirmed the basic parameters of their friendship. But the constancy of their devotion to each other, like their consistent pursuit of social and political change, did not preclude growth. Their relationship evolved with the maturation of each individual; and as the two women grew their public commitments took on new forms. As each developed an understanding of the complexity of the world, so too each elaborated and reinterpreted her aims. Both Stone and Brown Blackwell brought what they learned individually back to the nurturing, familial relationship between them, sharing their causes and campaigns, their daughters and dress patterns.

In their public lives, Stone and Brown Blackwell committed themselves to work for the social progress of women and the emancipation of black Americans from slavery and racial prejudice. Yet from the start of their friendship, their interpretations of the appropriate courses of action frequently differed. For Stone, the achievement of political rights for women and for blacks took primacy over concern with remedying social or cultural inequalities. Slowly, Stone adapted the organizational forms of the antislavery struggle to the woman's rights movement. Beginning her career as an itinerant lecturer for the American Anti-Slavery Society and its affiliates, she soon became an organizer promoting associational activity in the developing woman suffrage movement. Prompted by motherhood and age to retire from the lecture circuit, she maintained her ability to spread the equal suffrage message by establishing the *Woman's Journal.* In later years, she came to see suffrage as the essential right without which women would never achieve true equality, and she began to believe that the established political parties could be used as effective instruments to secure votes for women. The radical antislavery stance of her youth with its antiinstitutional premise thus slowly evolved into a pragmatic acceptance of the structures of politics and the need to manipulate them. Similarly, while she never abandoned her belief in the power of verbal persuasion, she became an adept journalist when she calculated it to be the best course for her to take. Her primary goals, the advance of women in general and women's political rights in particular, remained constant throughout her lifetime, even as her understanding of her work and her most effective methods evolved.

Brown Blackwell displayed similar continuity and growth as she matured. From the time in her youth when she declared her intention to enter the ministry, her desires to prove woman's intellectual capacity and to insure the social equality of women and men were framed in religious and theological terms. Her ordination in 1853 represented the culmination of the first stage of her development, marking for both herself and the world the competence of woman to pursue a pastoral role. Her subsequent resignation from this post indicated her recognition of the difficulty of reconciling traditional Protestant church doctrines and structures with her commitment to the equality of the sexes. But her later writings made clear that she never abandoned her belief in the power of Christianity, nor did she ever accept that religion and women's autonomy were antithetical. As her life circumstances changed, Brown Blackwell changed the manner in which she publicly addressed these interests. During the busiest years of marriage and motherhood, she used the pen instead of the pulpit to explore her subjects. As the works of Darwin and Spencer gained intellectual currency, she combined more scientific investigation with her longstanding interest in the theological explanations of gender difference. Working pragmatically to prove woman's abilities, she brought her theological concerns to secular women's organizations and her scientific concerns to religious audiences. By example and effort, she contributed to the acceptance of woman's intellectual abilities and demonstrated the necessity for new social outlets through which women could exercise such powers. When, at the end of her life, she became "pastor emeritus" of her local Unitarian society she revealed the consistency of her commitment to a clerical role, and her belief that her career, both inside and outside the organized church, had always included a ministerial dimension.

The correspondence between Antoinette Brown Blackwell and Lucy Stone reflects the ways in which the two shared the evolving concerns of their public lives, while looking to each other for support and celebration of their private lives. In their letters, the two discuss with great familiarity the details of their multiplicity of undertakings, repeatedly expressing hopes that they will be able to coordinate their busy schedules to allow for visits and further discussions. Their mutual appreciation for career achievements often led to reciprocal promotion, each attempting to provide for the other speaking engagements, publicity for writings or appearances, or solicitations for members for various organizations. Yet in their candid correspondence, they also revealed their tactical disagreements. Early in Brown's Oberlin years, Stone articulated her disapproval of her friend's choice of a ministerial career. When she made clear her criticisms stemmed from the love and respect she bore her "sister," she set the tone of affectionate cooperation that characterized even the most judgmental of their communications. As they matured and altered their personal strategies to accomodate new realities, each helped the other revise positions and reconsider actions without revengeful reminders of previous attitudes.

Over time their family lives as well as their political lives took on increasing complexity. Each established her own family and negotiated her ties to the extensive Blackwell clan. Sharing the pleasures and challenges of motherhood, the two expressed new feelings and explored together new situations. The kinship relation between the old friends enriched their daughters' lives as each offered to the children of her "sister" a second home. The letters suggest that the circulation of daughters between the households linked the two closely. While their husbands, the Blackwell brothers Samuel and Henry, shared business advice and ventures, the "sisters" collaborated on the rearing and launching of the next generation of Blackwell women. While their other sisters-in-law occasionally intervened, the sustaining relationship between Stone and Brown Blackwell retained its primacy; neither was as close to another female member of the clan as to her old and trusted friend.

Just as the friendship matured over the years, so too did the quality of the correspondence itself. More accurate and more readable documents slowly replaced the cramped writing and idiosyncratic spelling that characterized the early letters; platform and press provided each woman with the opportunity to polish her skills. Letters written in conjunction with school friends or abolitionist coworkers gave way to family documents addressed to whole households or notes appended to the letters of husbands, or mailings including the scrawls of children. Most notably, the long introspective letters of the early years disappeared as the lives of the women became more crowded with political activities and social commitments. In effect, the two learned an economy of communication, writing shorter notes and writing less often, but conveying as much vital news. The reflective, minutely detailed letters of the early years were replaced by the broad outlines of the issues each confronted in personal and public life.

The passions and intimacy of youth were replaced by loving, gentle solicitousness and care as the intense and energetic young friends aged into mature dignitaries.

Not all of the letters that passed between Lucy Stone and Antoinette Brown Blackwell have survived. Some of the correspondence may have seemed too confidential for either the sender or the recipient to feel comfortable preserving it; thus Lucy Stone, for example, in her August 1849 letter, begs Brown to "burn these letters, before anyone . . . sees them." Other letters may have seemed too mundane or banal for either to retain. Antoinette Brown Blackwell's notoriously inept housekeeping probably accounts for other lacunae in the collection, and some documents may have been lost or removed before the collections made their way to archival repositories. In addition, Lucy Stone's daughter and literary heir, Alice Stone Blackwell, blamed "repeated movings and one fire" for the loss of some of her mother's letters.[4]

The correspondence published here includes all known extant letters between Lucy Stone and Antoinette Brown Blackwell. For some periods of their lives, the correspondence encompasses several months of nearly weekly interchange between the friends; at other times, long gaps without obvious explanation separate letters. Correspondence authored by Antoinette Brown Blackwell dominates this collection, often without interruption for over a year. Yet despite such imbalances, Lucy Stone's presence is felt: indirectly, when her friend responds to now-absent letters, and directly, when Stone's own words have survived. Throughout, there is never any doubt that the correspondence is a dialogue, a two-way communication.

These letters document nearly half a century of friendship and sisterhood. In the volume that follows, we have divided the letters into four thematically distinct chronological periods: "Agreeing to Disagree, 1846-50"; "Actual Conflict with the World, 1850-61"; "Full to Overflowing, 1862-81"; and "Fruitage-Weighted, 1882-93." Each section of letters is preceded by an introduction that highlights key developments in the years covered. The letters themselves appear with notes supplying additional explanatory and contextual information. We intend this volume to provide a glimpse into the lives of two remarkable nineteenth-century women who combined family and careers and who sought to balance their personal and political commitments. Above all, we present the letters in order to illuminate the mutual love and respect that sustained two extraordinary women, enriching all aspects of their lives.

NOTES

1. The standard source on the American woman suffrage movement, *History of Woman Suffrage,* ed. Elizabeth Cady Stanton, Susan B. Anthony, Matilda Joslyn Gage, et al., 6 vols. (Rochester: Susan B. Anthony; New York: National American Woman Suffrage Association, 1881-1922), included little on Stone, in large part because she refused to cooperate with their efforts. Moreover, as Lucy Stone aged, she was increasingly reluctant to trust the details of her life or work to those outside her immediate circle. Her daughter, Alice Stone Blackwell, in an act of filial devotion produced an account of her mother's life and work; see Alice Stone Blackwell, *Lucy Stone: Pioneer of Woman's Rights* (Boston: Little, Brown and Co., 1930). More than three decades later, Elinor Rice Hays's *Morning Star: A Biography of Lucy Stone, 1818-1893* (New York: Harcourt, Brace and World, 1961) represented the successful efforts of a popular author to produce a full-length biography based on archival sources. Most recently, Leslie Wheeler explored the unique marriage of Stone and Henry Blackwell in *Loving Warriors: Selected Letters of Lucy Stone and Henry B. Blackwell, 1853 to 1893* (New York: Dial Press, 1981). No author yet has fully explored Stone's place in the fragmented woman suffrage movement after the Civil War, her relation to the politics of the Gilded Age, or her relation to the mores of Victorianism.

Like Stone, Antoinette Brown Blackwell left no published autobiography, although at the end of her life she did provide both her niece Alice Stone Blackwell and her New Jersey neighbor Sarah Gilson with reminiscences of her life. Gilson later wove together these fragments into a full-length manuscript, with ample although sometimes unreliable detail. Never published, the typescript of this manuscript is on deposit at the Schlesinger Library, Radcliffe College, Cambridge, Massachusetts. In 1951, Laura Kerr, a popular author, wrote a creative biography for young readers, *The Lady and the Pulpit* (New York: Woman's Press, 1951), skillfully inventing dialogue and motivations where sources were absent. The first contemporary feminist to recognize the intellectual contributions made by Brown Blackwell was Alice Rossi, who reprinted selections from Brown Blackwell's *Sex and Evolution* in *The Feminist Papers: From Adams to de Beauvoir* (New York: Columbia University Press, 1973), pp. 356-77. But not until 1983 did Brown Blackwell's life become the subject of a full-length scholarly biography, with the appearance of Elizabeth Cazden's *Antoinette Brown Blackwell: A Biography* (Old Westbury, N.Y.: Feminist Press, 1983), a volume that begins to suggest the significance of the subject's life and thoughts.

2. Elinor Rice Hays's *Those Extraordinary Blackwells* (New York: Harcourt, Brace and World, 1967) explores the kin network and notes that the remarkable friendship between Stone and Brown Blackwell predated their incorporation into the Blackwell family. Alice Rossi explored Blackwell family relations in "The Blackwell Clan," in *The Feminist Papers,* pp. 323-46. The other major study of the Blackwell family, Margo Horn's "Family

Ties: The Blackwells, a Study in the Dynamics of Family Life in Nineteenth-
Century America" (Ph.D. dissertation, Tufts University, 1980), recognizes
the significance of the Stone–Brown Blackwell alliance within the kin network, but focuses more on the patterns established by those born into the
family. Numerous other works celebrate the achievement of other members
of the family, particularly Emily and Elizabeth Blackwell, pioneer women
doctors.

3. Nancy Cott, in *The Bonds of Womanhood: 'Woman's Sphere' in New
England, 1780-1835* (New Haven, Conn.: Yale University Press, 1977),
discusses at length the relations between women established on the basis
of shared gender identity in her chapter 5, "Sisterhood," pp. 160-96, and
suggests their significance in establishing the sisterhood of feminism in her
conclusion, "On 'Woman's Sphere' and Feminism," pp. 197-206. Both Stone
and Brown Blackwell were familiar with the evangelical tradition in which
women addressed each other as "sister" after joining the church. Female
abolitionists subsequently adopted this form of address for co-laborers, and
some, like Abby Kelley Foster, even used stationery with an imprint of a
female slave in chains below which the lettering appeared: "Am I not a
woman and a sister?" See Blanche Glassman Hersch, *The Slavery of Sex:
Feminist-Abolitionists in America* (Urbana: University of Illinois Press,
1978). Nancy Hewitt, in *Women's Activism and Social Change: Rochester,
New York, 1822-1872* (Ithaca: Cornell University Press, 1984), explores the
differences between antislavery women and sisterhoods of women working
for other reform purposes.

Carroll Smith-Rosenberg, "The Female World of Love and Ritual: Relations between Women in Nineteenth-Century America," *Signs* 1 (Autumn
1975):1-29, reprinted in *Disorderly Conduct: Visions of Gender in Victorian
America* (New York: Alfred A. Knopf, 1985), pp. 53-76, suggests the significance of the quasi-kin relations established by female friends, but has
been more widely cited for the references she makes to the romantic implications of women's same-sex friendship.

Other authors have focused more particularly on the passionate relations
between women friends. See, for example, William R. Taylor and Chris-
topher Lasch, "Two 'Kindred Spirits': Sorority and Family in New England,
1839-1846," *New England Quarterly* 36 (1963):23-41; Nancy Sahli, "Smash-
ing: Women's Relationships before the Fall," *Chrysalis* 9 (1979):17-27; and
Lillian Faderman, *Surpassing the Love of Men: Romantic Friendships between Women from the Renaissance to the Present* (New York: William
Morrow and Co., 1981).

4. Alice Stone Blackwell to Robert Fletcher, Oct. 20, 1931, Robert Fletcher
Papers, box 1, Oberlin College Archives.

Editorial Method

In transcribing these letters, we sought to communicate to readers the character and style of the correspondence and its authors; therefore, with the very few exceptions noted below, we have made literal transcriptions of the letters and have restrained ourselves from intruding upon the text except where essential to preserve the meaning of the document.

Where we have made editorial interventions we deemed absolutely necessary for the sense of a letter, our insertions appear as italics in square brackets. We have made similar notes when the physical condition of a letter prevented its transcription, e.g., [*torn*].

We have supplied in bracketed italics places of origin and dates for letters in which such information was missing from the original. Where our research revealed that the date—usually the year—written onto the letter in a later hand was in error, we have noted our divergence. We have also noted several cases in which Antoinette Brown Blackwell unintentionally misdated her own letters.

When correspondence was conducted on printed letterhead stationery, we have noted this information following the body of the letter, although other italicized information on the dateline that does not appear in brackets was part of the letterhead. We have added to the first appearance of a locality the name of the state, but we have not repeated it in subsequent appearances unless there was a possible ambiguity; for instance, we differentiate between Rochester, Michigan, and Rochester, New York, but since the only Somerville relevant to these letters is in New Jersey, we do not repeat this information.

Words or individual characters appearing in brackets without italics and sometimes followed by a question mark are our best surmise of the content or markings on the originals.

Phonetic spellings (perhaps intentional during the early years of the correspondence), misspellings, haphazard grammar, and random punctuation appear in this volume as they do in the original documents. We have silently added periods not apparent on the original letters or the copies from which we worked when the writer had clearly concluded one thought or sentence and began another with a capital letter directly following; we believe that such marks faded from the originals over the course of time. We have also used our judgment in differentiating between commas and periods, at times nearly indistinguishable in the originals.

We have struck repeated words or phrases without indicating where they appeared. We have retained cross-outs made by the authors only when they appeared to be of substantive interest to readers; other cross-outs have been struck without notice.

Particularly in the early letters, the writers seemed reluctant to waste space, so they apparently used a long dash or an elongated space to separate the end of one paragraph and the beginning of the next on the same line. We have rendered these into standard paragraphs. We have also absorbed minor interlineations into the text without notice.

When the conclusion of a letter was scribbled onto the margin, we have incorporated the passage into the body of the letter. Marginal postscripts jotted on any page of a letter appear here after the body of the letter. When a writer appended her letter to the correspondence of another person, or when others added words to Stone's or Brown Blackwell's text, this fact has been noted, although the text of the other writers does not appear in this volume. We have not included minor postscripts of less than one sentence that Stone or Brown Blackwell added to the letters of others.

At the beginning of the correspondence, the authors occasionally continued writing a letter over several successive days or even weeks. We have treated these letters as single documents, while retaining the writer's notes on the passage of time.

All the documents printed in this collection were either in the handwriting of Antoinette Brown Blackwell or Lucy Stone, or were transcriptions of letters assumed to have been originally in their handwriting. Except where noted, we have worked from photocopies of the original documents as they appear in the microfilm edition of the Blackwell Papers at the Library of Congress and at the Schlesinger Library; when questions arose, our transcriptions were checked against the nineteenth-century originals. We have worked from typescripts or handwritten transcriptions only when originals could not be located.

We include here all extant letters written by Lucy Stone to Antoinette Brown Blackwell, all extant letters written by Antoinette Brown Blackwell to Lucy Stone, and those by Brown Blackwell addressed jointly to Lucy Stone and other household members— Henry Blackwell and/or Alice Stone Blackwell; we did not locate any letters by Lucy Stone addressed jointly to Antoinette Brown Blackwell and other members of her family.

In notes we have referred to Lucy Stone by her initials LS throughout; for Antoinette Louisa Brown Blackwell, we have used the initials ALB for the period before her marriage and ALBB for the years following. In our introductory texts, when we do not use full names, we call the adult women "Stone" and "Brown" or "Brown Blackwell." While this use of last names in an intimate history may seem jarring to some, we believed it important to avoid the infantilization or lack of respect frequently denoted by the use of a first name for a grown person.

Each letter is followed by abbreviations indicating the nature of the document from which it was transcribed and the location of the document.

Whenever possible, notes identify persons and clarify references made by the writers in their letters. Biographical information is supplied only at the first mention of an individual.

List of Abbreviations

Document Symbols

  A: autograph; written in author's hand
BFP: Blackwell Family Papers
  f: fragment
  g: Mrs. Claude U. (Sarah) Gilson, "Antoinette Brown Blackwell: The First Woman Minister," unpublished manuscript, BFP.
  L: letter
 LC: Library of Congress, Washington, D.C.
  S: signed by author
 SL: Schlesinger Library, Radcliffe College, Cambridge, Massachusetts
  t: transcript or copy made at later date.

Abbreviations

Personal Names

  ALB: Antoinette L. Brown
ALBB: Antoinette Louisa Brown Blackwell
 ASB: Alice Stone Blackwell
 HBB: Henry B. Blackwell
  LS: Lucy Stone
 SCB: Samuel C. Blackwell

Oberlin Collegiate Institute

OC: Oberlin College Department
OL: Oberlin Ladies' Department
OP: Oberlin Preparatory Department
OS: Oberlin Theological Seminary
The date following the department designation indicates year of graduation; date/s enclosed in parentheses indicate the years of attendance of nongraduating students. Enrollment in the Preparatory Department is not noted except for individuals who attended only that department.

Other Abbreviations

AAAS: American Association for the Advancement of Science
AASS: American Anti-Slavery Society
AAW: Association for the Advancement of Women
AERA: American Equal Rights Association
AWSA: American Woman Suffrage Association
BFP: Blackwell Family Papers
BMS: Barbara Miller Solomon
HWS: *History of Woman Suffrage*
ICW: International Council of Women
MASS: Massachusetts Anti-Slavery Society
NAWSA: National American Woman Suffrage Association
NEWSA: New England Woman Suffrage Association
NWSA: National Woman Suffrage Association
WASS: Western Anti-Slavery Society
WCTU: Woman's Christian Temperance Union
WJ: *Woman's Journal*
WNLL: Woman's National Loyal League
WSA: Woman Suffrage Association (preceded by name of locality, e.g., Ohio WSA)

Friends and Sisters

In the older days, to me she was a close friend;
in the later days, she was both friend and sister.

—Antoinette Brown Blackwell, at a memorial
service for Lucy Stone, January 21, 1894

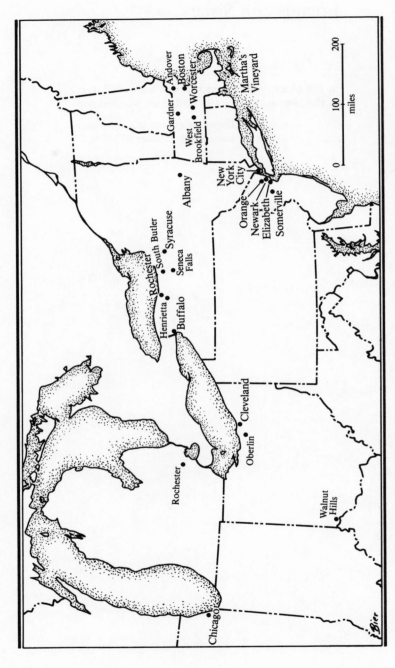

Important Locations in the Letters between Lucy Stone and Antoinette Brown Blackwell

Part 1

"Agreeing to Disagree"

1846-50

O dear! Lucy I do wish we believed alike. I wish somebody
believed as I do and some people are beginning to believe
so; but then we'll "agree to disagree" as you used to say
so often.
　　　　　—Antoinette Brown to Lucy Stone, early spring 1850

In the winter of 1846, twenty-year-old Antoinette Brown left her
home in Henrietta, New York, to begin her studies at the Oberlin
Collegiate Institute in Ohio. She later recalled that at the end of her
journey, a family friend and trustee of the Institute who was on the
same stage warned her to beware of Lucy Stone, "a very bright girl,
but eccentric, a Garrisonian, and much too talkative on the subject
of woman's rights. He advised me . . . not to become intimate with
her. . . . I resolved then and there to know more of Lucy Stone."[1] In
the next eighteen months the two women began the special relationship that drew them together as "friends and sisters" for the rest
of their lives.

Lucy Stone, the older of the two, had attended Oberlin for nearly
three years before Brown arrived. One of the very few women enrolled
in the only college course open to women in the country, Stone had
begun her quest for higher education many years before. Born in
1818 in West Brookfield, Massachusetts, Lucy Stone was the eighth
of nine children and the third daughter born to Francis and Hannah
Stone. Her parents, hardworking farmers, were committed abolitionists who believed in education for their sons, but saw little value
in advanced studies for their daughters. And they particularly opposed
Stone's desire to become a public lecturer on abolition and woman's
rights, siding with the preponderance of clergymen who condemned
public speaking by women as contrary to Scripture.

In contrast Lucy's older brother William Bowman Stone supported
his sister's quest. A graduate of Amherst College, Bowman was ordained into the ministry in 1842. He brought his outspoken abolitionism to the congregation he served until 1850 in Gardner, Massachusetts, and he applauded his sister's work on behalf of black
freedom and later woman's rights.

Lucy's younger sister Sarah also came to endorse her sister's efforts.
Married in 1845 to Henry Lawrence, a schoolteacher, Sarah frequently opened her home, also in Gardner, to her radical sister. In
addition, Lucy's older brothers Frank, who remained on the family
farm, and Luther, who became a merchant on the Illinois frontier,
both voiced their respect for their remarkable sister.

5

Like many young women of the time, Stone began teaching at the age of sixteen, instructing pupils in rural Massachusetts common schools. With the money she earned, she intermittently enrolled in local institutions of higher education, including Mary Lyon's rigorous Mount Holyoke Female Seminary in South Hadley. Her 1839 stay there was, however, cut short by the death of her sister Rhoda, which caused her mother to call Lucy home to assist her on the family farm. Young Lucy left Mount Holyoke with some relief, for her radical antislavery views were out of place at the seminary.

Stone's radical abolitionist ideology not only separated her from her Mount Holyoke classmates, it also unsettled her religious faith. In her teens, Lucy had embraced the Congregationalism of her family and had joined the West Brookfield Congregational Church. But her deeply felt sympathy with the antislavery cause soon placed her at odds with her own church and the Congregational association to which it belonged. In particular, she grew angry when her congregation voted to expel a deacon for his antislavery sentiments; and her indignation crested when she realized her votes on this matter of church governance would not be counted because she was a woman. Stone's antagonism toward the church deepened when in 1837 the Massachusetts General Association of Congregational Ministers reacted to the antislavery lectures of the Grimké sisters, Sarah and Angelina. These southern-born women spoke powerfully and from intimate knowledge of the evils of slavery, but a "pastoral letter" by the Massachusetts Association condemned their actions as beyond the boundaries of acceptable female behavior. Then nineteen years old, Stone listened to the contents of the document from her perch in the gallery of the nearby North Brookfield Church. As she later recalled: "If I had ever felt bound to silence by misrepresentation of Scripture texts or believed that equal rights did not belong to women, that pastoral letter broke my bonds."[2]

Freed from the trammels of the church, Stone thus developed an attraction for the anticlericalism of abolitionist William Lloyd Garrison, who had denounced the Protestant ministry for its association with slavery-tolerating denominations, which, Garrison claimed, like all organized religion, perverted true Christianity. But like many Garrisonians, Stone still maintained a hope for nonsectarian religious inspiration and she leaned toward a variant of the doctrine of Christian perfectionism in which the individual conscience was the supreme moral standard.

In 1843 at the age of twenty-five Stone entered Oberlin, where she hoped to combine her deep moral commitments with her desire to expand her intellectual and spiritual horizons. When she arrived, her allegiances to nonsectarianism, Garrison, and woman's rights set her apart from an institution associated with Congregationalism, Christian abolitionism, and the retention of woman's "proper" sphere.

Her first years at Oberlin were difficult. The Institute then counted fewer than 500 students, most in the Preparatory Department, a middle-level course that equipped students to undertake subsequent work in either the College, Ladies', or Theology course. While enrolled in the College course, Stone taught in the Preparatory Department and also did housework to earn her tuition and meet her living expenses. To economize even further, she often boarded herself for fifty cents a week rather than pay the one dollar required to eat at the common table. The Institute's long winter vacation gave her the opportunity to teach school in nearby Ohio towns. She thus saved both her salary and the cost of travel back East to the Stone home. Her hard work and commitment so impressed her family that first her brother and sister, and finally her father, agreed to loan her money to continue her studies.

Brown's path to Oberlin was less difficult; her family warmly supported the educational aspirations of both sons and daughters. Born in 1825 in Henrietta, New York, Antoinette Louisa was the fourth daughter and seventh of ten children in a large farm family sympathetic to abolition. Antoinette first attended school before the age of three when she insisted on accompanying her brothers and sisters to a country school; she moved through the district schools and then into nearby Monroe County Academy. The Brown family's active participation in the revivals that rocked the "Burned-over district" of upstate New York influenced Antoinette's precocious religious development and she became a member of the local Congregational church when she was not quite nine years old. As her interest in a life devoted to a religious calling took shape, both her local minister and her mother urged her to consider becoming a foreign missionary. Antoinette Brown embraced a bolder plan: ordination as a minister.

Combining parental support with funds saved from four years of schoolteaching, Antoinette Brown entered Oberlin in February 1846 in order to pursue her goal. The school was already familiar to the family; her eldest sister, Rebecca, a teacher, had considered attending some years earlier and an elder brother, William, had graduated from the Theological Seminary in 1841. Brown enrolled as a junior in the Ladies' course, in which she took classes with male and female collegiate students, but was not required to study the Greek, Latin, and Hebrew necessary for the bachelor's degree.

At the Institute, Antoinette Brown enjoyed the support of Lucy Stone, her elder by seven years. Stone's personal commitments and greater practical knowledge of the world, as well as her spirited defense of woman's capabilities, delighted Brown. As Brown later remembered, "Mine was the intense admiration of a younger girl for one much more experienced and influential."[3] The two enjoyed the camaraderie and privileged intimacy characteristic of nineteenth-century female friendships. Yet despite the closeness the two developed, their beliefs did not always coincide. Stone disapproved of Brown's pretty clothes and the "artificials"—handmade flowers—Brown displayed on her bonnet; Brown only slowly warmed to Stone's radical antislavery stance; and the two argued incessantly on matters of religion. They recognized the significance of these differences, but each found comfort in discovering a companion with whom she could discuss matters both weighty and frivolous. As the friendship burgeoned, each looked to the other for support; each claimed the privilege of integrating herself into her friend's kin network; and the two concluded that they would "agree to disagree."

The relationship between Lucy Stone and Antoinette Brown began at an institution founded in 1833 by Congregationalists who sought to prepare students to spread the evangelical message of the Second Great Awakening throughout the West. Located in rural Ohio, the school developed a distinctive interpretation of Congregational theology, known by the late 1830s as "Oberlin Perfectionism," which included a belief in human free agency and the ability of all to embrace God's grace. Isolated and egalitarian, the school also experimented with other reforms, including the Graham diet of vegetables, fruits, whole grains, and unbolted flour; a manual labor plan calculated to reduce student expenses and offset intellectual work with healthy physical exercise; and the education of women. At its opening, female students were permitted to enroll in the Preparatory and Ladies' courses. In 1837 women requested and received admission to the regular College course leading to the bachelor of arts degree, and thus, at Oberlin, began coeducation at the college level in America.

While both Stone and Brown came to Oberlin to pursue the rigorous course of study only the Institute then offered women, each also felt engaged in its theological debates—at least when she arrived. Although already nonsectarian in orientation, Stone was still concerned for her own spiritual state and her failure to experience conversion; but during her years of collegiate study, she became even further alienated from organized religion. Many years later she claimed that she became attracted to Unitarianism as a reaction against the evangelical Protestantism she heard preached by Charles Grandison Finney, the noted evangelist who was Oberlin's professor of theology and later its president.[4]

Brown, on the other hand, remained a Trinitarian Congregation-alist while at the Institute. She respected Finney and looked forward to studying with the man who had converted many members of her family during his successful revivals near her hometown. She had not yet experienced severe difficulties in reconciling her views on religion with the church's teaching on the role of women. Thus, because she intended to make her career as a Congregational minister, she studied traditional theology closely.

At Oberlin as elsewhere in the antebellum years, issues of religion and antislavery were intertwined. Oberlin pioneered interracial ed-ucation. In 1835 students dissatisfied with the prohibition of anti-slavery debate enacted at Lane Theological Seminary in Cincinnati moved to Oberlin after the Institute agreed to accept black students as a matter of policy and to permit free antislavery debate. The arrival of the "Lane Rebels" and Oberlin's subsequent "enlargement plan" received strong financial backing from Arthur and Lewis Tap-pan, wealthy New York abolitionists, and their support helped secure Charles Finney as professor of theology. Asa Mahan, a Cincinnati minister and Lane trustee who sided with the rebels, agreed to serve as president of Oberlin; and John Morgan, a popular professor of mathematics at Lane, agreed to teach New Testament literature.

Oberlin soon became the only educational institution in the coun-try where both races and both sexes received a college education. The area quickly became known as a "hotbed of abolitionism," as free black people began to settle in the village, and it soon became an important stop on the underground railroad. Oberlin-trained min-isters played leading roles in antislavery activities among western Congregationalists, and scores of Oberlinians served as abolitionist lecturers, teachers, and missionaries.

Most Oberlinians saw abolition as part of militant Christian reform and abhorred the views of William Lloyd Garrison and his supporters who demanded that all who would eliminate slavery disengage them-selves from institutions that included slaveholders. Oberlin's "Chris-tian abolitionists" refused to renounce their ties to the church and the Constitution and worked to promote change within institutions. They rejected the Garrisonian "come-outers" for a "voting antislav-ery" position, thereby aligning themselves with more moderate abolitionists. Thus during their student days Lucy Stone, already a committed Garrisonian, was "radical" even for Oberlin, while Antoinette Brown joined the majority of Oberlinians in sympathizing with the antislavery politics of the Free Soil party.

Oberlin's Christian abolitionism had a parallel in the school's attitude toward the involvement of women as public figures on moral issues. Although it had pioneered coeducation, Oberlin strongly opposed women speaking in public on the grounds that it violated scriptural injunctions as well as common standards of modesty and propriety. Oberlin, as well as most of American society, encouraged women to "stay in their place" and to effect reform through private influence in their families and genteel activities in local female benevolent reform organizations. Garrison's followers, including Lucretia Mott, Abby Kelley Foster, and later Stone herself and her Oberlin friends Sallie Holley and Caroline Putnam, endorsed public participation for women in all abolitionist activities, including holding office in their American Anti-Slavery Society (AASS). Interestingly, for all their differences on the role of women in the antislavery movement, both Lucy Stone and Antoinette Brown embraced moral reform, and both were, during their student years, officers in the Oberlin Female Moral Reform Society. But each, in her own way, pushed beyond its limits to a more public arena.

A few college authorities, most notably President Asa Mahan, supported Brown and Stone in their quest for equal female participation in college life and society. A champion of free antislavery debate at Oberlin, Mahan understood the injustice of denying women the opportunity to act for themselves in the reform movements of the day.

Soon after the two Oberlin visits of radical abolitionists Stephen and Abby Kelley Foster in 1846, Stone began to take her antislavery stand in full public view. She became an agent for the *Anti-Slavery Bugle,* a Garrisonian paper published in Salem, Ohio, and wrote an article that criticized Oberlin's interracial Congregational church for what she considered its inconsistent stand on fellowship with slaveholders.[5] A popular teacher at an Oberlin school for free black adults, Stone was invited by the town's black community to speak at an antislavery celebration held on August 1, 1849, the anniversary of West Indian emancipation. This was the only public address she gave while a student at Oberlin, and it resulted in some consternation in the minds of members of the Ladies' Board at the Institute.

The Ladies' Board regulated the conduct of all young women enrolled in the various departments. Composed largely of faculty

wives, the board maintained social distance between male and female
students by enforcing rules against room visitations and prohibiting
students of different sexes from strolling together without permission.
To Stone and Brown many of the board's regulations seemed rea-
sonable, but they chafed at their exclusion from the full range of
training for public speaking. For women who proposed careers in
which they would address mixed assemblies, this obstacle was particularly burdensome. When a sympathetic faculty member granted
them permission to share in the debates held by male students in
the coeducational classroom, the Ladies' Board intervened and ex-
erted enough pressure on the faculty to bar the women from further
participation. Looking back, Brown generously allowed that the
members of the Ladies' Board were "all lovely educated women,
much more conservative than their husbands."[6]

Determined to be effective public speakers, Brown, Stone, and
several other sympathetic female students organized their own secret
debating and mutual improvement society, inspired perhaps by
Brown's experiences at the liberal Rochester Academy in Michigan,
where she taught in fall and early winter 1846-47. There she had
learned new skills by working with a young women's debating society
and delivering her own extemporaneous talks at school assemblies
that were open to the public.

Both Stone and Brown hoped that their August 1847 graduation
would present the opportunity to demonstrate the oratorical skills
they had been secretly practicing. When the time came, Brown read
her essay, "Original Investigation Necessary to the Right Development of Mind," for the Ladies' Department graduation ceremony.[7]
At this public event, except for the presence of President Mahan,
only women occupied the speakers' platform and hence, the Institute
maintained, the female graduating seniors did not step out of their
sphere when they read their own essays. Stone also was invited to
write a commencement essay for her graduation from the Collegiate
course. But because the all-male faculty presided over these exercises,
at which her male classmates delivered orations, Stone was forbidden
to read her own address. Rather than allow a man to present her
work, Stone refused to write an essay.

On departure, Stone deferred offers to lecture as an antislavery
agent in Ohio and Massachusetts, and returned instead to her family
home in West Brookfield, for the first time in four years. There she
taught school one final term to help repay the loans from her family
and began to do some public speaking. Late in the year she gave her
first public talk on woman's rights from her brother's pulpit in Gard-

ner, and in June 1848 she joined Abby Kelley Foster as an agent for
the Massachusetts Anti-Slavery Society (MASS). Her lecture tours
soon took her throughout the Northeast, and she attracted attention
wherever she went. The *Liberator* offered an enthusiastic appraisal
of her efforts, noting her "conversational tone, without any effort at
display. She is always earnest, but never boisterous, and her manner
no less than her speech is marked by a gentleness and refinement
which puts prejudice to flight."[8]

Stone included woman's rights in her antislavery lectures until she
was admonished by the MASS to stop deflecting attention from the
antislavery cause. Insisting "I was a woman before I was an abolitionist," Stone arranged to speak for the society on Saturday evenings
and Sundays but spoke for woman's rights during the week on her
own responsibility.[9]

Back at Oberlin, Antoinette Brown was struggling in her own way
to advance woman's rights. Immediately upon graduation from the
Ladies' course she applied to the Theology Department of the Institute. The faculty allowed her the privilege of attending classes but
refused to enroll her officially. Determined to obtain training, Brown
accepted these terms and began her theological studies with eight
fellow students. She and the only other female, Lettice Smith, both
held the tenuous status of "resident graduates" for the next three
years.

While her theological classmates offered her sympathy, Brown
worked virtually without institutional support. The Ladies' Board
made known its opposition to her studies by promulgating a new
rule prohibiting resident graduates from teaching undergraduates.
This deprived Brown of her income from the drawing classes she
had previously taught for the school. And although she successfully
initiated a series of perspective-drawing classes in the town, she nonetheless confronted the social isolation resulting from her commitment
to a ministerial career. Drawing on her prodigious strength of purpose
and religious faith, Brown developed an emotional self-sufficiency
that permitted her to focus on her studies as well as attend to the
needs of her two younger sisters, Augusta and Ella, who enrolled
while she was still in residence.

At the conclusion of her three years of rigorous theological study,
Brown did not receive a diploma; nor did her work secure her ordination despite the willingness of at least two Oberlin ministers to
sponsor her and the efforts of her classmate James Tefft to arrange
an ordination service for them both. The resistance of most of the
community convinced Brown to stand aside genteelly while male

classmates stepped forward to collect their diplomas and calls to the ministry.

Brown was not silent, however; in the summer of 1850 she spoke from the same platform as Abby Kelley Foster and other come-outers at a Garrisonian antislavery rally in a small town near Oberlin.[10] Although she criticized their views of the church and the Constitution, she demonstrated her readiness to move beyond her academic training for action in the world.

Lucy Stone stood ready to welcome her friend Antoinette Brown into the coterie of antislavery and woman's rights workers in which she had made a place for herself. An organizer of the first national Woman's Rights Convention, held in Worcester, Massachusetts, October 23-24, 1850, Stone urged Brown to attend and to participate. While Brown insisted on maintaining her intellectual integrity and refused to silence her differences with Stone and her allies, she proved appreciative of her friend's pioneering efforts and soon made her own contributions to the woman's rights and antislavery causes in which they both believed.

Now was their time to establish themselves as independent women in their chosen fields. Their career aspirations preempted any marital ambitions, for they realized that nineteenth-century marriage demanded of women "purity, piety, domesticity, and submission."[11] While Brown might easily embrace the first two principles, and Stone at least the first one, the two women turned to each other for the courage to break with the larger framework of cultural expectations and to pursue instead their autonomous plans. In seeing the conflict between marriage and career, they renounced what they believed to be the restrictions of the marital state. The need for mutual support grew as each followed her perilous and unprecedented design.

The advice, nurturance, and sympathy the two provided each other augmented the emotional resources each used to continue her project. Not surprisingly, however, the rigors of their undertakings proved a physical as well as a psychological strain. The threat of illness loomed large in the lives of many young people, and especially young women, in nineteenth-century America. Early Oberlin with its swampy grounds, overcrowded boarding halls, and drafty public buildings proved a breeding ground for cholera, typhoid, and consumption; the life of an itinerant lecturer traveling sometimes by foot over rough roads and enduring often inadequate food and lodging also demanded exceptional physical stamina. Even women and men whose lives were far more sheltered than Stone's and Brown's succumbed with frightening frequency to a wide variety of complaints and illnesses; in fact, perhaps one-third of Stone's and Brown's female contemporaries did not live to reach age twenty.[12]

Thus, as the two women exhorted each other to take care and offered mutual support and solicitousness, they built between themselves a network to insure their physical and emotional survival. They shared their ideas, struggles, and visions for the future; "agreeing to disagree," they built the foundation of a lifelong friendship.

Although most of Stone's letters are missing for this period, her voice still speaks, albeit indirectly, through Brown's responses. Stone's long letter in August 1849 spells out her concerns, her respect, and her love for her cherished "Nette," while Brown's more numerous communications detail her isolation and her appreciation and admiration for her "Dearest Lucy."

The first two letters in this section, written by Brown from Michigan while she was teaching at the Rochester Academy, suggest Stone's presence and anticipate her responses. The letters written in the years 1846 to 1850 reveal the influence of classmates, friends and family, and the shared concerns for reform and woman's rights on the deepening friendship of two early college-educated women.

NOTES

1. BFP-SLg, pp. 48-49.

2. *WJ*, Apr. 14, 1888, p. 117.

3. Ibid., p. 49.

4. ASB, *Lucy Stone: Pioneer of Woman's Rights* (Boston: Little, Brown and Co., 1930), p. 59.

5. Her article appeared in the *Anti-Slavery Bugle*, Oct. 9, 1846.

6. BFP-SLg, p. 58.

7. This essay, an early example of ALB's developing ideas on woman's rights, was later published in the *Oberlin Evangelist*, Sept. 29, 1847.

8. *Liberator*, Aug. 25, 1848.

9. *WJ*, Apr. 15, 1893.

10. *Anti-Slavery Bugle*, Aug. 24, 1850.

11. See Barbara Welter, "The Cult of True Womanhood, 1820-1860," *American Quarterly* 18 (1966): 151-74.

12. This figure is derived from Peter Uhlenberg, "A Study of Cohort Life Cycles: Cohorts of Native Born Massachusetts Women, 1830-1920," *Population Studies* 23 (Nov. 1969): 407-20.

"My *own dear Sister*"

Here I am in Rochester, fairly settled for the winter in a land of strangers. And where are you, to night dear Lucy. Let me see. Yes! there you are, sitting in the old armed chair, happy & alone, no not alone either, for here I am, peeping over your shoulder into the Presidents Philosophy[1] which lies open before you on the table. But you are not studying ma chere amie what *are you* thinking about. If you would only look up I could read it in your face. How natural it does look here. If you would shut the window Lucy, it would be much better, for you will certainly get cold, now it is October. Now come with me to my home. There are three young ladies all studying by the table, two boys with books in their hands, & your friend Net, with pen in hand, but stopping to explain a problem in algebra to one of her studious pupils. Mr & Mrs Harris[2] are sitting near conversing on the various topics of the day, & all together it is an excellent place to practice doing three things at once. We have a pleasant sitting room you see. Now come into my own room. There is a stand bowl & pitcher, one chair, & a strip of carpet spread down in front of the bed. This room is occupied by myself & an interesting girl about 16. It will seem like a very small room to you, at first, but you will soon get accustomed to it. Look out of the window, & see what a fine prospect. The Clinton river winds gently & slowly along in the valley, just below the window. This beautiful stream with its green banks, & picturesk islands, is enough to compensate one for the want of many other conveniences. When I am sad or lonely I sit here & gaze out upon the beautiful scene, till my heart grows better & happyer. They are sometimes cheering moments & how I do wish my dear sister Lucy was here, to share every thought & feeling. I think of you then Lucy, & I think of *home* while a thousand strange thoughts, plans, anticipations, & emotions crowd around till my heart aches & my brain becomes almost giddy. But the low murmuring of that river, has power to sooth again till every thought is tranquil as its own pure water.

Now dear sis, would you like a description of Mr & Mrs Harris "mine host & hostess." Mr Harris is a lawyer, a graduate from Dartsmouth, & a right down Presbyterian Whig, who believes there is nothing new under the sun, except the new folly of man in chasing the [*illegible word*] [fortunes?] of strange doctrines. Mrs Harris has been for several years a teacher in Virginia. She says she is opposed to slavery, but if she were at Oberlin, she should feel like telling the colored people to stand behind her back, while she sat at table. You may think I have little sympathy from them & little opportunity for thinking myself, & yet thoughts will come, sad bitter thoughts sometimes, & sometimes full of hope, but all buried up to gether in my own soul. My boarding place is so far from the school, I am going to leave here soon, & if possible get a room to myself. We have now about 86 scholars, have no boarding house, almost every family has several boarders, & we are expecting *many* more. Mr Moyers[3] is an excellent teacher. He has a fine mind, vastly superior to what "that letter," would indicate. He is deservadly popular, is exactly adapted to the place, "off hand & little pollished." I have all the small children in my room, but have some very large classes, & frequently exchange with Mr Moyers. My children are all good, & pleasant, they are about 12 years old, & about 20 in number. It is an interesting class but it is rather hard work to keep them still, & sometimes I wish they were all mesmerised. Mr Moyers improves upon acquaintance, believes in womans rights, & tells me to act independently to give as many lectures as I please, to the young ladies, & to the whole school, upon any subject & at any time. We have Retorical exercises in the *church* every Saturday, & next time I am going to make them a regular speech. Have a bible class on the sabbath, & talk to the young ladies once every week, or lecture as miss Adams[4] call it on all sorts of things. So you see it is a good place, for improvement. It is something new & the girls like it. So do I, but after all so far as the school is concerned I have not the least ambition. God never made me for a school teacher. Mr Moyers is very much unwell, is tired of teaching also, & I verily believe we shall both give it up & go home, before the winter term commences. Dont tell of that Lucy, it is not at all probable, & I only think so when I am homesick. One of the young men, a student, assists also in teaching. We have no French class yet, & one of the young ladies in the village had a drawing class before I came.

The location of the village is perfectly delightful. In every direction it is hemmed in by green hills, Paint Creek & Clinton rivers, both pass through the village, & unite a little distance below. The buildings are all small, there is a distillery, two taverns, two church[es,] one Congregation, one Christian,[5] or rather a partnership church for all denominations. *Our* minister moved into the place last week, preached very passably last sabbath, seems a good man. His name is Parks, & he has been an Evangelist. We have a number of stores, mills, shops, &c. Mr. Harris is just managing a lawsuit. His office is near the house, & the men are all around considerably excited, & talking loud. One of them has just come out with the news, the jury have given a verdict "no cause for action." So here are the charges & all for nothing. There is a great contrast between this place & Oberlin. Very few of the people seem to be reformers, or to believe in improvement of any sort. Now Lucy you have every thing just as it is, & just as I feel. Write me in return as long a letter, & do please commence it the very day after you get this. I meant to have written you before but have scarcely a liesure moment, at least when I was not *so* tired, for teaching is new business & was very fatiguing at first. I am reading Scots poetry, The Reformation, Paleys Theology,[6] & the Presidents works, either, as the mood suits. You know I did not anticipate much pleasure here, & considdering every thing fair prospects are more than realized.

Has H. Cook[7] Gone home. Has—but I will not ask questions, you must tell me every thing. Now about the journey. At Cleavland went on board one boat, but not finding Mr Fairchild[8] finally left & took the Boston, & went in company with mr Safford[9] to Detroyet, arrived there early Thursday morning, had a delightful time, but no storm, left the city at nine—met Mr Fairchild in the cars, & went home with him. They told us there was no stage going out from the Oak as I expected (a mistake by the way) & Mr F. invited me to Birmingham with them, promising to send me to Rochester the next day. I had a pleasant visit at his home tell Eliza[10] she has got a good brother & sister at any rate. I have every reason to feel grateful to them. We arrived at B. about 10^{ock}, took dinner at Mr Ingersols, Lumans[11] uncles, the next day went as far as Troy, & spent the night at a Mr *Stones*. Their daughter had been teaching at Birmingham & boarding at Mr Fs. They were good Abolitionists, & had two children named after Angelina, & Sarah Grimke.[12] I like all *Stones* pretty well & they were certainly very good ones. Arived at Rochester Saturday morning & so here I am. The people all around are talking very happily but it is misery to talk of one thing, & think of something else. You cannot tell how bitter [*text missing*][13]

The people here are against all reforms. They would take their children and turn me out of doors if they knew what I believe and yet they are good to me.

Mr. Fairchild had a long talk about woman's rights. He was very kind and good natured about it but it put me into such an agony as I never wish to feel again, and for once I did wish God had not made me a woman (I do not wish so now). They did not know my feelings and I cannot tell them to you but heaven grant you may never know them by experience. It did me good after all. How I do want to see you dear, dear Lucy. Mr. Fairchild inquired after you;

he remembered us at Commencement. I wish I had not begun this subject, it calls these same feelings back again and makes me resolve not to spend two years in studying the languages but in getting a more practical knowledge.

Nette

ALf-LC/tLf-SLg

1. Asa Mahan, *A System of Intellectual Philosophy* (New York, 1845). Mahan (1799-1899) was president of Oberlin 1835-50. Earlier as a pastor and trustee of Lane Seminary in Cincinnati, he had vigorously opposed the prohibition of debate on slavery, and so moved to Oberlin. After his resignation from Oberlin, he became founding president of short-lived Cleveland University, and later president of Adrian College 1860-71. The author of numerous philosophical and theological works, he spent the last eighteen years of his life in England, where he edited a monthly magazine, *The Divine Life.*

2. Edward P. Harris (1802-68), an 1826 graduate of Dartmouth College, moved to Rochester in 1836 where he practiced law. After the death of his first wife in 1831, he married Elizabeth S. Gillet.

3. Peter Moyers (1818-47) founded the progressive coeducational Rochester Academy in 1845 where he served as teacher and principal.

4. Mary Ann Adams (d. 1871), OL 1839, was principal of the Female Department at Oberlin 1842-49. She married Charles Conkling, a minister, in 1850.

5. A Protestant denomination now called Disciples of Christ.

6. William Paley, *Natural Theology* (London, 1802).

7. Helen Cook (d. 1886), OL 1846, from New York, attended Oberlin classes after her graduation, and completed her studies at the Western College of Homeopathic Medicine in Cleveland in 1852. She later married Augustine Barker and was a physician in New York City and Buffalo.

8. Edward Henry Fairchild (1815-89), OC 1838, OS 1841, was then a minister in Birmingham, Mich. In 1853, he became principal of the Oberlin Preparatory Department, and in 1869 president of Berea College in Kentucky.

9. Jacob Safford (1795-1863), an early Oberlin settler, was a prosperous farmer.

10. Harriet Eliza Fairchild (d. 1891), OC 1847, taught at the Rochester Academy 1847-49 with her Oberlin classmate and future husband, Robert Kedzie, whom she married in 1850.

11. Luman Church Ingersoll (1823-97), OC 1846, OS 1849, became a dentist and lecturer on dental science in Keokuk, Iowa.

12. Sarah Grimké (1792-1873) and Angelina Grimké (1805-79) were abolitionists, woman's rights reformers, and lecturers. In 1838, Angelina Grimké married Theodore Weld, an abolitionist orator and writer.

13. The remaining extant text of this letter is taken from a transcription included in Mrs. Claude U. (Sarah) Gilson's "Antoinette Brown Blackwell: The First Woman Minister," unpublished manuscript, Blackwell Family Papers, Schlesinger Library, Radcliffe College, Cambridge, Mass., cited hereafter as BFP-SLg.

[Rochester, Mich., Winter 1847]

Dear Lucy,

You can not think how glad I was to hear from you. I had been wating very impatiently to hear from home, & thought I would have a long cry, if a letter did not come that night. But none came, & still I did not cry, for I found a long letter from *sister Lucy,* & it made me quite happy only you were so sad it made me sad too from sympathy. I thought you knew me better than to believe I could ever forget you, or cease to love you, but was glad to hear such a thought was not long cherished. And now my dear sister let me beg of you Never entertain such a feeling again, do not for my sake or your own. Time & circumstance may make great changes in us both, but never while we both live shall I cease to regard you with the same deep feelings; for *I* have not loved in vain. You tell me you do not wish to become acquainted with a very good & amiable young lady, because you are afraid you shall learn to *love* her, & then she will go *away* & leave you. Pardon me dear Lucy, but you do need a severe rebuke. Why are you becoming so missanthropic. Think you I feel more unhappy because I know that there are warme hearts somewhere in this bright & beautiful world, that would throb still more kindly, to learn of my wellfare; that would shed a tear of sympathy in commiseration for my sorrow, & deal with me in the faithfulness of true friendship should they see me departing from what *they* deemed to be the path of duty. Have I caused you more sad than happy hours, & do you regret having known me. Far different has it been in *my* case, & heaven send me a score of friends. I believe I could find room to love them all & still find my heart growing warmer & better by the kindly influence. It is now vacation & you have nothing to do but think. I know you will forgive my frankness but dear dear Lucy I do tremble for you. You feel almost alone at Oberlin, & your feelings are all pent up in your own soul. Have a care Lucy or your mind will become as hot as Cratons,[1] & as sad as Edwards. But your spirits are too buoyant to be always sad, &

you can not long cherish that feeling without a bitterness mingled with it, a bitterness & censoriousness arising from that very cause, which we have so often lamented. Do pray the Lord to keep you from the snares of the advisary who is ever eager to enslave the aspiring soul. You may think my caution unnecessary but there [*is*] fearful danger for you & me too.

Where is Miss Smith is she teaching. I am very anxious to hear from her. What is Miss Lovell[2] doing. What are you all doing in Oberlin. Where is Josephine.[3] If I knew where to write I would write to her. Ask her brother[4] about this Reporting Style in Phonography.[5] Are there any works I can get on that subject i.e. Reporting. I Have a class commencing phonography soon. If I knew who was at Oberlin, or where some of the young ladies are, I should write to them. You must tell me about every body. Write me two whole sheets full wont you sis because you will have time now & do be good to poor Nette. You did not say anything about the discussion in our class. I have been very anxious about it. Was anything more said or done about it & how much progress did your class make in their studies last term. What are you doing all vacation. How do Emeline[6] & Lettice[7] like keeping house. Is Craton lecturing & how does he get along. Give my love to brother. [Hurry] with that money . . . & to Edward. They are wating to take this to the Office. God by A.L.B.

Wednesday

Sis

Will you begin to think again I have forgotten you. Imagine yourself just in my situation & you will not wonder I have not writen you before. Think how incessantly I am occupied. You shall hear all about it but at present I am just in the mood for telling you about our "literary society" having just returned from there. It consists of about 50 members has been in opperation several weeks & is both pleasant & profitable to all who are members. We have a good constitution & the order of exersises thus far have been the following Two composition, thre declamation, two other composition, a discussion contents of the budget box. For discussion we appoint two chief disputants & these choose each two others making six in all. There are *some* young ladies here of superior tallent — *all take* a *deep* interest in the exercises & I must say I have never before improved so rapidly in my life in the use of the tongue. How I wish we had such a society at Oberlin such exercises & such fearlessness & eagerness in the path of improvement. We are all getting to be womans

rights advocates or rather the *investigators* of *WOMANS DUTIES.*
We are exceeding careful in this matter & we all move on together
step by step looking at principles & entirely forgetting the conclusions
we must at length come too. Some will undoubtedly shrink back
when they come to find where they stand & believe they must have
been mistakened. other will want moral courage to carry out what
they know to be duty, & a few I hope & believe will go out in the
world pioneers in the great reform which is about to revolutionize
society. You see my all hoping heart in this as in every thing else.
Mr Moyers is a very different man from what I expected at first he
has a fine mind & a warm heart & is a thorough friend of all reform.
The school now numbers more than a hundred. I will give you the
order of my classes this term. In the morning Philosophy there are
about 35 in the class all young men & young ladies next Robinsons
Algebra[8] & fine scholars they are some of them. You will have some
of them at O next fall. Next Grays Chemistry[9] a good class & lastly
writing. Penmanship is the last thing I should teach but have copy
plates give instructions &c & teach them how to make pens &c. In
the afternoon the order of rescitations are Grammar, Towns Analysis,[10] Davies Arithmetic,[11] Robinsons Arithmetic[12] Spelling. We have
three grammar classes all reciting at the same time each averedging
30 or 35. other classes in proportionate numbers. We have two assistant pupils a young man & young lady & still a plenty to do. I
teach in either room as it happens to be conveniant & am getting
quite at home though it did seem strange at first. You will easily
imagine there is little l[u]asure time for me either in school or out.
I began your letter several weeks ago & then laid it by to finish
vacation. Vacation which lasted one week was spent up in Washington
McComb Co. & so here I am writing the first spare moment after
10[ock] & in great haste. Do write to me immediately & I will answer
you this time with out wating so long. I have been having long
discussions with my friends at home about Womans duties, & expect
another letter soon. They tell me to act conciensiously but think I
can do more good in some other way. But I believe there is soon to
be a new era in womans history & the means to effect this must be
truth wielded in firmness gentleness & forbearance.

If I could only see you I should talk two days without stopping.
Oh that Spring had come. I have a hard lesson to lear[n] here though
everything does seem pleasant. I have a new boarding place a large
nice room by myself, pleasant & near the schoolhouse pleasant people

to live with, warmhearted scholars & good health. And yet I do wish Spring had come. Have enclosed 4 [#] for Taft.[13] Please give it him.

Your own Sister Nette.

ALS-SL

1. ·Samuel T. Creighton, OC (1846-47), from Springboro, Ohio, lectured in Ohio for the Western Anti-Slavery Society (WASS) in 1846.

2. Louisa Jane Lovell (1822-48), OL 1846, married Michael B. Bateham, editor of the *Ohio Cultivator,* in 1847 and wrote the "Housewife's Department," a column in his paper.

3. Josephine Penfield (1829-1901), OL 1847, married Richards Cushman, OS 1847, in 1848 and served with him as a missionary in Haiti until his death in 1849. In 1850 she married Michael B. Bateham and took over the "Ladies' Department" of the *Ohio Cultivator.*

4. Charles Penfield (1826-91), OC 1847, OS 1850, was Josephine Penfield's brother. He taught languages at Oberlin and later in Cleveland.

5. Phonography, a popular nineteenth-century reform, was a system of shorthand based on phonetics, or fonetics, which was the attempt to reform the spelling of the English language by using letters phonetically.

6. Probably Rebecca E. French (1822-72), OC 1847, from Adrian, Mich. She married A. G. Lawrence and late in life taught at Washington College, Oakland, Calif.

7. Lettice Smith (1823-1911), OC 1847, OS (1847-50), married classmate Thomas Holmes in 1847 and, with ALB, completed the Theological course of study. She taught at Antioch College 1854-56 and at Union Christian College, Merom, Ind., 1865-74.

8. Horatio N. Robinson, *An Elementary Treatise on Algebra* (Cincinnati, 1846).

9. Alonzo Gray, *Elements of Chemistry* (New York, 1841).

10. Salem Town, *An Analysis of the Derivative Words in the English Language* (New York, 1835).

11. Charles Davies, *Arithmetic Designed for Academies and Schools* (Philadelphia, 1841).

12. Horatio N. Robinson, *A New Practical and Theoretical Arithmetic* (Cincinnati, 1845).

13. James Cutler Tefft (1816-55), OC 1847, OS 1850, a strong supporter of ALB's ministerial ambitions, subsequently served as a missionary in Sierra Leone, where he died.

[Henrietta, N.Y., July 1847]
Sitting room at the old Stone mansion

Dear sister Lucy

Here I am at home & a busy happy home it seems to me. My friends are all usually well & happy. father is just finishing his haying,

Mother making a cheese & us girls all talking laughing or writing &
having a merry time.

My sister Rebecca teaches this summer about a mile from my
fathers & she comes home every night since my return. Gusta has
been up & taught for her three days this week. Elly attends school
but this is the last day of the term & then she has a va[ca]tion of
six we[e]ks. Doubtless you will feel very much interested in family
matters but you have heard so much about my friends that it is
certain you will know who I am talking about.

You shall now have a discription of my adventures since leaving
Oberlin. At half past two PM we sailed away from Cleavland in the
fine boat Hendrick Hudson. It was mild & pleasant all the afternoon
& just at sunset we had a grand thunder storm. The wind was not
very high but the waves tossed gladly around us & dark clouds covered
the whole sky while the sun seemed struggling through them &
shedding around his beams of glory as if hurrying away to seek a
nights repose beyond the reach of the tempest. The thunders raised
their voices & the ligntnings danced from cloud to cloud & sometimes
seemed as if leaping down upon the waters.

I wish you had been there Lucy & we would have watched all
night but as it was after remaining out an hour or two after sunset
I left the heavens covered with glory & was soon lulled into a sound
sleep.

All night I heard or dreamed that I was hearing the wild music of
the elements & it seemed as though I was floating among the clouds.
It was a happy fancy & the airy pillow upon which my head seemed
resting was a very different thing from the naked plank upon which
I was sleeping for I took a deck passage several ladies came with me
all the way to Rochester & we all shared the same fare & fared pretty
well too. At 5^{ock} Tuesday morning we were in Buffalo. & I might
have taken the cars & been home at noon but finally took the packed[1]
& reached R. early the next morning. The packed was crowded to
a perfect jam & afforded ample variety for the pen of Boz:[2] if he had
been willing to give the world the items of life on the "Erie canaal."
In the afternoon I reached the village & went directly over to the
peace convension[3] which was then in session. Gus. & Mary[be]th
were in the gallery & I thought they would jump once when they
saw me come in. Mr Goodell[4] was there & at my brothers at tea. I
told him all about Maria & he seemed very happy to hear. He said
two or three times over "So you saw Maria less than three days ago.
Well I am glad to hear she is doing so well." Poor Maria. If he had
known how sick she was going to be he would have been sad. Give

my best love to her, to Lottie⁵ & to all the young ladies who are sick. I am almost afraid to hear from Oberlin again lest I shall hear that some of those we loved so well have parted from us forever— no I hope not forever even if we should be called to part for time.

You see Lucy, I should make slow progress in telling you all I have done for the last few or even all the incedents which might be interesting. My aunt & two cousins from Hammond Where brother I.A. lives were here visiting when I came home & one cousin remains with us to attend school. I was glad they were here but sometimes used to wish the[y] had waited another week. Lucy I have wished you were here a dozen times a *dozen* times. It would not have been wasted time either & would have cost you but a little perhaps no more than to remain there, if you stayed as long as I expect to now. I was intending to leave home to day & about this time—to take the evening packet—spend the sabbath in Buffalo & monday visit Niagara. A company was going to the falls with me among which were my brother & his wife sister Rebecca. We had not certainly decided whether we should take the packet or wait till monday & then go in a steamboat by the way of Lewiston.

A few days since I received a letter from Jane Penfield⁶ giving some account of the sicknes at O. & now my friends will not consent to my returning at present. So the excursion is given up & I shall probably be at O not till about the first of Aug. Write to me immediately will you not dear Lucy & tell me again "all about every thing" & particularly the sickness. My mother would feel bad to have me go back till I hear. You know how careful our mothers are. I know how bad they would feel to have me return. So I have concluded to stay though I should prefer to be there & yet it is true I have not half finished my visit yet.

I have finished my first of August essay.⁷ The subject is West India Emancipation Prophetic of the Future. The piece for Commencement⁸ is written also but I have not revised it as I shall have to do considerably for I am going to vary the plan some. My subject is mind adapted to originality of thought or investigation. Something of that sort but I have not worded the ca[p]tion yet. Have not showed it to any one yet & shall not till I have rewritten it. If I had been going back this week it would have been all completend before this so you se I have not procrastinated. Have been studying Hebrew some & lotts of other things beside visiting till I am tired enough. I go out into the barn & make the walls echo with my voice occasionally but the church stands on the green in such a way that I have too many auditors when I attempt to practice there. The barn is a good large one however & the sounds ring out merrily or did before father had filled it so full of hay. Oh Lucy I wish I could see you only one hour. Good bye.

Didnt you get a letter for me from Rochester. If you did do not send it now but send me word. It should have been there long ago & what is more it has lotts of money in it so dont hook any out. Remember you are bound by the code of honor. The term closes at Rochester in a few days & I may possibly see Mr Moyers at Henrietta before I return as he is going out to Yale at the Commencement. My sisters told me to tell you they were getting very jealous of you for they are sure I talk more about you than I should either of them if I were absent. I am glad yo heard from Mercy[9] but she ought to have written me here before this give her my love when you write to her. I have not written you any thing relating to the paper[10] but really I have been vexed enough & sorry but I believe with you that it is not dead but sleepeth. I could get a fine list of subscribers here. Give my best love to Miss Adams & tell her am trying to be good. Remember me to Mrs Tracy[11] & to any who may inquire after me. Dont get sick dear Lucy & write a long long letter. I am so anxious to know what your friends said.

Your sister Nette

ALS-SL

1. Packet boat.
2. A reference to Charles Dickens, *Sketches by Boz, Illustrative of Everyday Life and Every-day People* (London, 1836).
3. In the 1840s many antislavery reformers became active in the peace movement in opposition to the extension of slavery by American annexation of Texas and war with Mexico.
4. William Goodell (1792-1867), a New York minister, editor, and radical abolitionist, was a founder of the Liberty party. His daughter, Maria Goodell (1826-98), OP (1846-47), married Oberlin graduate Lewis P. Frost, OC 1848, a minister.
5. Charlotte Farnsworth, OL (1846-47), from Boston, died in Oberlin, August 5, 1847.
6. Jane Penfield (1823-81), OL 1847, married Alonzo W. Hendry in 1848 and settled in Sandusky, Ohio, where he was a lawyer and judge.
7. On August 1, 1833, West Indian slaves were emancipated by the British government. Abolitionists celebrated this event instead of the Fourth of July as a festival of freedom.
8. ALB delivered an essay, "Original Investigation Necessary to the Right Development of Mind," at the Ladies' Department commencement, August 24, 1847. The *Oberlin Evangelist* printed the essay, September 29, 1847.

9. Mercy Lloyd, a Quaker from Lloydsville, Ohio, was active in the WASS and woman's rights reforms. In 1849 she married Jesse Holmes, also a Quaker.

10. In June 1847 members of the Oberlin Young Ladies Association voted to publish a newspaper, the *Oberlin Ladies Banner,* but the faculty and Ladies' Board "totally disapproved" of the enterprise.

11. Hannah Tracy (1815-96), OL (1847-48), a woman's rights leader, writer, and physician, taught school and wrote to support her three children after the death of her first husband. In 1847 she enrolled in the Ladies' course at Oberlin while running a boarding house. Remarried in 1852 to Samuel Cutler, she wrote and lectured extensively on married woman's property rights. In 1869 she received a medical degree from the Woman's Medical College of Cleveland and in 1870 she became president of the American Woman Suffrage Association (AWSA). She wrote frequently for the *Woman's Journal (WJ).*

[Oberlin, early September 1847]

Dear Lucy

It is a long time since you went away & it has seemed longer still to Sarah[1] & I. Do you remember Lucy that little note I sent you more than a year ago bringing against you such grave charges & telling the sad effects of your "art" upon myself. Well it is just so I feel now only much worse. I wish you were here but still am glad you are gone if you will only come back West again sometime. We have strange times since commencement & at least Every one else seems to moove onward very much like former times. Your classmates are nearly all gone. Kinney[2] Huyson[3] & Larison[4] leave tomorrow. Miss Adams is getting well rapidly takes charge of the young ladies & hears one recitation. Prof Finey[5] is Better & every one looks happy. So do I too when I am out of my room but here all alone sometimes look & feel the personafication of sadness & my heart feels "utterly lone & desolate." You have seen me have the "blues" often enough but you have never seen me quite as miserable as I feel now once in a while because I have never felt so sad before since I came to Oberlin & have never had so much cause to feel so. I dont know what to do, how to feel, or what think, will or decide about anything. But before I go any farther Lucy let me say once for all that it is not my heart that is troubled, but my judgement. You may shake your head & disbelieve me but it is true nevertheless. Much as I miss your society & feel the need of friends to advise & sympathize I am still glad of the privilege of standing alone in the wide world

with none but God for a supporter & every feeling of my soul
acquaisces with the decision of His entitling Will. Those rekindled
emotions of a few weeks since are all gone now, & gone I believe
forever. It was only the faint glowing of dying embers which flash
brightly before they expire & the next moment are extinguished. You
will ask what does [troub]le me then. Quite enough for ones to have
my plans for the next three years all destroyed & without being at
all able to learn the cause. You know Miss Adams told me I might
teach enough in the Institution to pay my expenses for the time I
chose to study here. While she was sick & th[e] Ladies Board disar-
ranged everything it seemed to be regretted & that was all I felt about
it. Now she h[as] recovered but she has not only not said anything
to me about teaching & given to others the classes I did teach but
she has avoided saying a word to me about it & when I have tried
to get an opportunity to at least find out the reason she complains
of being too much fatigued to see any one at present. It seems very
strange but I suppose s[he] has a good reason & I shall hear it
sometime. I love Miss Adams & as well now as ever. We have a new
principle coming this week to assist her, & next summer Miss Adams
does not expect to be here at all. It is Miss Atkins[6] who takes her
place. Have not heard from home yet & dont know whether they
will think it best to have me go to Michigan or not but [assume]
they will give no very definit[ive] answer but permission to do as I
think best. Probably I shall not go for these two reasons & these
only, Agustas health & leaving my studies this fall & winter. Most
of the people here seem to think it foolish for me to study Theology
at least before taking a college course & if they do not say so some
of them expect I shall not succeed very well & I have little desire of
fulfilling their presentiment by spending the time which should be
spent in studying in any other way. You will wonder then how I am
to get along. I dont know but shall trust Providence for means &
just go on as I have done since Commencement studying very hard.
Probably shall borrow the money from home or some where else &
pay again when the time comes to earn it. As for the teaching here
it would take a great deal of explanation to make me willing to teach
here again & I am glad I am not going to teach. Finally Lucy I am
getting all hopeful & hoping again I can study better think better &
talk braver for every thing that has happened & this discipline has
done me good. Missapprehensions & missunderstandings have done
it all & Sarahs sermons on Charity are much needed in this world
but all will yet be well for there *is* "a good time comming." If I knew
where I could rent so much money I would obtain till there was

means of paying again for it is much better to get on now than stop
& teach a year. I have just commenced a large drawing which will
probably be finished this week. The Hebrew goes finely & the lessons
do not seem hard at all now. Now Lucy I will beg pardon for troubling
you so much about my troubles but indeed it is hard to keep so
much perplexity to oneself, & to trouble Sarah *much* about it, would
be unkind for she is not *very* happy since you left & she takes so
much care of Mrs Henry[7] she will certainly be sick unless Edward
comes home. You must scold her Lucy & tell her to be careful of
her health for she wont mind me. Robert Kedzie[8] has gone to Rochester to see how he likes them.

We have fine weather now only very hot & the quiet times here
are delightful.

Sarah just came in with her note to you & let me read it. She tells
you I dont want her to be with me much in public &c & without
an explanation it may call down an honest rebuke from you particularly in remembrance of the past. The people have an undefinable
somewhat against me & as she is a stranger & just come to the hall
I refused only to her being only too much with me in the sitting
room &c. [I] told her if she wanted to see me she could come to my
room [a]s much as she chose & thus prevent the people from thinking
her exclusive ultra or any thing else that is bad & still sacrafise neither
principle nor feeling on her part or mine. Farther than this I would
never advise Sarah to act in that matter or do what might not be
honorably done in like circumstances. But Lucy I had never so much
need to [a]void your society as she has mine. The people always
[re]spected though they feared your influence. What they think [o]f
me is a mystery I guess even to themselves. At all events I am "strong
in conscious rectitude." Mr. Foot[9] preached last sabbath afternoon
on our duties to man or philanthropy & that was what called out
Mr Cushman[10] on Thursday. Lucy will you write every thing & paint
your heart as fully as I have mine every thought & feeling & motive
& wish too. Be good & get your heart full of love to every one &
dont love Nette any less than you do now will you

Nette

I wish you was here to sleep with me to night. We would have a
long talk wouldn't we. Give my love to your father and mother &
that good brother.

ALS-SL

1. Sarah Pellet (1824-98), OC 1851/58, from North Brookfield, Mass.,
attended Oberlin at the urging of LS, her childhood friend and neighbor.

Although she left Oberlin in 1852 and was not officially granted her degree until 1858, she was credited with graduating in 1851. In 1853 she traveled to California where she lectured on temperance and woman's rights, and later taught in North Brookfield, Mass., and New York City. She continued to speak and write on temperance and woman's rights.

2. Lester Kinney (1821-1918), OC 1847, was Oberlin railroad station agent and active in local government.

3. Simeon Hughson (1823-91), OC 1847, graduated from Union Seminary in 1850, and was a minister in New York and New Jersey.

4. William Larison (1823-72), OC 1847, considered lecturing for the American Anti-Slavery Society (AASS); later he became a lawyer in Newark, N.J., and Chicago.

5. Charles Grandison Finney (1792-1875) cut short a promising career as a lawyer in upstate New York to become the foremost evangelist and revivalist in nineteenth-century America. He came to Oberlin in 1835 as professor of theology, and served as president 1851-65.   .

6. Mary Atkins (1819-82), OL 1845, was the assistant principal of the Oberlin Female Department 1847-49, and principal and owner of the Young Ladies Seminary at Benicia, Calif. (later Mills College) 1854-65. In 1868 she became principal of the Female Department of Central High School in Cleveland and the following year married John Lynch, OC 1851, an attorney.

7. The mother of Edward Henry, OC (1845-48).

8. Robert Kedzie (1823-1902), OC 1847, taught at the Rochester Academy 1847-48. In 1851 he became a physician and served as a surgeon during the Civil War. Later he became professor of chemistry at the Michigan Agricultural College (now Michigan State University). He married Harriet Eliza Fairchild in 1850.

9. Charles C. Foote (1811-91), OS 1840, was an antislavery lecturer and preacher who helped establish settlements in Canada for fugitive slaves.

10. Richards Cushman (1819-49), OS 1847, married Josephine Penfield in 1848 and died the following year while serving as a missionary in St. Marc, Haiti.

Oberlin Sept 9th [*1847*][1]

Dearest Lucy

We wrote you some time since [i.e.] two or three days ago, but did not send the letters immediately & will now write a few lines more. I have talked with miss Adams. She did not know what the ladies board had done about the drawing but said they had been telling her how I believed &c & that they did not think it best to have me teach. She was anxious to have me teach that class at least she [*sai*]d but I told her I did not wish to now & so the ma[*tter*] ended & now I do not feel sad about it at all. But I will not write any more now or your letter will weigh to much & beside there is hardly time now.

Wishes
Nette

ALS-SL

1. This letter appears on the same sheet as a letter by Sarah Pellet written later on the same day.

[*Oberlin*] Sarahs Room, Sept. 22nd, '47

Dearest Lucy,

We received your wellcome letter this evening & you can easily we both felt very glad. Miss Pease goes to the office you know. I ran to see if she had a letter for me but she replied "no" & I turned away disappointed. I wish I had one for you she continued & I have one for Miss L. Brown[1] (a young lady who has recently come to the hall). O dear said I why wasnt it for A. L. Brown. "Why perhaps it is" she exclaimed holding it toward the light & sure enough it was. She had been accustomed to see my whole name written & did not notice. I felt glad she did not for a pleasant contrast is agreeable you know.

Sarah was visiting with brother Bart so I read the letter first & by that time Literary Society commenced. We went in & answered to our names & after staying awhile came out & here we are writing to you. I am going to stay & sleep with her to night & doubtless we shall both think & say two or three times over before we go to sleep How I *do* wish Lucy was here for notwithstanding all Sarahs theory about *wishing* she does wish once in a while.

The literary society prospers very well. Jose[2] is appointed to give the address in two weeks. She told me tonight she should write nothing but the heads & speak it. Isnt that good. Sarah has an appointment next week to discuss & I have one to read.

You had a multitudinous number of questions to ask about Oberlin & one of us will try & answer you but wouldnt you like to get a bit of other news that after all you have not included some good news too Lucy. Miss Lovell is going to be married not to [Dr]. Dean either or any other good person of our acquaintance but to a Mr [*blank in original*][3] a man who fell in love with her last Commencement kept her memory inshrined in his heart for a year without knowing where she was to be found—met her here at last commencement— made proposals—& kept the matter in consideration a week or two came here again & perhaps corresponded some in the interval & is now accepted. Miss L. still thought of waiting till spring & was going to teach in Mansfield but the other day she came to have me take the school & they say she is to be married soon & that she is going to have a real wedding with wedding cake—quite as much of a novelty in Oberlin as haveing mother & daughter married the same evening. Miss L.s intended is a noble looking man wealthy & tallented report says & of course she is very happy & I am happy for her & so are you I know.

Well Lucy so you think more than ever you must not get married. I am glad of it for so do I too. Let us stand alone in the great moral battlefield with none but God for a supporter & there will be a lesson of truth to be learned from our very position which will be impressed as deeply on the minds of the people as any we have to teach. Let them see that woman can take care of herself & act independently without the encouragement & sympathy of her "lord & master" that she can think & talk as a moral agent is priveledged to. Oh no dont let us get married. I have no wish to. I am sure I am not going to Rochester. You have reasons in my last. I waited for an answer from home, until it was time to write to Mich then sent word on my own responsabiallty that I could not go for the same reasons I gave you. That evening a letter came from my father & brother. They told me to act as I thought best & they would be satisfied but I guess they thought I should probably go & my sisters seem to feel but best they did not write themselves. Father told me to learn portrait painting if I chose & so I have commenced—tuition 16 dollars. When I went to see Mr Brocaw[4] the President[5] was there haveing his portrait taken. when I went in he noticed me & said soon after "Some people use it as one argument that womans mind is not equal to mans that she has never become eminent in portrait painting." "Yes" I replied "but I have just come over to see if Mr Brocaw will teach me how to paint." He laughed at me a little—wished me success &c & I wish I could but do not expect to do much because I cannot spend much of my time in that way & could never make a celebrated artist if I did. I received a letter from Mr Moyers a few days ago not hearing as soon as he wished & wanting the school to commence the 21st. he wrote me if I came to tell him when I would be in Detr[o]it & he would meet me there. The ride from Detr[o]it to Rochester would have "jibed on" oddly to the one from Rochester to Detroit would'nt it. Mr M. has been very sick.[6] Was taken ill at Cleveland & has hardly been out since I wrote back as cheering a letter as I could but told him I must remain here through the fall.

5 Ock A M

It is a good pleasant morning but my eyes are only half open for we talked some last night & I feel sleepy though Sarah has been studying for an hour & now she is writing you with all dispatch. All the time after she arose I have been dreaming about you & some of them were strange dreams too.

Last night I told many of the young ladies I had heard from you & was going to write you immediately many of them sent love &c &c & Miss Fairfield[7] said tell her to "guard against ever getting a bitter spirit" & I could not help thinging it was worth writing. She seems a very good girl & is feeling very sensitive about this womans rights question. She is so affraid educated women will get out of their sphere & thus make the world believe education unnecessary to them or perhaps injurious if carried to a great extent. Much as I disagree with the sentiment it seems like a worthy feeling & in one light a noble one & I love & respect her for it. For her injunctions I heed it with all dilligence & I know you will but if you had seen the different states of mind as clearly illustrated as we have here lately you would not wond[er] at the repeated injunction from your sister Nette.

Miss Atkins is here & we all like her. She of course came to my room & as I remai[ned] there two or three days became considerably acquainted with her. She is lovely good intelligent affable & self forgetful but she has not the firmness & dignity of charac[ter] that Miss Adams possesses. She will probably be very popular as a teacher & next sum[mer] Miss Adams will *probably* not be here. When I left my room there was no front room unoccupied & Mrs Right[8] told me I could have a front room with a room mate or any of [the] back rooms & so I have gone up into the attic again for I always liked tha[t] room & it is so pleasant there I am not sorry for the change though I felt bad at the time I mooved. Lettice is here at Prof. Fairchilds.[9] She has been taking care of Miss Holly[10] who has been sick with a fever but is better & nearly well. Lettice had a letter from Emeline the other day. She has heard twice. E. says she is happier at home than she expected to be. Her friends do not seem to reallize what it is to be expelle[d] & do not care much.[11] Her mother is now journeying East & she is keeping house. Father said when he wrote Agusta says she will tell you about her own health.

She did not write so I dont know exactly but if she had been sick
he would not have written so & probably she is about the same.

I have grown very happy lately & do not feel half so sad for the
good cause is prospering though we have hard struggles & *they think*
Public Opinion will prevent us from studying Theology very long.
They dont know us yet.

Nette

ALS-SL

1. Laura Brown, OL (1847-48), was from Bainbridge, Ohio.
2. Josephine Penfield.
3. The name omitted was Michael B. Bateham, editor of the *Ohio Cultivator,* who married Louisa Lovell in 1847, a year after hearing her antiwar and antislavery graduation address, "True Valuation of Human Interests."
4. David Brokaw, OP (1843-45), a portrait painter and daguerreotypist in Oberlin, served briefly as town mayor.
5. Asa Mahan was then Oberlin president, professor of philosophy, and associate professor of theology.
6. Peter Moyers died October 17, 1847.
7. Sarah Fairfield (1825-96), OL (1848), taught in Ohio and Michigan until her marriage in 1850 to Nathan S. Burton, a minister. In 1859 she helped found the Young Ladies' Institute at Granville, Ohio, and served as its principal 1859-61.
8. Susan Allen Wright, OL 1843, with her husband, William, helped supervise the Ladies' Boarding Hall.
9. James Harris Fairchild (1817-1902), OC 1838, OS 1841, taught languages, mathematics, natural philosophy, and theology and served as president of Oberlin College 1866-89. He wrote on theology, philosophy, and the history of Oberlin. In 1841 Fairchild married Mary F. Kellogg, OC (1837-38), one of the first four women to enroll in Oberlin's regular College course.
10. Sallie Holley (1818-93), OL 1851, abolitionist, educator, and woman's rights supporter, lectured regularly for the AASS. After the Civil War, with Caroline Putnam, OL (1848-51), she operated a school for ex-slaves in Northumberland, Va.
11. Despite this expulsion, French was later listed as an 1847 graduate of the College course, which suggests her violation was a minor one.

[Henrietta, late Winter 1848]

Dear Lucy

Streter[1] & I have been haveing a talk about womans right to public labors, — *speaking* in particular. He is a queer sort of a man more like Prof. Morgan[2] than any one else I can think of, but more genteel in his manners. He believes women have a right to speak in public [g]atherings that is social meetings, prayer meetings &C, but that they have no right to preach & the thought of a womans being ordained or becoming a pastor over a church seemed to him perfectly absurd. When speaking of particular passages of scripture after hearing my interpretation he would sometimes give his own, but would almost always laugh & tell me I should get righted at Oberlin—that I was just beginning my Theological Course & he had just finished his—that we would wait, & have our discussion when I got through— that he thought we should not disagree so much then as now—that he hoped I would spend weeks & even years in investigating the subject & if I could then find my present views supported by the bible why very well. He seemed, & I think *was* glad to have women study Theology, said he thought they could make it of great use to them in their sphere of action &C. After all I like him better than any man I have ever talked with on the subject who did not believe with us. Indeed I can hardly find any one to *talk with*. Some of them cant talk, & some of them wont talk on this question.

Associated as I have been this winter frequently with ministers I have not found one who has been both ready & willing to talk about the matter candely. The Baptist Elder in town has however promised to do so & I think is both willing & anxious for an examination of the subject. He says he has not canvassed the matter sufficient to know how to reconcile all the bible teachings but he is very favorable to womans *rights* & *duties*. He lives near us & I am going over in a few days to compare bible, commentaries, & common sense. Brother Wm[3] seems half afraid to talk with me for fear of making me worse but has promised when he could get time to take up the subject & talk as long as I pleased. One day when he was over to fathers he had just got ready to commence when *Peck*[4] came up from Rochester. After a while he proposed to have Peck look at the matter with us. The Poor fellow knit his brows, & shugged his shoulders, & replied he should'nt like to get into an argument on *that* subject & so it all ended with a laugh, but I must do my brother the justice to say that he really has not had time since for he has been engaged almost night & day ever since.

I tell you Lucy when ministers will do that way it means something they have not examined the subject much themselves & some of them around here at least, begin to feel a little uneasy at their old position, & are not *quite ready* to advocate that, nor *quite ready* to get a new standing point. I have a grand chance to bring the subject in in some form, almost every time I meet an old friend or a stranger, for generally the first question after finding out what I am studying is "Are you going to preach—be a minister—a public lectureer["] &C &C or else such remarks as "You can write sermons for your brother—or your husband["] or something else of the sort & so the subject comes in without dragging. Sometimes they warn me not to be a Fanny Wright[5] man, sometimes believe I am joking sometimes stare at me with amazement & sometimes seem to start back with a kind of horror. Men & women are about equal & seem to have their eyes opened & tongues loosed to about the same extent. A while ago the teacher of the academy[6] began to talk on the subject. He scowles enough at any time but now his face was twisted into a thousand shapes, & after we had got about half a dozen items of each others views the matter all died away a quietly as the evening twilight.

The scholars have been haveing discussions in the papers of their societies all winter on Womans right to vote. My sister Guss advocating the affirmative.

Nette

ALS-SL

1. Sereno Wright Streeter (1810-80), OC 1836, served as an antislavery agent and preacher in Ohio until 1848, when he settled in Henrietta, N.Y., to replace William Brown as minister of the Congregational Church.

2. John Morgan (1803-84), antislavery activist and minister, served on the faculty of Lane Seminary until he was dismissed in 1835 for supporting students who demanded to hold antislavery debates. He then moved to Oberlin, where he was professor of New Testament literature.

3. William B. Brown (1817-1902), OS 1841, ALB's elder brother, was pastor of the Congregational Church in Henrietta, N.Y., 1846-49, and later held pastorates in Sandusky, Ohio, Andover, Mass., and Newark, N.J. He wrote extensively on religious topics.

4. Henry E. Peck (1821-67), OS 1845, engaged in pastoral work in Rochester, N.Y., until returning to Oberlin in 1852 as professor of sacred rhetoric and associate in philosophy. In 1865 he was appointed U.S. minister to Haiti, where he died of yellow fever.

5. Frances Wright (1795-1852) was a British-born writer, lecturer, and reformer whose radical ideas on education for women and blacks often led to accusations that she stood for atheism and free love.

6. The Monroe Academy was a private secondary school in Henrietta, N.Y.

Henrietta, March 28th '48

Dearest Lucy

Here I am still in Henrietta. I presume you are aware of this for
Sarah is a better correspondent than I am; but after all Lucy she
does'nt love you any better nor *half as well*. I have been actually
haunted with duties labors & responsibilities ever since leaving Oberlin.

I talked about comeing home to rest but have never worked harder
a 4 months in the world, so you will not believe I have at all forgotten
you or loved you any less than I used to. You do not believe that I
know, for you know me too well to believe I can ever forget my
friends *such* a friend as *you are* at least, for though you dont know
how much I loved you you do know that I did love you a great deal
for I remember your telling me I *could n't help it if I tried.* This was
partly true in spite of my theory & yet it supports the theory after
all. We believed no more things in common than any other of my
classmates, perhaps *not as many* & yet I loved you more than all
the rest together. You say you laughed over what I wrote you, & so
did I when writing it but I dont know what it was for I believe I
did'nt read it over. But I think it was the truth & after all not very
far from a "golden mene."

Would you like a summary of the principle events that have taken
place in our family & community since I wrote you. You shall have
it & you must of course return as full an account of every thing
which interests *you.*

Several weeks since my brother went to Troy spent two sabbaths
& on his return commenced a series of meetings which continued
nearly every evening & sometimes in the afternoon, for anumber of
weeks. The degree of religious interest in the community had seemed
to demand such an effort for some time, & the result proved the
wisdom of making it at that time. The meetings were still, & solemn,
with almost no apparent excitement, & yet deeply interesting, — a
kind of interest which truth always produces when it is held up
steadily before the eye of the mind & examined intelligently.

Numbers were hopefully converted from *selfishness* to *benevolence,*
& though there have been no more than the usual meetings for the
last three weeks, a healthful state of feeling seems to exist here &
every few days some lingering one professes to have been "born
again."

I dont know whether you have any sympathy with these things or
not but dear Lucy if you had been here sometimes you would have
felt that it was good for true christians to meet together for week

after week when circumstances demanded it to promote *genuine revivals* of *pure religion,* & you would have felt too that the churches were not *all* corrupt: for *God was here.* My two youngest sisters were among the number who feel that they are changed, & indeed they are changed if we can judge from appearances. They have both united with the church but they have no sympathy with the "brotherhood of thieves"[1] nor I either. You are bound to believe us. Do you. Ha ha

Well L. we will not quarrel now after talking this matter over so often will we. I wish we could see alike but if we cannot let us both believe & examine our beliefs candedly & then look forward to the time when we shall see "eye to eye."

Walker & Jacobs[2] were here about 4 weeks ago talking on Anti slavery. I did not hear them but they were liked very much. About a week afterwards Douglas[3] & Remond[4] came. They talked one evening & the next afternoon at East Henrietta & then went to the west village. They did not touch the question of the Constitution but Douglas handled the church a little; but he only talked of slave-holding churches & such bodies as held direct fellowship with them.[5] He talked plainly about the Methodists which made the good minister *twist* a little; but as most of those present believed that [*torn*] such connection with slavery or its advocates as would at all [*sa*]nction their guilt, was to become equally guilty, & [*torn*] made no effort to prove that *many* of our northern churches did hold any such con-nection, there was not a great deal of discussion. My brother made a little bit of reply to some few points (most of them Douglas' positions) & Remond made a bit of areply, & then followed two or three other "one words" more by one or two others, & themselves, & if there had been time they might have got a little bit by the ears. But they did not & we parted proud of a meeting where people believing differently could meet together & not quarrel. If they would only use some epithet to distinguish between true *christianity* & its *counterfeit* & not violate terms which are in almost every mind sacred, they might denounce or mimic to their hearts content both the slaveholder & the slaveholders religion, &, if done in the spirit they manifested here, I would say Amen. So would the mass of all who here them, but when they will th[us] violate a proper feeling of reverence, & refuse to distinguish between things which differ, the mass at least must feel an *over* amount of prejudice. If public teachers will not discriminate how can they expect their hearers to do so. But enough of this.

My brother left this place for Troy last Thursday. Mr Streter of

Austinburg[6] arrived here the day before to supply his place. He preached us two good sermons last sabbath & we all like him. There was an amount of feeling at Wm's leaving that we had none of us dreamed of, & if he had realized how the people felt before he engaged to leave he would not have engaded to go to Troy, but after all I think it was for the best.

Prof. Morgan wrote br W[m] a strange letter a while ago designed I suppose for my special benefit. He first assumed that if women lectured in public then the male & female mind must be egsactly alike, & then went on to talk about lillies & roses, willows & oaks, men & women, &c & finally closed by saying, "If Antoinette will be a Mrs Sigourny, a Mrs Ellis or a Mrs Ingraham,[7] I will say Amen most hartely, but if she tries to be a Finney or a Webster[8] I must say Alas." "I hope she has too much sense to choose the latter course"— My brother had written to him to inquire what they would study for a month or two this spring, & this was a part of his answer.

For all this I like Prof. Morgan he is honest & I dont wonder at his conclusions when looking at his premises—I start for O. next week with Agusta. The ladies board will not admit Elly on account of her age.[9] Bad roads & a multitude of other things prevented my returning at the opening of the term but I shall loose only about 5 weeks & have been studying some at home besides.

I have been examm[in]ing the bible position of women a good deal this winter—reading various commentaries comparing them with each other & with the bible, & hunting up every passage in the scriptures that have any bearing on the subject either near or remote. My mind grow stronger & firmer on the subject & the light comes b[ea]ming in, full of promise. Lately I have been writing out my thoughts to see if they will all hang together but have not finished yet. It is a hard subject & takes a long time to see through it doesn't it. But "no cross no crown." You have seen the account of Miss Blackwell.[10] It was a noble step was n't it. Truly the watchmen *do* bring "glad tidings" & there *is* a "good time coming." Write & tell me everything wont you. Direct to Oberlin & send as quick as you can. You will not wonder I have not written sooner when you know how busy I have been, I attended meetings about half the time. Should not have gone as much under the circumstances but for the example sake though I should like to have been there all this time. After these closed my br. was packing & fixing for moving, then father rented his farm for two years & we had to give up part of the house & move the things & they are not all moved yet though the family come in in a day or two. We are so glad father & mother are released from the care of the farm.

We have had a fine Common School Celebration. Half the town were assembled together. The Academy e[xhibi]tions came off last Thursday & Friday. The ladies read prize essays. My Sister Guss took the prize—The Influenza is around here very hard. My father & mother are both sick with it & they have all had colds but me. We feel quite alarmed about father in particular & mother too.

You remember the money I told you about. It was stolen by the girl who took also a watch ring & other things. We had strange times with her in making her own it after we had found some of the things she carried off.

Someone says we always take pains in writing to any one we love but you will not think it a rule will you. I love you well enough if I do write badly.

[Antoinette Brown]

AL-SL

1. Following publication of Stephen S. Foster's *Brotherhood of Thieves: Or a True Picture of the American Church and Clergy* (Boston, 1843), abolitionists used this phrase to describe clergymen who did not make strong antislavery commitments.

2. Captain Jonathan Walker and John S. Jacobs, lecturers for the AASS, spoke in Henrietta on February 27, 1848.

3. Frederick Douglass (1817-95), black abolitionist, orator, and journalist, lectured for the Massachusetts Anti-Slavery Society (MASS) 1841-45 and in 1847 founded the weekly antislavery newspaper the *North Star.*

4. Charles Lenox Remond (1810-72), black abolitionist and orator, lectured for the MASS.

5. Abolitionists debated whether the Constitution could be interpreted as an antislavery document; they also argued about whether the church should extend fellowship to slaveholders.

6. Sereno Streeter had been pastor of the Congregational Church in Austinburg, Ohio.

7. Lydia Sigourney (1791-1865), American sentimental writer, and Sarah Stickney Ellis (1812-72), English missionary wife, wrote for largely female audiences. Their books addressed moral, religious, and domestic issues. Sarah R. Ingraham wrote the popular religious book *Walks of Usefulness among the Sinning and Sorrowful* (New York, 1843), which was published for the American Moral Reform Society.

8. Daniel Webster (1782-1852), statesman, congressman, and senator, was the outstanding orator for the Whig party.

9. The Oberlin Female Department required students to be at least sixteen years old for admission; Ella Brown was then only fourteen.

10. Elizabeth Blackwell (1821-1910), the first woman to graduate from a regular medical school, received her degree from the Medical Institution of Geneva College in western New York State in 1849. After further study in Paris and London, she opened with her sister Emily a private dispensary in New York City that became known as the New York Infirmary for Women and Children. Her brothers' marriages later made her a sister-in-law of LS and ALBB.

[Oberlin, June 1848]

Lucy Dearest

James & Sarah[1] have each handed me a note to inclose for you & now I am going to take just as much paper as I can & not make the package over weigh & write it just as thick as I can & not trouble you too much to read it.

Perhaps you will almost wonder at this when you think of the short & far between little notes that you have condescended to send me lately. Do you not stand self convicted on this point Lucy, & do you not think my forebodings of last fall may possibly be realized that you may yet cease to write from your heart. But no Lucy, dearest dear Lucy I do not believe this. I know if you were here now you would talk with me just as you used to & that you will write so too the next letter if you are not too busy. But somehow that last letter did seem to me to be just such a one as I often write to an *acquaintance* with whom *concience* & *custom* compells me to correspond. It had no soul in it & was just a statement of facts & incidents, cold & brief without any circumstances of interest connected with them.

But Lucy I dont know why I am writing in this way. It is not because I feel so for my heart has just been called back to the time when we used to sit with our arms around each other at the sunset hour & talk & talk of our friends & our homes & of ten thousand subjects of mutual interest till both our hearts felt warmer & lighter for the pure communion of spirit. Lucina Strong[2] was in here & we were talking of you, & when I looked out upon the airy floating clouds that we have watched so often together my heart was full & I would have cried for the visions of the past only I knew there would be no one here to sympathize with such tears as these. And so I have crushed them all back into my heart & have begun to write you but I can hardly banish the train of thought or rather feelings in which I am plunged & speak of subjects which will interest you more. But why need I banish them. It will do my heart good to speak its feelings

& you will love me no less to feel that my love towards you is all
unchanged. But I am changed & am changing constantly not in looks
or actions perhaps though my classmates sometimes remind me that
I am getting to look very grave & serious & hardly act like myself.
The other day Jane Penfield was here & a number of us were together
& they all joined in telling her how sober I was getting by studying
Theology & I could only defend myself by telling them if they could
convince me of looking sober they could not make me believe that
I had felt unhappy for this was not so & it is not so. I have never
been happyer in the world than for the last few months but it is a
new kind of happiness & I have kept it all buried up in my own
heart & shared it with no one. If you had been here it would not
have been so & it shal[l]not be now. You may look into the depts
of my soul but you must never reveal what you see not even to [*two
words blacked out*][3] will you, ha ha.

After you left here you know how the ladies board thought of me
& of my being prevented from teaching in the institution. Those
were dark weeks. I felt that I ought to study but had not a penny
of money nor any means of obtaining any except by working at 3
cents an hour or going away to teach. To add to my trials I took a
severe cold which lasted many weeks attended with a hard cough.
You knew about it, & Sarah attributed it to my not wearing wrappers
&c but all the wrappers in the world could not have prevented me
from taking cold while I was constantly exposing myself to the damp
air in such a state of mind. She knew nothing of this for I never
made her a confident. It could not be for we are not alike. I do not
mean she did not know of the circumstances but that she did not
know of my feelings. At last you know I decided to stay here & as
I told you "trust providence" for assistance & Lucy Providence has
assisted me. I learned then to cast myself on the Lord as I had never
done before & I learned to pray to him as I had never prayed before.
Perhaps you will think me superstitious but I have learned to talk
with God as I would talk with a friend & I feel that to have his
sympathy is all I need. You know we used to wish some times that
we could live on & feel no need of the sympathy of any one & I
have learned to feel so. I do not mean that I do not wish for sympathy
but I can feel perfectly happy without it, & when any thing troubles
me I can tell it all to God & he certainly does comfort me even in
the most trifling griefs, & see how he has helped me in pecuniarary
matters. Last fall I left here in debt more than 10 dollars & my
friends at home had assisted me to learn portrait painting beside all
they give me [*illegible word*] when I came from home at first. But

I painted all winter & so that was an equal exchange. In the spring
my brother told me he would let me have money enough to complete
my studies with. If I could find no method of earning it readily &
I might pay him when I get through, this was enough to make me
feel at rest on the point at least & I received from him a considerable
sum but since I came here I commenced a class in perspective
drawing. Last fall, I was ready to teach at 18 pence an hour & there
was a prospect of a small class at that but this spring I raised the
price to a dollar for 40 lessons & went on perfectly independent of
the institution. The class was full & I earned 20 dol in 8 weeks, 50
cts an hour. Another class, has now been continued for a week &
this is filled to overflowing so that we have had to bring additional
seats into the assembly room & I shall have earned enough by commencement to carry me through the whole winter for I expect to
remain here & study. Whatever you may think of this I certainly
regard it as a favor directly from the hand of God & I have no fear
now either of being unable to sustain myself during my studies or
of not being able to *talk* or do any thing else that seems duty when
I am through my studies.———

The cause of woman is moving on finely here. You know the
Theological students are all required to tell their religious experience
before Prof Finney. Once or twice when he called for those who
already had not done so Teft mentioned Lettice & I. Once he looked
as though he did not know what to say & the next time said "O we
dont call upon the ladies." They had all told me we should have to
speak & I felt so badly at what he said that I just began to cry &
was obliged to leave the room. It was the first & last time that I have
cried about any thing connected with this matter this spring but it
came so unexpectedly. After I went out they talked over the matter
& it seems Prof Finney did not know we were members of the
department in any other sense than the other ladies are who go in
to hear the lectures. You know he was sick last fall & we are not in
his classes 'till commencement so he really did not know about it.
He said he was willing any lady should speak if she wished to & If
we were members of the department he should like to know it &
know about it. I went over to see him & he certainly seemed to
forget that he was talking with a woman. We conversed more than
an hour sometimes upon the gravest subjects of Philosophy & Theology & he expressed himself freely upon the true position of women.
Said he did not care how much she was educated that her education
had been fundamentally wrong—that though he did not think she
was generally called upon to preach or speak in public because the

circumstances did not demand it still that there was nothing right
or wrong in the thing itself & that sometimes she was specially called
to speak—that he would not only permit us to take part in every
exercise in his classes but would aid & encourage us in doing so &c.
&c. But he said that Prof Morgan told him he thought every teacher
ought to have the right to decide what exercises the ladies should
take part in in their own classes & that he had consciencious scruples
in refference to our delivering orations & preaching sermons. So the
matter stood & each teacher was to decide for himself. A week or
two after Prof Finney called upon me to speak in the prayer meeting
& did so. Told them the exercises of my mind particularly in reference
to this subject & my determination to preach & speak in public when
I was prepared for this. They all seemed surprised & pleased too at
my speaking my views so plainly & surprised too that I was really
expecting to speak. Last week Prof Finney came along after the
meeting & told me he should like to have me take part in the prayer
meetings at any time. Lettice says she shall relate her religious experience but she has not done so yet. Mr Finney insisted upon Miss
Atkins talking at the next meeting one day when she was at his house.
She told him she would do so if she was a member of the department
but did not wish to now.

    Lettice has never taken part in the Litterary society.[4] She says she
has not time but I have had an exercise in discussion orations &
essays. They talked & talked about preventing me but at last let it
go. Prof Morgan said if he was the teacher he would not let me
sustain any other relation to the department than the ladies to the
college classes i.e. he would have no discussion or declamation from
ladies but as it was a society the members had a right to say what
I might do & they were too evenly divided to prevent me from
speakin[g]. He said he respected me none the less for my views—
that he would not critticise me any more severely than he would if
I were a gentleman. His remarks were kind notwithstanding his
strange "Conscience" & he has been in all respects very careful to
say nothing to wound my feelings. A great many little incidents ocur
that are full of interest but it takes so long to write them. The ladies
pray in the drawing classes & it begins to seem all right but at first
many of them whould whisper "I shouldnt think she would do that"
if I prayed myself or if I called on some lady they thought it was
[recess] using them almost but I always obtained the consent of the
lady before speaking to her in the class & then as no one ever hesitated
when called upon they began to think it must be right. So this ball
is rooling steadily steadily steadily. Lettice & I may have every priv-

ilege now promised us except delivering our own sermons. We have
nothing to do with that this year & though Prof Morgan says no;
we shall not do it he may change his mind or rather his *consience*
before then.

They have appointed the married Wadsworth[5] & I each to write
an essay on the 14 of 1 Cor. 34.35, & 1 Tim 2 11.12.[6]

How I do wish Lettice would take part in these exercises. She does
well in her studies but she has no confidence in herself & she never
talks at all in the class except when it comes her turn. Some of the
people here declare she is enceinte[7] & I am half tempted to believe
it but she denies it flatly. It will be too bad if it is so but a good
many would rejoice. Dont speak of it to any one.

Mr Cushman is in this country. Will be at Oberlin in a few weeks
& Jose leaves with him for Hayti in Aug.[8]

My sister Agusta is sick — not down sick but she has a hard cough
& is not able to study. I fear she will never be entirely well again
you know her health has been poor for a year. She is very anxious
to study & is doing well or was till now. She reads Compositions
with Sarah Pellet & you know they are haveing discussion in that
class. Sarah has told you about it I suppose. Guss was much interested
in them but what she can do now I dont know. She may have to go
home. I feel an anxiety about her that I cannot express for I was the
means of bringing her here yet I am glad she came even if she has
to return. You will begin to wonder dear L what wonderful secrets
I have communicated to you that must not be told to even your best
friend. I have wandered away from what I began to say & may
possibly return to it when I take up my pen in the morning.

                                              Henrietta June 28, 1848
Lucy you will be surprised to see the date of this last page is
Henrietta but here I am at home in the "old stone mansion." My
sister grew rapidly worse & I dared not let her remain at Oberlin
any longer. She could not travel alone & there was no one I knew
of going East so I have come home with her. She is fatigued with
the journey but is so excited now that she feels better than when she
started. When we reached home we found *Mother* sick with a kind
of intermitting fever. She is very weak but sits up part of the time.
We did not know she was sick though she has been down for two
or three weeks & I presume she has worried about it. We hope Mother
will be *better soon.* If they are all well enough they will take a journey
East after harvest.

O Lucy it is hard to have our friends afflicted. My heart feels sad to day. My Mother is trying to sleep & the "girls" are ta[l]king together so I am left to wander about where I please. I have just been into the garden & out down under a cherry tree & cried. How I should like to see you now but it cannot be. I expect to return to Oberlin next Thursday if Mother is better. Agusta is able to be around some & I shall not stay on her account now but shall come at Commencement[9] or in the fall is she is worse. It will be hard to return to O. under such circumstances & probably people will wonder at my doing so bu[t] dear L you can tell how I would feel under the circumstances. Inclination must be sacrificed to duty. It will be very doubtful now whether I remain there through the winter & study as I intended but it will be all for the best.

While Gus was so sick I neglected finishing your letter & indeed entirely forg[ot] it till I was about ready to start home & then concluded to bring it along & mail it here. James & Sarah thought I had sent it & I did not tell them I had not. S. came to see us start & she said we shall have a letter from Lucy before y[ou] get back. I told her I hoped so. You will write immediately wont you. I was to blame for keeping this letter so long but you will forgive me. Dont wait days before you write after you get this. Dont please dont Lucy.

                                                                            Nette

So L you are going to lecturing are you.[10] Well you had better have told us so & not said *Perhaps*. Success to the Truth, & to you Dearest Lucy so far as you preach it & preach in the right spirit. I am glad you are going to lecture.

Do you think you shall teach with Kedzie.[11] If you do we shall see you shant we but you will never stop to teach if you commence talking. Be good Lucy be good & dont be afraid of any body but speak as though you had a right to.

ALS-SL

1. James Tefft and Sarah Pellet.
2. Lucina Strong (c.1823-1905), OL (1839-40; 1846-49), from Portage, N.Y., married Henry Mills in 1850.
3. The two words blacked out appear to be "Samuel Brooke." Brooke (1808-89) was an abolitionist lecturer and agent for the *Anti-Slavery Bugle* and *Liberator.* He frequently appeared with LS on antislavery speaking tours.
4. ALB was the only female member of the Theological Literary Society in the history of the organization.
5. Elijah M. Wadsworth (1815-99), OC 1846, OS 1849, married Clara

Battell in 1840. He was an architect and builder in Berlin, Wisc., 1852-57
and school superintendent 1857-68.

6. 1 Corinthians 14: 34-35 and 1 Timothy 2: 11-12. Both texts discuss
the religious status of women.

7. Lettice Smith and Thomas Holmes had been married eight months,
hence speculations about her possible pregnancy had arisen.

8. Josephine Penfield married Richards Cushman in Oberlin, July 20,
1848.

9. Commencement took place August 23, 1848.

10. LS began lecturing for the MASS in June 1848.

11. Classmates Robert Kedzie and Eliza Fairchild taught at the Rochester
Academy 1847-49. LS considered teaching there for a year to help repay
money borrowed from her family to pay her college expenses, but chose
to became an antislavery lecturer instead.

                                          [Oberlin, December 1848]
Dear Lucy.

Helen[1] called last evening & left the little note you sent in her
letter. Do not fear my getting married. I have neither opportunity
nor inclination at present to take such an irredeemable step & have
so little confidence in such a plan for either of us that I am glad to
respond most hartily to your emphatic *dont DONT DONT* & send
it back like an echo to your self. At the same time I am not prepared
to regret as you do the engagement of Mercy Loyd.[2] From what I
know of her it seems to me she will do as much good in that relation
as in any other & probably more. Certainly if she has a husband
worthy of herself there is no reason why this should not be so. She
would not lecture as you will or do any thing else which cannot be
much better accomplished by the aid & Sympathy of a husband.

How glad I am that you are going to lecture for the Womans Rights
Convention or Soc. rather.[3] Helen forgot to bring her letter last
evening so I have not seen it & dont know exactly what you are
intending to do, when, how, &C. but I am so happy to think you
will leave the antislavery field to the hundreds of others & labor for
the elevation of woman but do be careful & remember there are two
extremes & one glorious mene. Put your sandals from off your feet
& walk lightly for you will be treading on holy ground & yet walk
fearlessly for the God of Moses will be there to instruct you in regard
to what you must do. O Lucy if we will only hear his voice he will
surely teach us how to lead the people out from their cruel bondage

but without his assistance we can never effectually strike off the chains of prejudice ignorance & sin.

The town is now nearly closed here & then I shall commence examining various practice questions, reading, studying, &c. I feel as though I had never improved as much in a whole year as during the last 3 months. We are learning to take in comprehensive views of things, to see their bearing & relations & to turn them over in all possible ways & look at them in various lights. H[ave] such grand thoughts as we are haveing developed & the discipline of talking, discussing &c. I am in extecy half of the time. but after all this is a world of trials & I have plenty of them. Dont you. I do wish you had time & inclination to write me everything. Tell everything about your new society when do you commence lecturing with them. Would they employ me & let me believe as I do. O I expect to have to stand alone—all alone in the world. On what conditions, terms &c do you lecture & in what field. Do do come to Ohio. If we could have a visit of only 2 hours it would make my heart a year younger than it is, & my head much older no doubt—Sarah has been doing to much this summer but begins to see her fault so she will probably improve.

Miss Blachly is married to Dr Bradly.[4] Cox is engaged to Helen Cochron[5] & he has gone home to spend the winter. Write very soon wont you.

Your own sister
Nette

ALS-LC

1. Helen Cook.
2. Mercy Lloyd married Jesse Holmes December 15, 1848.
3. In late 1848 LS began to devote more public speaking time to woman's rights, lecturing on the topic five days a week, while continuing her work as an antislavery lecturer on weekends; no formal woman's rights society yet existed.
4. Sarah Blachly (1817-93), OC 1845, taught in Wisconsin before marrying Dan Bradley, a minister, in November 1848. The couple served as missionaries in Siam.
5. Jacob Dolson Cox (1828-1900), OC 1851, lawyer and antislavery politician, helped organize the Ohio Republican party and served in the state senate. He was a major general in the Civil War; governor of Ohio 1866-68; secretary of the interior 1869-70; and U.S. representative 1876-78.

Helen Finney Cochran (1828-1911), OL (1844-46), the eldest daughter of Charles and Lydia Finney, married William Cochran, a professor of philosophy at Oberlin, in 1846. He died the following year. On November 29, 1849, she married Jacob Dolson Cox.

[Oberlin] Feb 25th '49

Dearest Lucy

It is a beautiful morning warm & pleasant as Spring & about as muddy in the roads. I have just come in from a walk over to Sarah's room at Mr Hills.[1]

When I was passing along the board walk on Pleasant street I thought of our evening strolls together & your favorite quotation "how shall two walk together except they be agreed" sounds so naturally in my ear that I half looked around expecting you were beside me. Thoughts of you steal over me every time I walk that way particularly if it is evening & at no time is your memory brighter sweeter & dearer to me than then. O how glad I should be to have your arm around me & my arm around you & to walk with you again on that narrow plank even at the risk of slipping off into the mud.

Dear dear L. when shall I see you again & when shall we walk together & talk together as we used to. Will it be ever again—ever in this world or in the next. When will it be. Every one is beginning to ask when will Lucy Stone be here. They are anxious to hear you lecture. You would have a house full & overflowing. Sarah says the papers report you as haveing said [things] which you did not say & that you ought to have it publicly corrected.[2] I have not seen the paper & dont know what was stated there or in what respects you felt yourself misrepresented but one day Mr Wright was speaking about it & I told him that the public print did injustice to your statement & that you had corrected the matter in a letter to Sarah. He said he was glad it was a false report but that a private correction of the mistake for this place would not do—that it was a publicly asserted slander against the place & ought to be publicly corrected. I think so too in justice to yourself as well as to Oberlin for I find already that there is an idea creeping into the minds of many persons here that you are becoming bitter & denunciatory & it seems much of it to have arisen from misunderstanding on that one point. The people here love & respect you & so they will continue to do while you manifest a sweet noble spirit however much you may differ in sentiment but when you become like Mrs Foster[3] they will think of you as they do of her. O dear! Lucy *dont* imbibe her spirit or fall in with her manner for if you do one half of my love for you will be turned into pitty & you hate to be pittied you know. Yet I am sure your friends would all pitty you.

March 25 '49

Some one asked me the other day if I thought Lucy loved me as well as ever & I replied emphatically that I *knew* she did. I shall not ask you if that *is a truth of certain knowledge* for my own heart will answer. If my punctuality as a correspondent was the test of friendship or rather of love one might suppose it to decrease but if that *is* a test then I am surely becomeing a loveless being for I verily believe I have not written six letters in six months & all without the shadow of an excuse for appology till within the last few weeks when my eyes have been diseased in some way—a kind of contagious disease seems to be in the place here which I caught on my first arival. It is not at all severe & my eyes are nearly well again. This is why my letter is a month behind its earliest date. But dont think I have ceased to love every body—your self in particular. I believe my heart never was so full of love before but it is a love that scattereth & is concentrated on no *particular* object. I do love you dearest Lucy better than ever but I sometimes think of you just as I used to think of my brother Addy—that he was going wrong, all wrong & it makes me feel sad. You dont think it even right to pray that it is wicked & sinful for an enlightened mind at least, & is mockery to God. You dont believe in an overruling Providence.

Well Lucy say what you do believe candedly & honestly & believe with true honesty of heart & we'll all love you just as well but take care that you are not like those we read of in Hebrew yesterday "blind people that had eyes." How I do wish I could see you & talk with you but it cannot be now. You talk about cause & effect. I do believe that effect will always follow its cause but I believe also that a God to whom past present & future time is all present to whom eternity is an eternal now can so conditionat[e] certain blessings which he would bestow upon his children upon their asking, that, their asking in a proper state of mind is indispensebly necessary to obtaining. Why should we suppose that God has put in operation a certain chain of causes which must work out certain effects independent of other causes which may come in to modify the effect. This might have been Gods plan certainly so far as we know & again it certainly might not have been. We cannot affirm that there is any thing absurd in either supposition but since we are free moral agents we must be able in some way to affect our own destiny & why could not God in some sense conditionate his favors upon our own conduct. Nothing could be more natural or better fitted to make us feel the responsibility or right doing ourselves. Certainly there is that in prayer which prepares the recipient of a desired favor to receive it in a spirit which will benefit him. It seems to me that your error lies in supposing God at the beginning of time established a certain changeless order of things so far as his interference at least was concerned (for of course you dont make man a necesitated being) & now he has nothing to do but look on & see what is done & let holiness & sin work out their own consequences according to his changeless laws. This makes God a cold hearted lawgiver & not a benevolent father. It does away with the atonement of Christ & with every other feature of christianity. We have then no need of Holy Spirit & the bible is not an inspired book it is utter nonsense & the wickedest lie that was ever told. O Lucy weigh the matter well before you take such a stand. O I do want to see you. Our views were different enough when you were here but they are widening all the time & if you do believe as I have just supposed you did your God & mine are as different as our views & as far apart as the East from the West. This was not for surely dear dear L. this cannot be. I must have misinterpreted your views. Write & tell me what you do believe on those points.

But I must leave this subject now for there are other things to say & you are going to have so many letters in one or are all obliged to write but little.

Our class are all here & have been here ever since the term commenced with the exception of Thomas & Lettice.[4] We have spent the whole time in discussing the subject of the Trinity & have nearly finished on that question. All have regretted that Thomas was not here. He knew it was to be the first question & that we adjourned last fall leaving the question to come up in the Spring sooner than we should if he and others had not expected to leave soon & could not be here to hear the discussion. It has been deeply interesting & the amount of evidence in favor of the Trinity has seemed to me truly astonishing. Our next question will be the humanity of Christ.

Martha Rawson[5] is in town again she says give her love to Lucy tell her she has written several times & received no answer. She sprained her ankle in her journey homeward & has not been able to go out much since. Looks well & acts just as she always did.

Miss Gates[6] is our Principal now. Sh[e] is pleasant but very different from Miss A.[7] & I feel as though I had lost a good friend tried & true. Miss G. is only Assistant Principal & they will get some one else as soon as they can to fill this important office but I should not wonder if miss G. remained. She will doubtless do well.

The new Mrs Finney[8] is agreeable & affable. She comes to our recitations frequently & talks—i.e. makes remarks if she feels like it. The Proffesors are all kind to me & very careful not to injure my feelings but some of them like to tease me pretty well & Some of the people are still afraid of my influence.

I left Agusta with a bad cough. They said she might get well yet— that she might remain in the same state in which she now is for a long time or she might not live through the season but thought I had better come here at any rate it was so uncertain how she would. She thought I had better come but felt very bad to have me leave & I—you may [know] I felt for I cannot tell you. If she should be worse it is possible I might go home even now but I dont know.

The people in H[9] invited me to make them a "speech" on womans rights. So I did give a regular lecture to a crowded house & did not disgrace myself. Our folks agreed to every thing I said & were glad to have me speak. I did not think they would feel so.

Every one seemed pleased & urged me to stay & speak again in our own Church (the lecture was in the Baptist house near my fathers) offered to let me talk as much as I pleased. Some of your Garrisonian friends from Rochester were up & invited me to go down to R. & promised me one of the public halls & a full house but my things were allmost packed to start for O. the next Monday & it was then such fine going & there was so much prospect of muddy roads if I waited that we thought it best I should not stay. But I told them I should be at home again in a few months probably & then would talk for them.

You asked what about my falling downstairs. I walked off in the night in a fit of abstraction with all the dignity imaginable & found myself suddenly landed at the foot of the sitting room door. I struck my back but did not feel it till the next day when I was about unable to move & was shut up for two or three weeks that was one reason for my going home last winter. I needed rest & found it too for I did absolutely nothing all winter.

I thought you knew about it. It has nearly recovered but is rather weak yet & will not endure close study for a long time. Write immediately & then I will agree to answer in at least 4 days after I receive your letter.

> With much love your own sister
> Nette

Heman[10] was going to write you but has not done so I suppose because he thought you ought to have written him before. James Monroe[11] says give my love to Lucy & tell her I hope she will do well. You know he is now Prof. here. He says does she know I have two little ones! He seems very proud of them.

ALS-LC

1. Sarah Pellet then lived in the home of Hamilton Hill (1794-1870), secretary and treasurer of Oberlin 1841-64. He and his wife, Anna, moved to Oberlin from London in 1840.

2. On November 20, 1848, the *Liberator* printed a letter by Edward Morris of Cape Cod who reported that during a speech in North Dennis, LS ridiculed revivals of religion, Oberlin professors Charles Finney, Asa Mahan, Henry Cowles, "and indeed all I knew connected with Oberlin." A correction by LS appeared in the *Liberator* on April 3, 1849.

3. Abby Kelley Foster (1810-87) was a radical abolitionist lecturer and woman's rights activist. Married to radical reformer Stephen S. Foster (1809-81), she spoke twice along with her husband at Oberlin in 1846, where the couple's views were unpopular.

4. Thomas and Lettice Smith Holmes.

5. Martha Rawson (1825-1912), OC 1847, taught school until her marriage to George Congdon in October 1849. She later owned and managed a greenhouse in Oberlin.

6. Clarinda Gates (d. 1889), assistant principal of the Female Department in 1849, later married Gilbert S. Northrup.

7. Mary Atkins.

8. Elizabeth Ford Atkinson Finney (1799-1863) became Charles Finney's second wife in November 1848. The widow of a businessman, she was the founder and principal of the Atkinson Female Seminary in Rochester, N.Y. In Oberlin she served on the Ladies' Board of Managers 1851-63, and participated with Finney in his revivals in the United States and Great Britain.

9. Henrietta, N.Y.

10. Heman Bassett Hall (1823-1911), OC 1847, OS 1850, married Sophronia Brooks, OL (1844-46, 1849-50), in 1849; with her he served as a missionary in Jamaica for ten years. He later held pastorates in Ohio.

11. James Monroe (1821-98), OC 1846, OS 1848, lectured for the AASS before enrolling at Oberlin and subsequently served as professor of rhetoric and belles lettres 1849-62 and professor of political science and history 1884-96. His political career included terms in the Ohio house 1856-60, the Ohio senate 1861-63, and the U.S. House 1871-81; he was U.S. consul at Rio de Janeiro 1864-70. In 1847 he married Elizabeth Maxwell (1825-62), OL 1846, of Mansfield, Ohio; and in 1865 he married Julia R. Finney (1837-1930), OL (1852-53), daughter of Charles Finney.

[*West Brookfield, Mass., August 1849*][1]
No. 1

Dearest Nette

I am sending a lot of letters by Sarah, and it makes me feel heart sick to think how little can be said in them, when so much wishes to speak itself. This letter writing is a miserable way of communicating, after all, though I would not on any account be deprived of it. But when ones soul is full, and only a little sheet, to put it into, it is *so* aggravating. There are so many things I want to *say,* and *feel* with you, that I dont know where to begin — First I hope your brother Wm. will come east and settle in Westminster. It is in the association to which my brother[2] belongs, and the towns join. Of course you know I do not agree with all your brother's orthodoxy but then, he has some spirit of progress, and would have a great deal if he were not in clerical trammels.

My brother has had to battle alone with all the proslavery ministers of the Association, and it was through his agency the question was stirred this year in the Massachusetts General Association of continuing in fellowship with slaveholders. Our brothers would be mutual help to each other I think. I hope Wm. will come east, tho I have but little confidence in the good that can be accomplished by ministers, while they remain such, still if I have not mistaken Wm's character he will one day be a *man,* and not a minister in the common acceptation of that term, and his *visible growth,* by a "sympathetic emotion of virtue" will aid others. Besides Nette, if Wm. settles in Westminster, he will be only thirty miles from Brookfield and seven from Gardner where my brother and sister reside. And I *guess* you'd come to visit your brother, and if *we* would not visit too, it should be no fault of mine. O Nette when there are so many good reasons why he should come, wont you encourage him to do so.

I wonder if you have any idea how dreadfully I feel about your studying that old musty theology, which already has its grave clothes on, and is about to be buried, in so deep a grave that no resurrection trump can call it into being, and no Prophet voice, clothe its dry bones with *living* life? Even now, it prolongs its existence only by a kind of *galvanism.* The *quickening spirit* is *wanting.* The Centuries that are gone, "with outstretched arms," stand waiting to bury it in the deep darkness from which it came, while all the voices of the Ages that are beyond us, are saying "Give up" — ["]Give up" — The Great *Soul* of the Present, hungering and thirsting, for the bread and water of Life, falters by the wayside, finding no green pastures, or living fountains, that are not all polluted with the horrid stench which goes up from the decaying corpse of such a theology, with which Humanity, and God himself are weary. Yet *my own dear Nette* is spending *three* precious years of her life's young prime, wading through that deep slough, from the stain of which she can never wash herself, and by which I *fear,* her vision will be so clouded that she can only see *men* through *creeds,* while her ear, will only hear God's voice speaking in the *written* book, unconscious of the *unwritten* revelations so grand and glorious which stand out, in "living light" all over God's creation—Your *heart,* it cannot spoil I know, for God has made his own impress there so indelibly that it *cannot* be effaced. Your heart will *ever* feel after the heart of its fellows—to drop healing where sorrow's wounds are made,—to purify, where Crime's viper brood nestle—to cheer where adversity lowers—and to banish Hate by its Love—You have honesty & candor *now,* more than most others. I dread to see these noble qualities trimmed, and your generous soul belittled to the defence of an outgrown creed—O Nette it is intolerable and I can think of it with allowance only when I think that the loss of what is *invaluable* in *you* will purchase apparatus to batter down that *wall* of bible, brimstone, church and corruption, which has hitherto hemmed *women* into *nothingness*—The fact that you have entered a field forbidden to women, will be a good to the sex, but I half fear it will be purchased at too dear a rate. Sometimes I think that you will leave, Oberlin with the same *free spirit* with which you entered it, and blame myself for ever thinking otherwise, then it creeps over me again, like the cold sense of "coming ill," that you will be *only* a *sectarian,* and never dare to throw yourself out like "incense to the breeze", careful only that the healing fragrance shall be spread abroad—but you will have to be politic so as not to injure your *sect,* and to keep in, with your craft, and not losse caste with the clergy, (if you ever get it (!) which God grant you never may) &c. &c. &c. &c.

Now Nettee dear, do you think I am a monster? Wait forty years and see—Why Nette you would get as much discipline, in a thousand ways, with far less danger to yourself and you would learn more of the world, in one month, by *actual conflict* with it, than you possibly can in the three years you will spend there.

I am not crazy Nette, nor getting wild, and you must not think because I write as I do that I am any less your friend, or that I love you less than formerly. It is because we are *real* friends, and because I love you so much, that I speak so freely.

The idea is horrible to me, that you shall ever be in the predicament of the poor things I meet with almost every day, who dare not speak fearlessly, against the giant sins of the time, *because some of their church* would be implicated! And almost any where, let a clergyman speak boldly as his heart, and conscience prompt and how soon, he is ostracized, and so they go, dumb dogs. Nette I would far rather see you in the grave, for then I should know your spirit was free, than to see you the poor victim to *sect,* and *party.* But some good Angel will I hope guard you, from the *tendencies* around and enabled you to come out, like gold tried. You have been tried there, and the trial, has brought to light noble traits in your character, and I love you all the better for what you have so nobly suffered. But do keep a *free* spirit my dear dear Nette.

No. 2³

Dear Nette

I have written you one sheet full and have not *begun,* to say what I would if we could sit down as in days of "old lang syne," — or if we could sleep awake: Nette *dont DONT D-O-N-T,* when you "settle as a pastor" take any *children.* It will seem just like an old clucking hen, who shows her setting propensity, without having any eggs to the merriment of all the roosters, and the shame of all the hens. I would a great deal rather let you have one of *my* children to take care of you, when you are old. Not that I think you would not make as good children as *one, alone* can. indeed I think you would do far better than the majority with *two,* but the fact that God has made father's as well as mother's necessary to the *existence* of children, is conclusive evidence, to my mind, that the influence of *both* is *necessary* to their best development, and whatever comes out of your hands *ought* to be *best.*

I dont like the idea of your "settling"—I am afraid you will settle into just what other min[is]ter do. No not *just* what they are, for you will always be *more,* but I am afraid you will settle into something *less* than *you* ought to be. I tell you all that I do not like in your plans Nette. And you want me to dont you? for tho we may not *like* each others plans, we do *love* each other, and can speak just what we think without being so politic or afraid of giving offence. I can to you, and I guess you can to me. Nette I have not felt the influence of the prayers you were going to make for me. Have you been too busy to make them? I shall pray the *effectual* prayer for you, if free, plain dealing will accomplish any thing. Nette dont cling

to that chimera about prayer. Sarah will explain my view of it to
you, and it seems to me you cant fail to see its correctness. And
when you do, wont you own it to me?

Sarah and I wish the cholera would go to Oberlin a[*nd*] take off
quite a number. We regard it as a pious wish. Sarah will explain.[4] I
am glad Cushman is dead[5] i.e. I feel no war, with the "special Providence" which removed him. Josephine will be as much again of a
woman without him, as with him. I sympathize with her grief smitten,
desolate heart, — but his loss, — will be her gain. I should thought
more of her regard for the heathen there, if she had staid, after her
husband's death, and not left them to lie in their heathenism, and
burn in hell forever, as she believes. But she was young to be there
alone. She did nobly at his death.

It required a great deal of fortitude for her to go through the funeral
ceremonies — Josephine is a noble girl, and has the elements of real
greatness, and now that she is free, she may make something. You
must keep hold of your influence of her. What are you going to do
next winter? I wish you could spend it reading something on Womens
Rights. You ought to read Mandsfield's ["]Legal Rights of Women."[6]
It seems to me that *no* man who *deserved* the *name* of *MAN,* when
he knows what a *mere thing,* the law, makes a married woman, would
ever insult a woman, by asking her to marry. It is horrid to live
without the intimate companionship, and gentle loving influences
which are the constant attendant of a true love marriage — It is a
wretchedly unnatural way of living, but nothing is so bad as to be
made a *thing,* as every married woman now is, in the eye of Law.
Nette let us get down these laws, and then marry if we can. We could
do so much more good, in a natural, than in an unnatural position —
My heart aches to love somebody that shall be all its own. I have
not yet reached the place where I need no companionship as you
have. Do you think I am silly? Say so if you do: Dont give yourself
any uneasiness on my account, for I shall not be married ever. I
have not yet seen the person, whom I have the slightest wish to
marry, and if I had, it will take longer than my lifetime for the
obstacles to be removed, which are in the way of a married woman,
having any being of her own, and though it is sad and desolate to
live unmarried, it is *worse,* to be a *thing*—I mean to live and love,
all that is loveable, whether in men or women, and I will let them
know it too. I will talk with men as well women, on *all* subjects,
that pertain to the good of the race. Not with *all* men, nor with *all*
women, but with such as are of an "understanding heart" — Is'nt it
right that I should? I will every where, make *humanity MORE* than

women, but with such as are of an "understanding heart"—Is'nt it right that I should? I will every where, make *humanity MORE* than *sex,* and I will extort from those who look on, the acknowledgement that no animal or unworthy motive prompts me.

But I am giving you more than your share of letters perhaps, but then I love you most, so you can forgive most scribbling. But may be you are weary by this time, and I will stop. You had better burn these letters, before anyone unless it is Sarah, sees them, for to some they would be foolishness, and to others a stumbling block.

Take care of your back and not *think,* a great while at a time. I feel anxious about you, for you have not always been careful enough, but I will not blame you, for making no special effort, to keep from the bosom of the Father.

Sunday Aug. 19. Dearest Nette I have been almost two days alone! Father has gone for my Mother who is on a visit to my sister—They will be here tomorrow—I shall be glad to have them come, but I have been very happy all by myself, and today it is so still and quiet. I almost wish, it would *always* keep so. It reminds me of those early days, when I seemed to hold converse with the winds and find companions in the clouds. The blue of the sky is deeper, than its wont, and, moving slowly, like spirits, the clouds—vast masses of light, fringed with darkness, are stepping toward the sun, moved by those winged *messengers,* who show no *commission,* and who need none for they do *His* bidding, who holds them in His hand, and whose *right* to rule, heathen, and Christians alike, acknowledge— The day is calmly beautiful. The Wind, though it write no word, speaks to the souls in whispers as it passes on, and leaves its impress like the *shadow* of a *sigh.*—Such days now and then, come to sooth the spirit, and make it bend in meeker reverence to the Diety, teaching those lessons of quiet truthfulness, which in this world of falsehood, and turmoil, so often need to be repeated. I sat by my window today, admiring the beauty, and harmony with which the *inanimate* cr[e]ation conforms to its laws . . . half sad that man so disregards *his* laws. But then *Man,* even in his ruins is nobler than they. Take him up from his degradation,—wash him from his filth, and with reason en-throned, how truly it may be said of him, that he "wants but little from Angels." None need ask a nobler mission, than to *help* man, to be what God desidned he should be.

I shall send you a Liberator with the speeches of Phillips,[7] Theodore Parker,[8] (so spoken against at Oberlin) R. W. Emmerson,[9] Burleigh,[10] Follen.[11] I hope you will read them all, especially the three first mentioned—When I listen to so good speeches, I want *somebody*

by me, who can *feel* it with me—you understand. Nette dont you
remember how we laughed over Emmerson's Essays. Well, I see now,
a deep meaning, in almost every sentence. I read the same passages
over and over again, and some new beauty gleams out every time.
May be we will read it together again sometime, and we should find,
that what was before a *sealed book,* is now full of light, of beauty,
and of glorious truth. Emmerson found it difficult to speak, at the
meeting. The "spirit" seemed wanting, but he has been more accustomed to reading lectures prepared before hand.—But here I am
almost at the bottom of the last page of another sheet. Are you
provoked with me for taking so much of your time. I cant help it—
but I wont write again very soon, but I shall write a little more now
on another sheet.

Nette dont ever apologize when you write to me because it has
been so long since you wrote, for when you apologize, you add sin
to sin. If weeks, or months or years even intervene between your
letters dont make any excuse about it. Let me have a line that shows
your mind and heart truly, and tis all I ask.

No. 3[12]

Aug. 21 I have torn this sheet in two so as not to give you two long
letters. But if they should be too long, just dont read them now, but
put on an envelope to each, and drop them in the P.O., about three
months apart, and you will get new letters from me once in so often—
It is *four* months since you have written me. I am not finding fault
but stating a fact, which you would do well to take into *serious*
consideration. Is it a fact, that the course you are pursuing is robbing
you of your regard for human kind? or only, for *some* of the race?
O Nette how I do wish we could meet and talk, all that our hearts
want to so much, for notwithstanding some of the Oberlin friends
(?) query whether I love you as much as formerly, *YOU know.* and
I know to the contrary.

Just as I wrote the last word my brother put into my hand your
letter, of nameless date. O Nette how glad I was to get it, and how
eagerly I have read it, twice over and more than ever, I felt, how I
wish we *could* meet. But Nette dont dont pretend that you have no
need of human sympathy in the sense explained, and in which I
understood you at first. No doubt you feel so now but depend upon
it, tis only capping a heaving volcano. Your large social nature, with
the deep movings of your soul, were never designed to be all shut
up to yourself, and you do violence to the best department of your

being, when you make the attempt. Sure there are few, *very* few who can understand, and enter into the soul's holy of holies, but those few, or that human one, *is needed*. and any one is *better* who *shares* his souls holiest emotions, aye, and *stronger* too. I never had a friend like you Nette, to whom I wished to *trust everything,* and who could understand me. I had friends, who came into the "outer cour[t]." But into the *sanctum,* none but you ever went, and I do not feel more of "pain, than pleasure, on account of our previous intimacy." The sweet memories that cluster around it, and the knowledge that in the wide world *one* heart understands me, can *feel* what I feel, and sympathize with me, is an infinity of good to me. Is not our *soul* sympathy, an *eternal bond?* And is there not then a life-long bond, or tie, between us?

You say you are lively and cheerful, and laugh as loud as ever, and a great deal oftener. I remember you *used* to laugh most, when you was saddest, from the generous wish not to make others sad. Is it so now? I cant help feeling sorry that you wear artificials. You are not *small* enough for them, or they are not *large* enough for you. "Sed non disputandem de gustibus."[13] Your hair curls *naturally.* So I shall have no war about that. Indeed I think curls would be very becoming to you, and hope you will not think that it costs more than it is worth to look pretty.

If you will be politic as you say, it will be just the way I wish you to be—It is exactly my idea of *true policy*—Stick to it—Sarah and I have had good times. She will tell you just what she thinks about me, she will tell you too, of my father and mother, as she became very well acquainted with them, while spending a few days here. She will tell you too, about my hilly, rocky, home. I dont mean she shall keep you from your lessons to talk of me and mine, but sometimes between sundown and dark and when old memories are stirred. She will love to tell, and you will love to hear. I hope to see her once more before she goes West. May be she wont go so soon as she expected on account of the cholera,[14] though she said she should not wait. She dont think she should have the cholera, as her mission is not yet complete. May be too she believes in special Providences— I am sorry about Augusta. I loved her and hoped good to the race from her talents, but she will die. It is not the perfection of the Almighty's plan, when the young die. This being, I mean its mechanism, was manifestly designed to continue three score years and ten, and I always feel a painful sense of *incompleteness,* when it fails

before its ti[*m*]e. The soul, in so short a time, cannot attain the
growth desirable before it goes to the Spirit land.—

[Lucy Stone]

AL-LC

1. A later hand has added incorrectly "undated (early) 1850." Internal
evidence indicates this letter was part of a series of three letters written in
August 1849.
2. William Bowman Stone (1811-90) graduated from Amherst College
in 1839 and studied theology until his ordination in 1842. An outspoken
abolitionist, he was pastor of the Evangelical Congregational Church at
Gardner, Mass., until 1850, when he returned to the Stone homestead in
West Brookfield to farm. He served on the West Brookfield school committee for thirty-five years and was elected state representative in 1873.
He married sequentially three sisters, Phoebe Robinson (1813-52), Sa-
mantha Robinson (1810-84), and Martha Robinson (1814-85).
3. A later hand incorrectly dated this portion of the letter as 1850 and
treated it as a separate document.
4. Sarah Pellet, a native of North Brookfield, visited LS before returning
to Oberlin for the fall term.
5. Richards Cushman died of typhoid fever June 9, 1849, in St. Marc,
Haiti, while serving as a missionary. Without assistance, Josephine Cushman performed his funeral service in French and arranged his burial.
6. Edward Deering Mansfield, *The Legal Rights, Liabilities and Duties
of Women* (Salem, Mass., 1845).
7. Wendell Phillips (1811-84), Boston abolitionist, woman's rights advocate, labor reformer, and orator, became a friend and supporter of LS.
His speech and those of the others whose names follow appeared in the
Liberator, Aug. 17, 1849.
8. Theodore Parker (1810-60), Boston-based abolitionist and controversial Unitarian clergyman, was disliked at Oberlin because of his transcen-
dental theology, which replaced biblical revelation by personal intuition
and direct experience.
9. Ralph Waldo Emerson (1803-82), transcendentalist, essayist, and poet,
moved to openly support abolitionism soon after LS heard this speech.
10. Charles Burleigh (1810-78) was a lawyer, Garrisonian lecturer, and
woman's rights supporter.
11. Charles Follen (1796-1840), born in Glessen, Germany, lectured on
jurisprudence and metaphysics in Switzerland; he came to the United States
in 1824 and taught German and ethics at Harvard until his dismissal in
1835 for antislavery activities. He then became a Unitarian minister.
12. Two later hands have added on this sheet, "1848-1850" and "LS
1849-8?" This sheet is clearly a continuation of the preceding letter.

13. LS has incorrectly written the Latin phrase meaning "There is no disputing about taste."

14. Cholera was reported through the Midwest in the summer of 1849.

Henrietta Dec. 28. 1849

Dearest Lucy

You have been expecting a letter from me I know and perhaps have almost given up expecting. But really I am not much to blame. At first I waited to hear the decision from Oberlin about my being admitted into the Institution[1] then engaged to teach in our Academy for the winter and had so short a time for preparations and so many new dresses to make (being destitute of old ones) that I waited till I should get to teaching then I felt so nearly sick and at last so quite sick that I could not write and now it is holidays and I am just recovering from a severe Influenza and nervous headache so I will have apologies and write you a long long letter. But where shall I direct it. I know nothing of your present location or what you are doing and so will direct to West Brookfield.

Your good kind long letter of nameless date for I have left it at the village and so cannot answer all your inquiries was received from Oberlin soon after I reached home in the fall. Sarah has perhaps told you that we started the same day she for Oberlin and I for Henrietta so I have not seen her since she left O. in the summer. How I do wish I could have visited with you as she did. Lucy why cant you come into this state this winter and so come to Henrietta. You may lecture here as much as you please and shall have a large audience attentive and intelligent. Besides some private learners or listeners one at least who will be glad to devote her time to you for no matter how long. Do come dearest L. *do DO DO.*

Are you lecturing this winter. I hope you are and for a new society and that you are doing much good—and having fine success every way. How I do wish I was doing something besides teaching this winter but the time has not come yet for me to do much as a public teacher.

I came home for Agustas sake and ought to remain here till Spring. She is a great deal better and we are really beginning to hope she may yet recover. Her health is better every way but her life is yet hanging upon a slender thread. We hope for her and with increasing confidence.

I shall teach only one term and am only a mile and a half from home. My situation is a pleasant one in many respects. I board in the Institution have my youngest sister for a roommate—a pleasant recitation room of my own opening into my room that is warm from [6] in the morning till 10 at night and is lighted in the evening by a large lamp suspended from the ceiling have the charge of a number of pleasant merry hearted girls from 14 to 22 years of age boarders; and teach classes principally of ladies but including some gentlemen. We have about 30 in the family and nearly 96 in the school. There is one large schoolroom for the whole school which is under the superintendence of the principal and recitation rooms for all the other teachers. One of my former playmates an old schoolmate many a day in these same Academy walls who graduated last fall from Dartmouth Is teacher of languages and some of the higher branches of mathematics we have a native French teacher a gentleman and a pleasant young lady who teaches music and drawing all boarders in the family and altogether it is quite pleasant. I teach Algebra Geometry Physiolog[y] Philosophy &C. &C. expect to have a class in Mahans Intellectual Philosophy but do not know but we shall take Ab [*blank in original*]. We have a class in French in the evening and I am learning to speak the language. It is better than studying at home and doing little or nothing as I am not now needed there to take care of my sister. My salary is 3 dollars per week and the privilege of learning French with several other privileges of teaching some kinds of painting and drawing on my own responsibility so that if I could feel strong and well I have no doubt I should be able to do a considerable towards discharging my debts or assisting myself in future. But Lucy I am almost sick this winter and as nervous as I can be almost. It must be a part of it at least occasioned by my fall. I say as little about it as possible for it makes my friends so anxious but I shall get to be as figety as can be if I am not careful so I have given up all hard thinking for the present and have very little to do with the subject of Womans Rights or any other exciting question. All I need is rest and no excitement and yet I never was so anxious to do something as now and there would be opportunities enough if I sought them.

Do you know anything about my thinking of applying to some other Theological Seminary for admition. I had concluded to do so if the way seemed prepared for this but although my friends would not oppose me in this and even favor it to some extent yet they see but little reason for my leaving O and are anxious to have me get through my studies. So they will not think it best to assist me to means and as I am anxious to get through studying also and am so very nervous already have about concluded not to spend any more time and strength for the sake of what might be gained by going to some other Institution. Besides it is so uncertain whether I could be admitted elsewhere and yet it would do good to make the application. But it is best as it is. You will not care I suppose you are so much opposed to my studying Theology so long. I am glad I have studied the discipline has been such as I could have obtained no where else even if that were the only advantage to be gained. Then it has made me better to contemplate those "great truths" and my heart feels larger and warmer. Oh I love that class of studies.

And you are afraid I am getting bigoted exclusive and narrow minded. No no I am not—I *am not* at any rate I think so. One thing is certain I am not afraid to act as my conscience dictates no matter what the world may think and Dearest Lucy I am not time-serving. I am not 'Politic' in the bad sense of that term. But what use is there in saying what one is when actions speak louder than words and at present I cant act in such a way at least as to vindicate myself. But dont think too hardly of me my dear sister "wait a bit" and see. I am going to tell you all about my plans on another sheet and you will not think me egotistical for writing them to *you*. My father and mother have gone to attend the funeral of an aunt who died suddenly a few days since with inflamation of the lungs. She and her husband died both in one week of the same disease. What a lonely house that must be. My poor cousins how much I sympathize with them. There are 4 daughters unmarried—all young ladies and a large family of other children. How could I bear to loose both my parents so suddenly. But the ways of God are mysterious and "He doeth all things well.["]

We have good sleighing now for a few days but it is beginning to disappear.

Oh A Happy New Year to you. A bright happy year from the first of January to the 31 of Dec inclusive. Write me as soon as you receive this for I am very anxious to know what you are doing this winter and how you are prospered and all about every thing you please to tell me. Tell me all about your plans for the future wont you in return for mine.

Ever your own
Nette

ALS-SL

1. ALB had reapplied for admission as a regular student to Oberlin's Theology Department, but the faculty again denied her request.

Henrietta Stone mansion almost 1850

My own dear Sister

I have just finished one sheet and now for another crowded full.
There are so many things to tell you! If you were here I could talk
continually for a week unless I should grow unspeakably happy in
your presence. We certainly ought to write oftener at least I ought
to write three times as often as I do for I forget what I want to say
or what I have said and my heart remains crowded full of things I
want to say and have no one to say them to. O if we could only
talk together as we used to. You wrote that you did not like the plan
of my adopting children, Sarah[1] told you about it I suppose.

It must seem strange to you without knowing all my other plans
or enough of them to make them harmonize. Well Lucy I am coming
to the confessional so have patience and remember that like all father
Confessors you are sworn to secrecy. I do not think with my tem-
perament health &c &c I can do as much good by giving up my
time exclusively to lecturing or preaching as I could by doing various
other things in connection with these. Besides much is to be accomplished in reforming the world by writing: more persons are accessable
by this means than by any other and it seems to me that almost any
one can accomplish more by both methods than by being confined
to either.

I know a person needs to be talented to write any thing which is
worth reading and yet the truth even if plainly told will produce an
effect and the novelty of many of my subjects will ensure a reading
for a time at least. Then I love to write and by taking great pains—
more than I have ever done yet, shall I do believe do passably well.
Then again I cant go wandering up and down in the earth without
any home. Not *cant* because it would require too much self denial,
but because I should get to excited and too downhearted from reaction
to accomplish any thing. Perhaps you will think this is all nonsense
but I do not think you quite know me yet and besides I am not
quite as I was two or three years ago. I need a pleasant happy home
to rest in and some pleasant happy children there to keep me from
becoming a misanthrope. Dear Lucy I do think we are in danger of
this: it is my greatest temptation and some times I almost feel as
though it did not good to try to make people better. They are wedded
to their idols and it would be a thankless task if doing good was not
"its own exceeding great reward." Then I find little sympathy in the
thoughtless aimless multitude and even thinking people have little
sympathy with my views and feelings and I really dare not *pray* to
be kept from a wrong spirit unless I make such efforts as common

prudence would dictate to enable me to overcome the evil. But give me a quiet home surrounded by trees and flowers and there I can worship God and love the world and can make as many and as long lecturing tours as seems best and go when and where Providence makes an opening. Besides I shall need a good reference library and many other things that home alone can furnish. Then with a good matron and a good housekeeper many a little ragged starving outcast would be glad to accept even such a retreat and though you say a child needs a fathers care yet he can better do without that than without the care of both father and mother and even if they sustained to me the relation of little brothers and sisters that would be far better for them than living in the world destitute of relatives.

But you will point next to the great additional responsibility arising from housekeeping. It will be great. I have counted the cost and tried to weigh it before deciding upon such a step. But I have found already to my cost that the mind cannot be employed constantly upon the same subjects without great injury to all its powers and a change of cares will do me good. My love of order is becoming more developed than formerly and though not remarkably good yet, as I intend to do most of the planning in household matters while others are to execute I have no doubt we shall have a very tidy well ordered establishment. It may be you will ask as some others have done why I cannot with great proffit and propriety take a *husband* into the establishment to assist in lightening my responsibilities. Well in the first place I could never expect to find a man who would sympathize with my feelings and acquiesce in my plans. And it would require nothing less than a miracle to make a man of talent and heart who would be willing to be a coworker in such efforts. 2nd we can do very well without the husband. Lastly such a personage would threaten the over throw of all or many of my arrangements or else the ma-trimonial alliance would have to be placed on a different basis from the common; and on the whole it is deemed entirely inexpedient.

Next I am always asked where I am to get *means* for carrying out all my plans. Well I have a rich father who can supply me with money enough if that is the only thing wanting without the least inconvenience to himself and since he is very wise and good I am sure he will assist me if it is for the best! if not why then I dont wish to succeed. But as it now seems best to me I have already picked out a building spot somewhere in the neighborhood of Cincinatti — a mile or so from the city. There are many things in favor of this location. The climate is good — it is on the borders of slavery and I believe the time has come for efficient missionary labor both with the slave and the slaveholder and that a woman can be more successful perhaps in that field than a man. It is a large and growing place full of crime and misery and there will be always *enough* at hand to do. It is a central location and is well connected with all parts of the country by rivers & railroads. It is a literary city—has good libraries and other means of improvement. In short it is in almost every respect a very disideratum of a location. So dear L. I am expecting to go to Cincinatti as soon as the necessary arrangements can be made probably next fall not to a permanent home at first and probably not for some years yet, but to the city to do good and get ready to do good as fast as I can.

I think now of leaving Oberlin as soon as vacation comes for the Theological services which will be some time in July. Perhaps visit at my brothers awhile if he is then in Sandusky and then go directly to C. where there will probably be some opening for earning a living.

Commencement will be little to me as I have no connection with the Institution and our class is miserably small at the best: though there will be a good College class. Indeed I may not go to O. at all. Prof F.[2] is now in England and may remain there. It is doubtful whether the Pres. will be at Oberlin next year and alltogether the prospect is not very flattering for the next season. But Prof Morgans Exegesis is invaluable and I suppose some one will take the place of any absent teachers. Prof. F. will doubtless return a year from Spring if not before. But enough of planning. They the plans may all be very far from being executed and I have no great partiality to them if I can find better ones. So write and tell me what you think. Suggest improvements or suggest new ones.

It is now late at night. I am writing in my sisters room. They are sleeping soundly. Guss. still breathes short and hard but she is so much better even in that respect we take courage.

O about my preaching last fall. I spoke only twice—had large and attentive audiences and was much encouraged[3]—was invited to send them word when I returned to O. in the Spring and they promised to come out after me any time and take me back again if I would go there and speak. I have written some since I came home have not spoken in public am teaching a large and interesting bible class—made some remarks by invitation at the reorganization of the sabbath school & bible classes. The cause of woman is progressing slowly and steadily here in town. There is not room to write how much I love you but it is a great deal.

Write Lucy very soon—a long long long letter—tell me every

thing and let us be sisters forever wont we. How I do wish I could hear from you to night. What *are* you doing?

In love
Nette

ALS-LC

1. A later hand has added "Pellet."
2. Charles Finney preached in Great Britain for eighteen months in 1849-50.
3. ALB gave her first sermon in a schoolhouse in Henrietta, Ohio, a small town about eight miles from Oberlin.

Oberlin [*late February 1850*]

Dearest Lucy

It is a fine pleasant afternoon just such an one as makes me think of you. Dear Lucy if you were here now in this pleasant little room in the old boarding hall why then — I dont know what would happen; but I believe I should sit down and cry for joy. Yes here we are in the same room that I occupied at the time I came from home with the artificials in my bonnet, and you came in and cried over me for sorrow. Dear dear L. I love you better for those tears than I should have done without them, and I have no artificials in my bonnet now; but am just as much determined as ever to think them pretty and may perhaps wear them again sometime, but not to tease you though. I said "we are in the same room," but poor room! it has almost lost its identity, through the abundance of paint, white wash, and paper till not a particle of its former brown countenance can be discovered. In a word the old boarding hall looks almost like a new one. Then under the administration of Treas. Hill and wife together with Mrs Hopkins our Principal[1] it is quite another place.

My Sister Ella is here with me and helps to account for the plural "we" used above. She is a good girl but has "fallen on evil times" as far as regards her studies here and is obliged to wait two or three weeks yet before she can go into any classes.[2] She is reading and studying with me but was crying half an hour ago and was almost inclined to wish she had never come to Oberlin. It has all gone now though, and a moment since she was laughing heartily at some thing she was reading.

Now Lucy where are you and what are you doing. Laying out your plan for the lecture this evening? Success to you. I'll fancy I hear you talking when the time comes; and perhaps some good spirit will bring some of your thoughts to my ears and I'll try if I can to distinguish them from my own musings. So take care what you say, for I dont want to attribute naughty thoughts to you. Are you a believer yet in the spiritual presences of living friends? Its a good doctrine, but I had rather believe in special Providences if as you think they will enable us to meet sometime within the year. Why can we not meet at O. It will seem like old times to us both and then you may take your degree at Commencement.[3] Do you not intend to do so. Do do do come. Sarah and I and all the rest of the *good* people — will wellcome you with hearts larger and warmer than ever.

Lucy I thank you for your present of the Liberator. I have read carefully every number but the last, and that will be forwarded to me from home. It contains many good things, some noble ones some sweet ones, and some *bitter* ones. The *refuge of oppression*[4] is exelent, and invaluable as a history of the times — a thermometer of the public pulse. The Editor certainly shows skill and tact in his selections and the hardest sayings are sure to find an antidote near at hand. Will you please send them now to Oberlin for notwithstanging all your "dont gos" I am here and will give my reasons for this hereafter.

How busy you must be in your lectures about congressional proceedings and how hopeful the times are. The world *is* going on to perfection and though the waters are turbid from agitation they will certainly settle to a calmer clearer purer state, than they have ever been in before Poor Daniel Webster.[5] W[m] Day[6] was too noble to be his *grandson* and it is better as it is.

You are informed doubtless that we are having some trouble about our *President* and *Principal* here.[7] H. Cook calls it all childs play but though it looks serious enough to me it seems not to be alarming.

Mrs Burk will never be Principal again. President is to remain and if the world is turned upside down it will be for good. — Helen has been quite sick and is far from well now. She is keeping house and seems to be quite comfortable there with her neice. You know I suppose that Hyman[8] is trying to weave his golden snares around her and in due time he will doubtless be successful — more so I suspect than his friend and ally Dan Cupid. I wish some of my good friends would give to her their allegiance to the *little blind God* and so become again "in maiden meditations fancy free" Ha ha! Do you agree with me?

"Dont go to Oberlin Nette" those words are ringing in my ears.

Thank you L. for your kind advice. I would have heeded it but suspected you did not know all the circumstances. First I was anxious to have my sister Ella come here and she probably would never have done so if I had not returned here this Spring. My Mother would never have consented to her coming alone. She is the baby and Agusta was taken sick here. By the way she is much better, so much that we now think she will recover if she is careful. It is the *cod liver* oil that has done it. Again Providence did not open the way for me to go elsewhere. I had neither money nor health for this year, and was anxious to get through studying that I might commence acting. There are but few months longer and I shall be greatly profited by them every way. Our studies have never been more interesting, Prof. F.[9] gone notwithstanding. We hope he will return soon.

What shall I do Lucy when my studies are finished. I dont like the idea of teaching at all and am some in debt for my education. Please suggest something if you can. May be I shall go to Cincinatti but what can I do there at first. Work for the Lord and he'll board you is Prof. Finneys motto and I believe it but I must work better than I have done if I shall have to get in debt for a part of it.

How glad I am that you are going to spend the summer at Providence and glader still that you are going to write. What do you think of Elisabeth Wilsons book.[10] I have not been able to obtain a copy. I searched Rochester over for one but they had not received any there at that time. Of course you do not care for her defence of the bible except so far as the influence upon community; but is it not hopeful to think a woman is the first to write upon that subject very extensively. She is old school I suppose in her views from some things she said in the Liberator.

You see dear L. I have made no appology for not writing you before. It is because I have no good one. Some of the time after writing you last I was teaching, some of the time quite sick some of the time resting and thinking absolutely nothing, some of the time waiting to know whether I should come to Oberlin this year or not and for the few days since arriving here waiting to get settled. All this time have not forgotten you but I do believe have kept loving you better and better at least I have thought of you more than usual not thinking of so many other things perhaps. Your letter and the *Paper* showed me you had not forgotten me either and as it came Valentines day I received it as friendships gift. It was very kind in you Lucy and I know I ought to have thanked you before.

Are you not getting 'worn and weary' by your labors. Do be careful of your mind and body both for I suspect you need more rest than you are disposed to give them.

If you will only come you shall be one of my children in Cincinatti the oldest too—mamas favorite you know.

O dear! Lucy I do wish we believed alike. I wish somebody believed as I do and some people are beginning to believe so; but then we'll "agree to disagree" as you used to say so often. Some people here do agree with me in sentiment near enough now, only we have no tasks and heart sympathies in common and it seems almost as bad as though we were Jews and Gentiles.

How I wish ladies would act and talk as sensibly as gentlemen no matter what they thought if they would think sense nor what they said if it had some meaning to it, but as it is I really like the "gentlemen" better than the 'ladies' and as Ella my sis, says "I half wish I was a boy so I could have somebody that I liked to talk with." Dont you feel just so when you are traveling about from place to place and see women so little interested; or do they think they must talk with you upon important subjects. I like Mrs Hill Mr Hill too that is they are kind pleasant sociable intelligent &c. I sit at this table you know. Mr Hill said once that if I wanted to be a man I should be one and go to Tappan Hall to room.[11] He does not talk so now maybe he thinks it though but I suspect he never knew either me or my sentiments and probably never will. No one hardly has patience and interest enough to learn at least the latter so they set up a straw man and quarrel with it and as it is neither me nor my effigy they beat it without affecting me at all. So I get along as nicely as you please. H. Cowles is sick, with consumption it is to be feared, her voice sounds badly.[12] She was engaged to Mr. Kendall[13]—What is Mrs Foster doing and what does she intend to do.

How many children has Lucretia Mott.[14] Please give me a brief sketch of her history. I have a particular use for it. Are her children intelligent respectable and well trained. How did she manage to bring them all up and still speak so much in public. If you can tell me a few things about her I shall be much obliged. I admire her character [as] far as I know it.

Elihu Burritt[15] will be here in a few weeks.

Sarah is going to write you too and enclose her letter with mine.

In much love ever
Your Sister
Nette

Dont give "Measure for Measure" but write immediately and You shall see I am grateful.

ALS-SL

1. Mary Sumner Hopkins (d. 1897) was the principal of the Female Department 1850-52.

2. ALB tutored her youngest sister, Ella, after she failed to meet entrance requirements for the Ladies' course.

3. OC graduates were eligible for a master of arts degree three years after graduation if they had pursued professional study or its equivalent during the period. LS did not receive an A.M. although her classmates Thomas and Lettice Smith Holmes did receive A.M. degrees in 1850 at the completion of their theological studies. However, Lettice Smith Holmes, like ALB, was not recognized as a graduate of the OS.

4. "The Refuge of Oppression," a regular column in the *Liberator,* reprinted articles from proslavery or antiabolitionist periodicals.

5. Webster incurred the wrath of abolitionists when he backed the Compromise of 1850, arguing that states had the right to regulate local institutions, including slavery.

6. William Howard Day (1825-1900), OC 1847, was a black abolitionist orator and editor.

7. An experienced and popular administrator, Emily Pillsbury Burke, principal of the Female Department, was dismissed by the board of trustees in April 1850 for giving a male student a kiss. President Mahan defended her although this undermined his already waning support among the faculty.

8. The Greek god of marriage.

9. Charles Finney.

10. Elizabeth Wilson, *A Spiritual View of Woman's Rights and Duties* (Philadelphia, 1849).

11. Tappan Hall contained dormitory accomodations for men.

12. Helen Cowles (1831-51), OL (1845-51), died in Oberlin of consumption on May 4, 1851.

13. Sewall Kendall (1823-53), OC 1850, OS 1853, from Litchfield, N.Y., died in Oberlin November 3, 1853.

14. Lucretia Mott (1793-1880) was a Philadelphia Quaker abolitionist, active in woman's rights and temperance. With Elizabeth Cady Stanton, she organized the first Woman's Rights Convention at Seneca Falls, N.Y., in 1848. She and her husband, James (1788-1868), an abolitionist and reformer, raised four children.

15. Elihu Burritt (1810-78) was a peace reformer and promoter of the free produce movement. In 1846 he formed the League of Universal Brotherhood to work for abstinence from all war. The peace movement and Burritt were very popular in Oberlin.

West Brookfield June 9 1850

My dear Nette,

It is Sunday. I have been worshipping all day on the hills around my Father's dwelling, with a good friend, from Boston, who is out to enjoy the beauty of the country. He is more ultra[1] than I am, but we agree in many opinions and feelings, and had a very very pleasant visit. I have learned to harmonize more readily than I used to, with those whose views differ widely from my own. I have met a great many honest people, who are real believers, in what to me, seems humbug and I love them, because they are sincere and live up to their highest hight. I have met others, who seem to me, ultra beyond reason; and I love them too, for their manifest integrity. So with the friend to day. After he left, and "the *dishes washed,*" I took up "Emmerson's Representative Man",[2] intending to have a feast of reason, and the first object that met my eye was *your last letter* shut up in it and Emmerson at once was excused for a visit with *you.* But Nette I am so sorry you are at Oberlin, on terms which to me seem *dishonorable.* They trampled your womanhood, and you did not spurn it. I do believe that even *they* would have thought better of you if you had staid away. O Nette, I am sorry you returned, but for all this, you *KNOW* I *love you dearly,* and will say no more about it. You are there, and it cant be helped. I shant ever take a second degree and regret, deeply regret that I ever took any. I should love to be in that same room with you, I dont know but it is possible that I may be. An iron necessity seems *compelling* me to Cincinnati this summer. And I shall, in that case go by Oberlin. There would be so many things to talk about, that there would be no time to cry, for joy or sorrow, tho' I am not certain that we should not do both. I should be so glad to see you. You say you wish we believed alike, but while it would be pleasant if we could, still it dont make much difference, while we have heart sympathies in common, and love each other so much. I am glad you read the Liberator carefully. If you could only have been at the anniversaries at N.Y. and Boston[3] it would have done your soul good—I love the Abolitionists better and better. It seems to me there is no class of people so free from selfishness, so really magnanimous. But you think that I am blinded— Now Nette I have a plan by which you can see for yourself whether what I say is so.

We are to have a Woman's Rights Convention in Worcester, next Oct. *We want you to be there to make a speech or two.* The Convention will pay your expenses from Henrietta to Worcester. You shall stop at my Fathers and make me a visit, and after the Convention, go to

Andover, and spend the winter with your brother, and *finish* your theology, and at the same time attend *some* of our Anti Slavery meetings, and become acquainted with *some* of our Abolitionists. Is not that a good plan? Now Nette wont you come to the Convention. It will be an important occasion. We *need all the women* who are accustomed to speak in public—every stick of timber, *that is sound.* I wrote to Lucretia Mott this morning, and to Elisabeth Jones[4] of Ohio to secure their presence. We want to know upon whom we can *rely.* In *old* times, it was not good to number the army, but it is necessary now. Please let me know as soon as you make up your mind. I expect to go to Providence in a few weeks, and shall have access to the Library of the Athaeneum. Twill be a grand opportunity to improve, but I expect to be interrupted by the necessity of going West.

I hope Helen Cook wont marry. Tis next to a chattel slave, to be a *legal* wife. Elisabeth Wilson reasons too much from the particular to the universal, but her work will meet the wants of a large class of persons who go to the Bible to know what is right. It does not find much sale among the Abolitionists who make all questions rest on their own merits. They buy it, if at all, for friends who need it. Garrison bought 50. If I go West I will carry you a copy. You ask after Lucretia Mott. She has four children, all of them intelligent, respectable, and proud of their mother. She is a Quaker and Quaker, men & women, preach, when the spirit moves. She preached while she was bringing up her family, being in perfect unity with her husband, who aided in the care of the children. She will, in all probability, be at Worcester. Come and get acquainted with her.

You apologize for not writing to me. Dont do it Nette. It seems as though we were not the same dear friends that we used to be, when you waded through mud and rain, after 9 o'clock P.M. for the sake of sleeping with me. If you should'nt ever write me, I should still *know,* that it is not because I am forgotten, then *dont* apologize. You ask if I am not worn and weary. I was, when I came home, three weeks ago, but am rested now, and as well as ever.

The Anti Slavery women I think are more intelligent than most women, at any rate they have *thought* more, and they talk good sense. Still many of them, are not accustomed to take comprehensive views, as men are. How long it will be before Women will even *begin,* to be what they ought to be. Still a great change is working, and the right *will come uppermost.* I dont now, ever wish that I was a man. Tis better as it is. I can do more to help elevate women.

Tell Sarah Pellet I thank her for the scrip she sent me, and shall look for her letter sometime. I am going to write Wm. Day soon. I hope Ella will learn so much, as to make your Mother glad that she sent her to Oberlin—Central College,[5] is in advance of Oberlin. It has a colored man, and white woman, filling, each, a professorship,[6] and there is *no* difference on account of sex. May be you will be Proff there some day. S. Broke[7] was here a week ago today. He expects to go to O. this summer, and said he should call on you. I told him about your back, and he thinks he can help it, by [palliation]. Wont you let him try. Twill do no harm. I feel anxious about your back. Do come east in Oct. dear Nette *do*. It is too late to write now, but if there is time in the morning, I will add a word. Give love to Sarah, Alonzo,[8] Ella, Mrs. Henry, Hellen, and kind regards to Mr. and Mrs. Hill.

Monday Morning

Nette dont pay postage when you write to me. Tell Sarah that Addison Merril, (Mrs Hodge's brother)[9] stopped over night at her fathers last Friday. He said they were well, Charlotte was not at home, nor any of the children except the two little ones. I believe Charlotte was with Anctis—My mother says she will be happy to welcome you to our house next fall when you come to the Convention, *do come Nette.*

I suppose you are washing, and I am just going to do the same. Love to Lettice and Thomas & Tefft. None of them write me.

Most affectionately

Lucy

Saw Adams,[10] and Miss Ingraham, Livingston[11] & Skinner[12] at Boston the other day. It was pleasant to meet them—. Saw Robert Gray and his wife[13] at N.Y.

ALS-LC

1. "Ultra" described radical come-outer principles.

2. Ralph Waldo Emerson, *Representative Men* (Boston, 1850).

3. The AASS celebrated its fifteenth anniversary in New York City in early May 1850. The New England ASS met in Boston in late May 1850.

4. Jane Elizabeth Hitchcock Jones (1813-96), abolitionist and woman's rights reformer, lectured in Ohio in the 1840s. From 1846 to 1849 she and her husband, Benjamin Jones, edited the *Anti-Slavery Bugle,* the official organ of the WASS.

5. New York Central College in McGrawville, N.Y., founded in 1849 by the American Free Mission Society, admitted men and women of both

races. It went bankrupt in 1858, was sold to Gerrit Smith, and reopened for a year before finally closing.

6. Charles Lewis Reason (1818-93) was professor of belles lettres, Greek, Latin, French, and mathematics at New York Central College 1849-50.

At least two women served on the faculty of Central College: Eliza M. Haven, who taught French, music, and drawing; and Sophia Lathrop, who taught English literature.

7. Samuel Brooke.

8. Alonzo Pellet (1835-64), OC (1849-56), Sarah Pellet's brother, died of camp fever after the Civil War Battle of Vicksburg.

9. Addison Merrill (1820-57), OS 1849, was an agent for the *Oberlin Evangelist* in 1850, and later a minister in New England and Canada.

Mary Merrill Hodge (d. 1884), OL (1841-43), married Nelson Hodge, tutor of languages in Oberlin's Preparatory Department, in 1842; she served on the Ladies' Board of Managers 1851-53.

10. George Athearn Adams (1821-1903), OC 1847, graduated from Andover Seminary in 1851. After his ordination to the Presbyterian ministry in 1852, he was a minister in Indiana and Ohio.

11. Harriet C. Ingraham (d. 1900), OC 1847, married Charles Livingstone (1821-73), OC 1845, missionary, traveler, and brother of the explorer David Livingstone.

12. Edwin Smith Skinner (1824-1913), OC 1849, graduated from Andover Seminary in 1852. After several years in the ministry, he became a businessman in Chicago.

13. Robert Gray (d. 1860), OC (1843-46), was married to Angeline Skinner (d. 1893), OL (1846-49). He later studied at Union Seminary and preached in Boonton, N.J.

Oberlin June 2[0?] '50[1]

Dearest Lucy

I have just been reading over some of your old letters and among others that long one you sent last fall.

It seemed so much like an excelent talk with your very self that I could scarcely believe that I did not hear your voice as well as see your words.

And you really think you shall be here this summer. What kind of an 'iron necessity' can it be that is drawing you hither. I had hoped you would be guided here by the cords of love but come at any rate no matter what brings you and you shall have a most cordial well come at least from some of your friends. We heard you were to be at Columbus as a representative of our Ohio women.[2] So we looked and longed for your arrival here also and talked and thought about you. I will not say how much but enough to flatter if you are at all vain of being loved. O Lucy I do want to see you so very very much but I wish we could meet somewhere in a little green country town where there are woods and flowers and rivers and waterfalls and rocks and where we could wander away all day by ourselves and have no body to disturb us and could sleep at night in some quiet cottage where the people would not be disturbed but alow us to sleep awake as much as we pleased. Well but this cannot be so let me beg a favor of you. Dont dont dont come here expecting to go away again almost as soon as you get here for if you come at all we must have a long *heart* visit that we can remember all our lives with pleasure. There are holy happy memories twined brightly together in my thoughts of our past intercourse and I would not have them displaced by less pleasant associations. I loved you Lucy as I seldom loved any human being and as I much fear I shall never love another and now dont come and take away my beautiful picture of the past and substitute one that has any less bright and lovely coloring. Am I writing in a strange mood. Oh I feel all I say and sometimes I fear we shall seem changed in heart as well as sentiment just because we shall not have time to take a peep into each others souls as deep down as we used too — There were friends that I loved when I left home at first not as I loved you but with a debth of feeling that they never dreamed of. We parted and we have met again but we were each changed not so much I am persuaded internally as externally but there seemed some barrier that would not let us associate upon the same terms of former years and though we are friends still there are broken memories that were twined with my heart fibers and I can only say would that we had never met again. It has snapped assunder the golden chain of the past and the present is less beautiful. But dearest Lucy we must not will not meet thus will we. I had rather we should never meet again—-never, much as I long to see you until we meet either to part no more or to part forever upon the shores of the spirit land. Now Lucy my own dear Lucy forgive me that I should doubt that we can ever be less to each other than we now are but you are bound up in so many pleasant and so many powerful memories too that seem almost beloved to me that I do some times fear that the spell will be broken. Will you think me too sentimental. No I know you will not though I still believe you never loved me half as I loved you yet you can *feel* all I say. I know you can. Now Lucy write me [a] long letter before you come and tell if you can how much time you can afford to spend here and you need not say whether you will be just as warm hearted and frank and sympathetic as usual for neither of us can tell that till we meet and find whether we have still the same heart sympathies or not; but one thing is certain. I have just as loving a heart for somebody and a soul that thrills to the music of kindred emotions more vividly than ever so if you still have posession of the key of my soul you shall be reinstated there more firmly than ever. 'I do not need human sympathy' but I love it only too well and I have little enough of it certainly. Yet I have many many dear friend but they all come only to the outward courts of the inner being.

Ever your own
Nette

ALS-LC

1. Internal evidence indicates this letter was written in response to LS's letter of June 9, 1850. ALB appears to have left a space after the numeral 2 on the dateline.
2. Shortly after a woman's rights convention held in Salem, Ohio, in April 1850, northern Ohio women asked LS and Lucretia Mott to speak for the enfranchisement of women before an upcoming Ohio constitutional convention; both declined.

[Oberlin, July 1850][1]

Dear Lucy,

It is late in the evening and every body are asleep but I had much rather talk with you than go away to the stupid land of Nod. It is almost three long years since we met and I am so impatient to see you; yet I believe if you were to come now I should sit stupedly staring in your face and say not a word, Do you think then I am half asleep? Oh no! I should be unspeakably happy.

You think I have come back to Oberlin upon dishonorable terms? Then you dont know me. I never did a dishonorable public act that could make me blush to look any body in the face, never!

I came back here just upon no terms at all. They refused to receive me into the Institution. I came back to study Theology and get knowledge. I do get it, they dont interfere. I am not responsible for their conduct or decisions. I have nothing to do with them but I am bound to put myself into the most favorable position for improvement possible while the day for improvement lasts, and when I go out to work I shall work in the field where I think I can do most good and what if they, or any body else think I act unwisely, or dishonorably, or foolishly what can that be to me. I respect their advice but I do not abide by their decisions. Why should I? I never spite myself for their errors and I would scorn myself for resenting injustice done me for there is no time to spare for such things. If I had money and health doubtless I should have applied to other institutions but I had neither and no time to spare in regaining them. So I believe I acted wisely and if they respect me any the less it is because they dont understand me else it were the more shame for them.

Lucy if I believed I should one day throw away the bible—should one day come to believe that prayer to God was impious—that the sabbath was an ordinance of man that the church was the great resovoir of iniquity and that the present system of Theology was composed of blasphemous dogmas still I firmly believe that I should continue to be thankful that I had spent three years in the Theological investigations at Oberlin merely for the sake of the mental discipline I have acquired and which I believe could be obtained in no other way. "Actual contact with the world" will have its benefits but I was not fitted to be profited by it three years ago. There was need of a preparatory discipline and I have obtained it. Now come the sterner conflicts of real live and God helping me I am ready for them. I am no more conservative, creed-loving, timeserving or bigoted than I was three years since—am no less of a free thinker or independent actor; but I *have* more settled and consistent views and more self reliance or rather more implicit reliance upon an arm that will never fail me and will hold me up in opposition to o[ur] mistaken world if need be. In short I have a great deal more individuality so please dear Lucy dont lecture me any more about the folly or danger of my course or rather do lecture me for it can do no harm and may do much good. I like to have you speak what you think. If you did not do it with our great differance of views I should think we had ceased to be true friends.

You urge me to go East to the Convention in Oct. I should like nothing better than to be there but there are great obstacles in the way and I fear they may not be removed. First I have partly concluded to go to Cincinatti soon after Commencement. Of course I shall need *some* money to sustain myself with there for a little time and if I do not pay my brother what I owe him but take what I am now earning by teaching I shall perhaps have enough but if I should go East it would take it all even suppose the Convention should pay my expenses as you propose. Then I do not now want to spend any more time at present in the study of Theology. So Andover would have no other inducement than my brother being there and that by the way is very uncertain as he will be likely to remain at Sandusky though I think it is not quite as probable as that he will leave. Then why should your Convention pay any portion of my expenses. I might go there and speak against them in many things for I do not believe exactly with your party even on the subject of womans rights and I would not be bought to silence. So I suppose I cannot go but I should like to write them a letter if they will receive it.

Now you will ask what I am intending to do. I dont know except that I am going to follow the leadings of Providence. The probability is I shall go to Cincinnati and do whatever I find to do there and in that great city there'll be enough. As for a support I have not the least idea where it is coming from except it will doubtless come from the Lord. Am I following a chimera and depending upon a bubble. *I* think not but there is not a friend in the wide world so far as I know that can feel that I am acting wisely and at the call of God. O dear! Well I must stand alone. I preach and lecture occasionally as the way seems opened but do not try to take much of that kind of work on my hands at present.

Henry Whipple[2] is more blunt and harsh than ever when speaking about women. Many of the people are getting liberal and others are getting firmly set upon the oposite side.

We write skeletons[3] now twice a week and read to President. This is a happy pleasant and profitable summer to me. We do not study hard but have time to think and read. Elly is well & doing well. It is now getting late and I will leave the last page till morning. Pleasant dreams to you. If there is any communion of spirits to living beings one with another I think you must have been here mentally this evening. Think of it and tell me when you write if it is not true. Remember it is Tuesday night between 10 and 11 Ock.

Wednesday 4 O^{ck} PM

It is a lovely day and every thing is still and beautiful. I have just come from the Theological Literary Society and have for the first time to day an hour to myself. We are now occupying the room overlooking the garden oposite your little room in the corner. Every thing is pleasant and my heart is so full it is almost running over with happiness and yet I sometimes feel a vague sensation of dread or apprehension when I think of the dim unknown future. When you come here I have so many many things to tell you but there is no time to write them and I must tell you some of the news—Eliza Fairchild and Kedzie were here a few weeks since—were married a

day or two after and went to Michigan. Robert said tell Lucy I wrote
her last and should be glad to hear from her. Cinthia Coffin[4] started
this morning on a visit home will be gone till Commencement. Her
health is very poor. Hamilton Hill has been home some weeks on a
visit, left this morning. How conservative he is is'nt he. Martha
Rawson has turned into a farmers wife 'out West.' Prof. Hudson[5] will
leave soon for the East on an agency for the Institution. The boarding
hall is full this year. Sarah Pellet is going to board at Prof. Hudsons.
Dear Sarah she cries too easy and her heart is too full of trouble.
She ought not to board at Mr Hills any longer. It is the worst place
in the world for her but she has almost no money and on that account
it is better for her to be there. She is poorly fitted to contend with
an unsympathizing world *alone* and *I* wish most heartily there was
somebody who would appreciate and love her and was worthy to be
her husband but I dont know whether she will ever find such an
one. There is no bondage in real marriage notwithstanding legal
disabilities. I am going over to see Sarah now and will get her to
write you a letter but I dont think she will write much just now for
she has to study hard and has little time.

I do not know but that it is possible I may go to the Convention.
Certain things seem to make it look best but I shall not be able to
decide till Commencement or near that time, and do not expect to
go though it may be so. I am to address the Ladies Literary Society
next. They have a monthly address from some lady. Mrs. Hodge read
us an address last evening upon Moral courage, very good indeed.

My brother Addison has gone to Calafornia. Gusta is getting well
apparently. She plays on the piano. My father and Mother are about
going East perhaps have gone already and Gus and Rebecca will
keep house at home. How I wish we could be there at a cherry feast
this afternoon. So you dont think much of the present Peace movement. Consistency *is* a rare jewel; but I would go to London next
year[6] if I had money. There will be so many object of interest there.
If we could only go together but may be we will some time.

                                                                    Nette

ALS-SL

1. Although ASB subsequently dated this letter "1847?" internal evidence
clearly indicates it was written in July 1850.

2. Henry Whipple (1816-93), OC 1848, OS 1850, served as librarian of
the college, tutor, and principal of the Preparatory Department 1848-53
and, at the same time, as a minister in nearby Henrietta, Ohio.

3. Skeletons were outlines from which ministers extemporized sermons to their congregations.

4. Cynthia Curtiss Coffin (d. 1856), OL (1845-48), married Lorenzo F. Coffin, OP (1847-49), while he was a student at Oberlin. The couple taught at Geauga Seminary in Ohio until shortly before her death.

5. Timothy Hudson (d. 1858), OC 1847, tutored in Latin and Greek at Oberlin 1838-41. While still a student he lectured for the Ohio ASS then returned to Oberlin to graduate and become professor of languages 1847-58. In 1841 he married Betsy Branch, OL 1839, who served on the Ladies' Board of Managers for twenty years.

6. A World Peace Convention took place in London in July 1851. Oberlin sent a delegation to the convention and LS's and ALB's classmates Hannah Tracy Cutler and Josephine Cushman Bateham served as delegates.

Oberlin Aug 13th 1850

Dearest Lucy

I am at Sarahs room where I had come to spend the night and have your letter that I have just been reading lying before me. Dear dear Lucy you have lost a brother.[1] No not lost him I hope but have parted with him till you meet again on some brighter shore. Oh how glad you will be that you were with him when he died and do you know that I believe this was Providencial and all ordered exactly so by a wise kind God. Your sister will be so happy to have you with her it will do her great good but dont get sick.[2] You will be careful I know.

I feel sad from reading your letter and thinking how deeply your heart has felt & all that it has enjoyed and suffered since we parted but I cannot mourn for the loss of your brother as though it was a grievous thing for I feel that it was all for the best and doubtless you feel so too. I would love to sit down and weep with you and feel with you all that you have suffered but this may not be and yet there is a weight of sadness upon my spirit that I cannot and would not shake off. My own dear sister I do love you and though you do "differ from me in opinion" I can still say with that man off East somewhere God bless Lucy Stone & even add also God bless Parker Pillsbury too.[3] You do not understand me yet but I dare say you will some time at any rate we will love each other still at least I will love you.

We have thought & talked about you often since you left[4] and I have wondered where you were and what you were doing and thought of the sickness and of the danger to which you were exposed and

wondered when and where we should meet again. At last after much
deliberation I concluded to go East to the convention and visit you
at your fathers on the way. My brother is going to Andover. This
evening I had just written a letter to my brother telling him I would
be ready to go home with him at any time, when Miss Holly came
into my room and told me about your letter to Sarah. So I came
down here brought the letter and have added a postscript telling him
it would still be uncertain about my course & the reasons for this.
I should still like to attend the convention but do not know that it
will be best.[5] I should be a stranger in a strange land and it would
be hard for the people to understand me. You remember Sam'l Brook
wanted me to go to Litchfield and you answered it would be near
commencement time and I should be bussy. I thought you imagined
I would not like to go and answered so to give me an excuse. The
people at Liverpool have invited me to go there and lecture on
Temperance the day before the convention. So Miss Holly and I are
going out and as it is only [*illegible word*] miles from Litchfield we
shall go on then to the meeting not to speak but to see hear &
speculate. I only wish if it were not for its being a disgrace to the
state that Miss H. could have the pleasure of being mobbed. Would'nt
it be glorious but I suppose there is no hopes of it. When I see Mrs
Foster & Pilsbury can perhaps [*page torn*] better about going East.
Will write you again soon & tell you my plans for the winter. I am
happy & hopeful and all the world looks bright. It is late and as there
is so much to be done tomorrow I had better not write any more.
Sarah will write too. Do be careful of your health & of your sisters
and do what you can for those poor ignorant women. If I do not
write you again within a week from this time then direct me a letter
to Oberlin if you write within 4 weeks & please do if you can.

In love ever
Your Nette[6]

ALS-SL

1. Luther Stone (1816-50), LS's eldest brother, died of cholera in the
summer of 1850 in Hutsonville, Ill., where he was a country merchant.
2. Phebe Cutler Stone (1821-56), Luther Stone's widow, returned to West
Brookfield accompanied by LS. On the trip Phebe Stone had a miscarriage
and LS contracted typhoid fever.
3. Parker Pillsbury (1809-93), Garrisonian abolitionist, woman's rights
supporter, and public speaker, left his Boston ministry in 1840 in order to
speak out more freely on reform topics.
In a letter to Sarah Pellet, written Aug. 1, 1850, LS wrote: "Last evening
a minister in Foxboro gave his pulpit all day and evening to Pillsbury and

me, and said before all the people, 'God bless Miss Stone; God bless Parker Pillsbury.' " (BFP-LC)

4. LS had stopped in Oberlin in July on her way to visit her brother.

5. On August 17, 1850, ALB attended a WASS convention in Litchfield, Ohio, where she shared the platform with Garrisonian abolitionists and gave her first public antislavery address.

6. ALB's letter was followed on the same sheet by a letter written to LS by Sarah Pellet on August 14, 1850.

Part 2

"Actual Contact with the World"

1850-61

"Actual contact with the world" will have its benefits but
I was not fitted to be profited by it three years ago.

—Antoinette Brown to Lucy Stone, July 1850

By the time Brown completed her theological studies, Stone had already spent nearly three years as a public lecturer. Over the next decade, as the country moved from sectional crisis to civil war, the two explored new emotions and ambitions, new challenges and new comforts. Jointly and individually they expressed their continuity of commitments, while seeking new modes to realize consistent goals in a changing world; together and separately they struggled to fulfill both private and professional goals. Each first found for herself a position of public prominence and then grew into new personal and family relationships.

At the beginning of the decade Stone had already secured for herself a place within the network of antebellum reformers who shared her concerns for the antislavery, temperance, and woman's rights issues. In the years that followed, Stone sustained her commitment to radical Garrisonian abolitionist principles, while working more exclusively for the woman's rights cause. Using the annual May antislavery meetings, or "anniversaries," as models, she promoted the organization of the woman's rights movement around yearly conventions, beginning with the first, held in Worcester, Massachusetts, October 23-24, 1850. These gatherings obviated the necessity for a national society with potentially cumbersome machinery or embarrassing disagreements between factions, while making visible both the extent and variety of support for the cause. Speakers addressed the issues of the social, religious, and economic inferiority of women, the relationship between temperance and woman's rights, dress reform, divorce, and marriage. Stone herself expressed her special concern with woman's legal status, particularly the two issues of woman suffrage and the civil disabilities of married women.

Stone found enthusiastic listeners at these national meetings, as well as at the local conventions called to encourage state legislative change, and at the myriad of meetings she held in order to support herself. Her success as a lecturer was remarkable. As Henry Blackwell later remembered, "Certainly if ever there was a person *inspired,* who spoke as never woman before or since, it was Lucy Stone from 1849 to 1857."[1] Her 1853-54 western tour alone netted her over $5,000, a substantial sum for a farmer's daughter who, while a college student only five years before, had made her own candles in order to save her pennies. Her courage to strike out on her own as one of the first American women to support herself as a public lecturer on the "woman question" had, quite literally, paid off, earning her ten times the salary of a well-paid schoolteacher or antislavery agent.

Less through choice than circumstance, Brown soon joined Stone on the lecture circuit. Although she had hoped to obtain official recognition as a minister upon completion of her theology course, Brown deferred her ambition. Without theological diploma or pastoral call, she accepted the invitation of the Female Guardian Society to minister more informally to the wants of the urban poor in New York City. Before taking up her post, however, she traveled to join Stone at Worcester where both spoke at the first national Woman's Rights Convention; when her New York employers discovered that she combined what she called "limited orthodoxy" in religion with woman's rights activities, they cooled to her, and Brown, prizing her integrity and autonomy, broke with them. She struck out on her own, speaking and preaching throughout the Northeast, often accompanying fellow New York State resident Susan B. Anthony, working for the causes of woman's rights, antislavery, and temperance. Whenever appropriate, Brown made her case for female clergy, female activism, and an interpretation of the Bible as a document in support of woman's equality.

During these years, Brown accepted invitations to visit the pulpits of various churches; but despite the obstacles to her attainment of full clerical status within Congregationalism, she did not desert it for a denomination with a more liberal policy toward the participation of women in church affairs. Indeed, rather than accept the offer of $1,000 per year tendered by Horace Greeley and Charles Dana to preach at an interdenominational free chapel in New York City, she opted instead for a more traditional pastoral post when it was finally presented to her.

In the spring of 1853 Antoinette Brown accepted the call to a church in the tiny village of South Butler, New York. This isolated, rural congregation had displayed its abolitionist spirit when it had previously engaged the services of a black minister, and its desperation when it had accepted the efforts of a theological student. Now the village offered Brown their church at the modest salary of $300 per year. On September 15, 1853, friends from as far away as Boston gathered to watch as area ministers officiated at the ceremony by which Antoinette Brown became the first woman ordained in a regular Protestant denomination.

Even with her new religious duties, Brown remained active in the woman's rights and temperance movements. She soon became the center of a controversy dividing these two usually allied movements. In the fall of 1853 she traveled to New York City to attend a meeting advertised as the World's Temperance Convention. Her friend Lucy Stone, who had attended the planning meetings for the event in May 1853, had predicted that the gathering would be tumultuous, but the uproar exceeded all expectations. When Brown presented herself as a credentialed delegate from two temperance societies, the men running the convention refused to allow her to speak. To them, she was a "radical woman," stepping outside of her sphere. Horace Greeley, a sympathetic observer, chastised the managers of the convention in his paper, the *New York Tribune,* charging that the business accomplished by the meetings consisted of:

> *First Day*—Crowding a woman off the platform.
> *Second Day*—Gagging her.
> *Third Day*—Voting that she shall stay gagged.[2]

Once again Brown faced the difficulties of combining essentially conservative causes with woman's rights work. Although she struggled to keep both her faith and her woman's rights commitments, striking a balance became increasingly difficult for her. Woman's rights supporters attending the annual convention held in Cleveland in October 1853 debated sharply whether organized religion could be reconciled with support of the doctrine of equality between the sexes. Brown, who had unwittingly raised the question when she opened the convention with a prayer, staunchly defended her interpretation of the Bible as a document in support of equal rights. But old friends, including Stephen and Abby Kelley Foster, attacked all organized religious societies for the absence of any denominational endorsement of the right of women to preach. Brown thus found her own situation within the woman's rights movement to be an anomaly; she endorsed regular religion and was proud of her position as a member of the clergy, but the larger movement questioned the efficacy of religious affiliation and asserted the impossibility of women attaining positions like that which Brown already held.

Thus, Brown's uncomfortable and ambiguous position within the woman's rights movement, her rising interest in metaphysical and speculative topics, and her growing theological uncertainties all combined to undermine her confidence in her commitment to her ministerial role and ultimately her faith in traditional religion. Her theological beliefs deeply shaken, she left her South Butler pastorate in the summer of 1854 to rest and recuperate at the family home in Henrietta.[3]

At the same time, Brown, like Stone, began to reevaluate her personal and political positions on singlehood and marriage. The friends had entered the decade of the 1850s committed on both levels to the efficacy of remaining single. Yet they soon openly disagreed on the politics of the "marriage question," perhaps the single most controversial subject addressed by the antebellum woman's rights movement. When Stone and Brown had differed on other issues, their quarrels lacked the serious intensity that this crucial topic generated. Stone, for example, took up the bloomer costume, both in theory and in practice, while Brown dressed more conservatively and evaded the issue. But on questions of marriage and divorce, their discord was significant, reflecting a divisive schism that woman's rights leaders alternately discussed and avoided in their annual conventions.

The divorce question grew out of issues raised by women in the temperance movement and spurred some women to a more conscious commitment to woman's rights, just as woman's activism within the antislavery movement had aided the emergence of the woman's rights movement in the previous decade. Yet while antislavery advocates pleaded for a recognition of the humanity of the slave, some radical temperance women asserted the inhumanity of the drunkard and demanded that women be released from matrimonial bondage to such "beasts." To Stone, the logic of their position was compelling. She believed, above all, in woman's self-sovereignty, and found herself reconsidering the words of one of her Oberlin professors, "Women are more sunk by marriage than men."[4] Marriage, she recognized, annihilated woman's legal existence and wiped out her civil identity, her right to her own earnings, even her birth name. Thus Stone spoke in support of more flexible divorce laws, in addition to working for the elevation of women in marriage.

While Brown, like Stone, believed women to be penalized by the laws of marriage, Brown's theology led her to see marriage as a divinely forged and hence indissoluble lifetime bond between two people. She believed the husband-wife relation entailed a permanent connection analogous to the inseverable parent-child tie, and hence Brown could not countenance any move to undermine it, even when one spouse proved an unreformable drunkard. Brown thus found herself in opposition not only to Stone, but also to Elizabeth Cady Stanton, Susan B. Anthony, and other prominent woman's rights leaders, all of whom advocated the liberalization of divorce laws.

Although Brown joined these women to work on petitioning state legislatures for the extension of the legal rights of married women, she remained adamantly opposed to facilitating divorce, even when her position forced her to take a lonely minority stance in the tumultuous debate on the subject held at the 1860 Woman's Rights Convention in New York City.

If the question of divorce continued to pose abstract problems for Brown, the question of marriage proved a more immediate and personal concern. Previously, both Brown and Stone had speculated upon the difficulties of actually achieving equality between the sexes in the intimate marriage relation. An awareness of such obstacles coupled with early career commitments and goals had led each to personally disavow matrimonial ambitions. Stone rejected several suitors, but she was the first to review her attitudes toward marriage, in light of the attentions of the indefatigable Henry B. Blackwell (1825-1909), who wooed and eventually won Stone with visions of an egalitarian marriage founded on woman's rights principles. "Harry," as he was known to his family, was an English-born Cincinnati hardware merchant seven years Stone's junior. When he met Stone, he was already committed to both abolitionism and woman's rights. He had become a Garrisonian under the tutelage of his father, a sugar refiner distressed by his participation in the trade of slave-produced goods; and he had been introduced to woman's rights by his remarkable sisters. His elder sister Elizabeth (1821-1910), the first woman to graduate from a regular medical school, had already received her degree by the time he began to court Lucy Stone, and his younger sister Emily (1826-1910) would follow in Elizabeth's footsteps also to become a physician. His sister Anna (1816-1901), a poet and translator, became a newspaper correspondent, while his sister Ellen (1828-1901) was an artist and author. In fact Ellen and Anna had attended the 1850 Worcester convention, where they heard both Stone and Brown speak.

Henry Blackwell first met Stone when she stopped at his Ohio store to cash a draft from the American Anti-Slavery Society in 1850, but he did not pursue her seriously until May 1853, when he followed her to abolitionist and woman's rights conventions. He sought to demonstrate his suitability by acting on his antislavery and woman's rights principles. In October 1853 he accompanied Stone to Cleveland, where he spoke at the fourth annual Woman's Rights Convention, advocating the equality of women and endorsing the quest for the ballot; and in September 1854 he played a key role in the rescue of a slave passing through his own city of Cincinnati. Touched

by his courage and eloquence, and finding her deepest emotions
stirred, Stone assented to their union; they were wed on May 1, 1855.
The ceremony included the signing of a document the two wrote to
protest the legal and social inequalities of the traditional marriage
relation.

Yet even as they embraced a new personal bond, new challenges
emerged; the couple sought to demonstrate their ongoing commitment to their causes while deepening their commitment to each other.
Shortly after their wedding trip from Stone's family home to the
Blackwell family residence in Walnut Hills just outside of Cincinnati,
Stone and Henry Blackwell undertook the first of the many separate
travels that would punctuate their long marriage. In addition, Stone
shortly reclaimed her birth name, refusing to be known as "Mrs.
Henry Blackwell," although adding the suffix "wife of Henry Blackwell" to her simple signature "Lucy Stone" when the situation war-
ranted. In so doing, she recognized and celebrated her affections and
her partnership while maintaining both her identity and her political
stand.

At first surprised by Stone's decision to marry, Antoinette Brown
was nonetheless thoroughly delighted by it. Moreover, she watched
with interest as Stone and Henry Blackwell negotiated the difficulties
of the new relation, for she too came to face similar circumstances,
as Henry's older brother turned his attentions to her in the summer
of 1854. Samuel Charles Blackwell (1823-1901), known as "Sam,"
also supported feminism and abolitionism; moreover, he communicated to Antoinette Brown his understanding of her religious crisis,
offering her comfort and an alternative to her life as a single reformer.
Brown, having returned again to the lecture circuit, and perhaps
experiencing difficulties with her voice, saw the romance of the po-
dium growing dim. With Samuel Blackwell, the prospects for equality
in marriage grew bright as her affection for him deepened. On January
24, 1856, the two were wed. For both Brown Blackwell and Stone,
the occasion had an added joy, for the friends at last became kin
relations—"sisters."

As they had shared singlehood, so Stone and Brown Blackwell
now explored together the parameters of their married lives. Neither
withdrew from her public career immediately upon marriage, nor
did either believe that the birth of children should necessarily force
long retirement from the platform. Brown Blackwell had long hoped
for a large family, and it began after only eleven months of marriage
with the birth of Florence, November 7, 1856. A second daughter,
Mabel, followed less than a year and a half later, on April 13, 1858.

For Stone, both the desire for progeny and the actualization of her hopes required more time. After six months of marriage, she admitted that she hoped she and Henry Blackwell could "blend our lives in one who can take up the work when I lay it down, and who will inherit some of the qualities, which make us workers in the world's wide field."⁵ Stone waited nearly two and a half years from the time of her wedding until September 14, 1857, for the arrival of her only child, her daughter, Alice Stone Blackwell.

When Alice was less than eight months old, and her cousin Mabel barely one month, the sisters-in-law and their infants assembled in New York City for the annual Woman's Rights Convention in May of 1858. Both still hoped that their new maternal responsibilities would not prevent their pursuit of public careers. Yet Stone, anxious to resume her lecturing, shortly found that her resolve collapsed. She embraced instead the role of homemaker and mother, rarely appearing in her professional capacity until her daughter reached the age of five. As Brown Blackwell later commented, Stone was "an almost too careful and self-sacrificing a mother."⁶ Caring for her daughter in her first years became the centerpiece of Stone's life, and uncharacteristically Stone agreed to follow Henry Blackwell as he sought to establish himself in business. First the family went to Chicago, where he intended to make his fortune selling agricultural libraries to midwestern communities; then they returned to the East where he took a bookkeeping job. When Henry Blackwell reentered publishing in Chicago, Stone again followed him, and she returned with him when he once again settled in northern New Jersey. Amid this geographic and emotional upheaval, Stone suffered a miscarriage. Only when the Stone-Blackwell household reestablished itself close to other members of the extended Blackwell clan, especially Antoinette Brown Blackwell, did Stone seem to regain her balance and seek again a public role.

For her friend Antoinette Brown Blackwell, alternation between professional and personal concerns wove a different pattern. When her second daughter, Mabel, died at the age of three months in August 1858, Brown Blackwell threw herself into platform appearances, first on a temperance lecture tour, and then preaching weekly at a New York City hall she hired for the purpose. Her husband, Samuel Blackwell, supported her ambitions while welcoming any financial contribution she might make to their struggling household as he attempted unsuccessfully to establish himself in real estate. In the end, her Sunday meetings cost more than they grossed, and only with the help of a woman's rights fund were Brown Blackwell's losses covered. Although her life continued to be economically unstable for many years, Antoinette Brown Blackwell turned away from public speaking as a source for income, finding the lecture circuit difficult to reconcile with the needs of her growing family. After Mabel came four additional daughters: Edith in 1860, Grace in 1863, Agnes in 1867, and finally Ethel in 1869. Brown Blackwell was increasingly bound to her home by domestic duties, but she nonetheless found outlets for her energies. She claimed to spend at least three hours daily in "brain work" during these years.[7] By 1869 she had her first book, *Studies in General Science,* to show for it.

As their private dramas unfolded, however, neither Stone nor Brown Blackwell lost interest in the events taking place on the public stage. Although they had differed on the precise methods to follow to end slavery, both watched closely as the Civil War drew near, hoping that the battle for the Union would be accompanied by the achievement of freedom and racial equality for blacks. Events drew toward a crisis while Stone's and Brown Blackwell's voices, which had once rung out on behalf of the slave, were instead lowered in soothing lullabies. Over the course of the decade, neither abandoned her political commitments or renounced the fullness of family life; rather, each established new patterns in the interweaving of public achievements and personal growth, sharing with her intimate friend the triumphs and challenges, the hope and despair, of her efforts. Mutual support and celebration, expressed in these letters, provided reciprocal nurturance and helped each find emotional strength in a difficult personal and political era.

NOTES

1. HBB, "Memoirs," BFP-LC.
2. *New York Tribune,* Sept. 7, 1853.
3. Late in life, ALBB described this crisis as one in which she suffered "a loss of all belief" (BFP-SLg, p. 155), but her attempts to find pulpits from which to preach even as early as the fall of 1854 suggest that she may have subsequently exaggerated the depths of her despair.
4. ASB, *Lucy Stone: Pioneer of Woman's Rights* (Boston: Little, Brown and Co., 1930), p. 62.
5. LS to Susan B. Anthony, Nov. 2, 1855, BFP-LC.
6. ALBB, "Lucy Stone at Oberlin," *WJ,* Feb. 10, 1894.
7. ALBB, *The Sexes throughout Nature* (New York, 1875), p. 166.

Andover [*Mass.*] Nov. 20, 1850

Dearest Lucy

By some strange chance your sisters letter found its way into my satchel and came with me to Andover.[1] The little intruder was discovered soon after I reached here and I hasten to return it home for she will doubtless wonder what has become of it and feel sadly tried at the loss. Tell her I had no intention of pilfering it and can hardly imagine how it could get here and tell her I ask pardon for my carelessness.

Lucy you will hardly think me improved in care and pains taking about my things, after so many evidences of old bad habits, but I do believe a part of it must have arisen from the principle of association in finding myself again with you; and being carried back again into the past. So you see I am for throwing a part of the responsability upon yourself. Can you bear such a burden? Well no matter! you had better not try with your poor weak back.

I had a very pleasant time yesterday. Met some of the Andover people at Boston, and some at the depot here, and one good friend with a wagon brought my trunk up for me to the house. The friends here had almost concluded I should stay at the meeting for Mr. Thompson[2] at Worcester on Thursday as they did not know this meeting was deferred till a future time. They were glad to see me but the first question my brother asked was Why did you not bring some one with you. I told him Lucy said they would not want to see a Come outer, and Mary[3] said Why! didnt you give her the special invitation we sent for her to come here? I had forgotten she did send such a word but I remember it now. Of course you were only joking Lucy but [*don't*] ever say such things again for you will be thinking them bye & bye.

There was a letter here for me from Lettice Holmes—a long good one. They are for the present in Portsmouth NH. and think some of remaining there, but are not yet decided. Thomas was not at home when she wrote. They had not heard much about the Convention at Worcester. Lettice says "Where we stopped in N Y., it was considered a foolish operation, & when we came to Boston I heard it called a feminine affair. Will you write to me all about it, and tell just how it passed off in your view of it. How many times I have wished that I could see Lucy. I thought I could judge from her version of it how I should have looked upon it . . ." In another place she says "Give my love to Lucy when you write to her. I should like to hear from her, but she said she had concluded not to write to me any more."

If you chose to write her it would do her good. They will be at Portsmouth about four weeks.

Write me Lucy when you feel like it for I *do* love you dearly.

Yours affectionately
Nette

Give Love to all your family.
I had a nice ride with your father.

ALS-LC

1. ALB's brother William was then pastor of a free church in Andover, Mass.

2. George Thompson (1804-78) was a British abolitionist closely linked to the AASS. In 1850 he toured New York and New England with William Lloyd Garrison and others.

3. Mary Messinger Brown (d. 1878), OL (1837-41), became the first wife of William Brown in 1841.

New York Dec. 19, 1850.

Dear Lucy

Here I am in this great city but not to remain for the winter. You will be glad of this. Well so am I for it seems to be providencially ordered otherwise. The three ladies who were to have worked with me have been every one of them confined at home by sickness of either themselves or families so there was no one to labor with me. This was one circumstance. Then Pres. Mahan who has been here since I came still advised me not to labor in this field—the Guardian Society Ladies[1] are of course not in perfect sympathy with my views & would not cordially endorse the idea of my preaching on Sundays which was the plan we had formed. & all together the faith of my employer seemed to me to be shaken by circumstances, & I acknowledge my own, pointed me away from NY. So we called a council talked over matters & after due deliberation gave up our contemplated enterprise—the money will be applied to foreign instead of home missions & our energies bent in other directions, though Mrs Barns[2] herself will still labor as a Missionary when she is able. She is a noble woman, has really liberal views & would gladly sustain me in the contemplated labors notwithstanding any prejudice on account of my womananity. So would Mrs Weed.[3] I admire many traits in her character very much. Neither of them would have fettered

me in the least, yet they do not *fully* feel prepared to adopt all my
views, & since there must be some prejudice against me I felt oppressed with the idea of compelling them to bear the credit of views
which were not wholy their own though they had no hesitation about
it. The society ladies are kind courteous & pleasant, but they cannot
with their views encourage my preaching. So taking all things together
we all thought it best to relinquish the enterprize. Mr Weed is daily
expected home probably to die, of course his wife could not labor.
She has also two children sick one with measles. Mrs Barns herself
is sick quite ill with cold & being an old lady could not expect to
do a great deal herself except in pleasant weather. The converted
catholic woman has a daughter very ill. I am particular in mentioning
the circumstances that you may not misunderstand the matter. There
is prejudice in regard to me doubtless in the minds of the christian
community & there must be so long as they believe the bible forbids
woman's being a public teacher.

For my own part I am glad to be again free from any connection
with any one in laboring, for I believe with nobody, & I could not
work perfectly well with any one. I will for the present at least, be
employed by no society not only, but by no individual in particular
either, & will make no engagements for any length of time. Then I
shall be free to believe what I please, & to act as I please responsable
to my own concience & to God. Then I can go and come when &
where I please can lecture write or rest as the Spirit move me; and
above all can feel free—as free at least as it is possible in a world
where we must more or less involve others in our trials cares &
rewards, our honors or disgraces.

Oh I like to have an unfettered spirit & I will knowingly put no
more weights upon it. I can think of no person in the whole world
that I would sooner have for my employer than Mrs Barns, I love
her very much; but I feel relieved that our engagement is broken.
There are Noble women here in NY. & I think Lucy you do not
give them credit for what they really are. Of course the Guardian
society feels as all societies feel more or less, that 'ours is the cause'
& that 'we are the people'. Antislavery people feel that in some degree,
& sometimes not a very limited one. So do Womens Rights advocates.
Well! let them feel it. The mind can not from its constitution be so
intensely absorbed by all subjects as by one, & of course that one
grows larger as it develops itself in all its various phases. Yet there
would undoubtedly be less narrow mindedness if people had fewer
hobbies.

I for got to tell you Lucy that my lecture had neither the beginning

nor ending on the paper you saw. I wanted to end it with a verse of
poetry by, I dont know who, in regard to the final prevalence of right,
& as it was not at hand I ended by an unwritten close. & of course
began it for the Lyceum. The Lecture was very unfinished & is the
last one I hope ever to deliver in quite so crude a state, for I will
extemporise first, yet I like those thoughts for the times if they can
only be followed up by something more definite. You have probably
given the manuscript to Sarah before this. If not can you send it
down to the Depot on Monday next. I shall leave here at 8 that day
shall be at ~~North~~ West Brookfield in the afternoon by the express
train. so if you should have the manuscript give it to Mr. Gilbert &
ask him to have it ready for me & I will get out & get it.

I have been sight seeing considerably—am well paid in experience
for coming here, & not a looser pecuniarily, have been hearing as
many distinguished men speak as possible, have not labored at all
in the missionary work—decided to give up the enterprize in a few
days after reaching here & have since spent the time as I pleased. If
I knew where Mrs Rose[4] was I would call on her, shall perhaps find
her out. If I can affort shall write most of the time this winter. That
bible question is the one for me to fully settle in all its bearings in
the very out set of my investigations.—I am very happy Lucy but
I do wish I would see you. I wish you were here to sleep with me
to night.

My eyes feel very weak from going in the wind & looking so much
so I will write no more.

Yours in Love
Nette

ALS-LC

1. Founded in 1834 as the New York Female Moral Reform Society to
promote moral uplift, the American Female Guardian Society, as it came
to be called in 1839, was part of a national network that included over
250 local women's evangelical organizations.

2. Almira Porter Barnes (d. 1858), widow of Blakeslee Barnes of Troy,
N.Y., when already a mature woman frequently visited theological classes
at Oberlin in the 1840s, where she met ALB. A vice president of the
Guardian Society, Barnes offered to pay ALB's salary to work for it in the
New York City slums. Barnes subsequently provided funds for ALB to
begin her career as an independent lecturer.

3. Zeruiah Porter Weed (1809-70), OL 1838, was the first woman to
complete the Ladies course at the Oberlin Institute. She taught in Ohio
and New York and later worked for the *Advocate of Moral Reform* and

the Female Guardian Society in New York City. In 1844 she married Edward Weed, a widower and a minister. At the time of this letter she was living in New York City awaiting her husband's return from a trip to England undertaken in hope of improving his health. He died in 1851.

4. Ernestine Louise Siismondi Potowski Rose (1810-92), a Polish-born woman's rights activist who immigrated to New York in 1836, petitioned the New York State legislature for the extension of married women's property rights in 1840, and later spoke regularly on temperance, antislavery, and woman's rights.

Andover Monday [*December*] 30 1850

Dear Lucy

Your letter reached me saturday and I was glad to have even a few lines from you. Do not feel troubled about my manuscript. Sarah undoubtedly has it and I shall write her to send it by express. I do not need it at present and it will make no difference at all with me. I am glad you are with your sister for it will make her so happy but dont you get sad dear L. I thought you seemed a little so by your writing. This world certainly has more joy than sorrow in it after all its trials and I enjoy living better than I ever did before.

Take care of your health Lucy and dont, dont expose yourself to the cold until your system has recovered from that dreadful attack of the fever. You and your sister must take good care of each other. Give her my love and best wishes.

R. W. Emerson lectured here last Friday to the Lyceum. His subject was political Economy—a curious Emersonian affair was the whole lecture but rich beautiful and musical. He said we were all made to be rich and ought to study how to become so and that riches consisted in being able to avail ourselves of the labors of others, and thus to enjoy every thing which supplied a want of our nature.

His appearance did not meet my ideas of him but his lecture was so original it well atoned for any other disappointment. I do want to be rich dont you and as Sarah Pellet says 'we will be sometime' at any rate according to Emersons deffinition of wealth.

I am writing a half century sermon[1] and expect to go to Worcester and preach it in a week or two.

Sojourner Truth[2] has been here and lectured in Fry village about a mile from us. We did not hear her as it was the same evening of the Lyceum but she says she had a "blessed meeting, a blessed meeting." It was well attended & she had a good many books purchased of her. She had been at the Antislavery Fair.[3] I entirely forgot about the Fair or I should have attended it, was there nearly all Tuesday in Boston. I had a great mind to go back after I came home but could not well afford the time, just now particularly.

I went into several large bookstores in Boston to find Parkers Sermons[4] for a christmas present for my brother but could not find any of his writings, and it was so biting cold, that, after riding all night in the cars which were detained 11 hours behind the time, I was so chilly that it seemed as though I should actually freeze to death. so I gave up looking and purchased one of Upham's works.[5]

Yours
Nette

ALS-LC

1. A sermon marking the end of the first half of the nineteenth century.
2. Sojourner Truth (c.1797-1883) was a black abolitionist born into slavery in New York and freed in 1827. After working with mystical and evangelical religious groups, she became active in antislavery work around 1846, and in 1850 began to speak on woman's rights as well. The sale of her biography, *The Narrative of Sojourner Truth* by Olive Gilbert (Boston, 1850), was her major source of support.
3. Local and regional antislavery fairs raised money by selling goods provided by women sympathetic to the cause. The seventeenth national Anti-Slavery Bazaar was held in Boston, beginning December 19, 1850.
4. ALB probably sought Theodore Parker's *A Discourse of Matters Pertaining to Religion* (Boston, 1842).
5. Thomas Cogswell Upham (1799-1872), a Massachusetts Congregational clergyman, wrote extensively on theology, philosophy, and metaphysics.

Warren [*Mass.*] January 30. 1851.

Dear Lucy

Here I am at your friends, Mrs Blairs. We are having a fine visit. Have talked about you in particular and the Garrisonians in general. Mr. B. has been in the house most of the time, and has joined in the conversation, I like them both very much, but I suspect your friend thinks with you that I am *bigoted*. O well I cant help it.

I am out here lecturing on Temperance. Have spoken three times, and am to speak again this evening. Tomorrow shall return to Andover. We are having a regular Temperance revival. Last evening had an old fassioned experience meeting at the close of the lecture, some

confessions & resolutions made. The ladies have formed a society &
are making the gentlemen honorary members, by giving them a
gentlemens pledge to sign. I came here through the influence of Dr.
Cutler. How I wish you were here. If you were at your fathers now
I would go over and spend the Sabbath with you. Write me Lucy
about your health. I am quite anxious to know whether you are
getting well or not, and also how your sister is.

Have you heard Mr Thompson speak yet. I hope you have. I was
at Worcester and heard him there on English Politics—then afterwards attended the convention at Lawrence held by Mr. Garrison
and himself.[1] T'was a fine meeting. They both spoke nobly, and used
very nearly such language as a good orthodox man might have used;
but with a little different construction upon their words sometimes
as I took it. Then there were some few things said by way of sweeping
assersions; and statements which though true used in such connections seemed to me designed to mislead that I objected to in my
own mind, but on the whole it was a glorious good meeting and I
was glad to be there. Mr. Thompson is an eloquent man. I liked him
and Garrison both. You know I have seen but little of Mr G. personally, less than of allmost any of his party, so it was pleasant to
become acquainted with him. We all stopped at the same place.
James Buffon[2] was there and that Miss Kenny from Salem & others.
We had a pleasant time, your people are certainly many of them
very agreeable & I am not afraid of them of any truths being disolved
by the views of any particular class of people, but frankly I am not
converted yet from any of my views, either by Andover Theology,[3]
or abolitionists but alas! doubtless my views are being sapped at the
foundation, at least so every one is telling me. What will be the result
I dont know, but certainly some new light seems to be dawning slowly
in my mind. Well never mind I'll pledge myself to follow all the light
I get.

What are you doing this winter. Are you studying much, are you
writing or examining any questions. I am not studying the Bible
question as I expected, am lecturing more. Next week am going to
Abington. Shall preach on the sabbath and lecture several times
during the week on womans Rights.

Adams, wants I should get you to go out to Andover. He wants
to see you very much. Really he is improving or else I judged him
rather harshly. He does'nt seem so much afraid of some of the good
people as he did at first. I have become aquainted with several of
the students, & they condescend to talk, very respectfully with a
"woman preacher." Wont you go to Andover some time this winter

& spend a week or two. We'll have nice times & it will do you good. Your sister can spare you by and by. Give my love to her.

I do wish you were here to day for I have not been more in the spirit of visiting with you in a long time. Henry Whipple has been at Andover. He said he should visit you before he returned West. You may have seen him before this. We had a good visit. He wanted to see you very much, & he likes you after all your views. Prof. Hudson & father Keep[4] were there also—Have you heard anything from Sarah Pellet. I wonder what she is doing.

[*Antoinette Brown*]

AL-LC

1. Both Garrison and Thompson spoke at the quarterly meeting of the Essex County ASS held in Lawrence, January 18-19, 1851.
2. James Needham Buffum (1807-87), a housebuilder by trade and a Quaker, was an active abolitionist and an advocate of woman's rights, temperance, and peace.
3. The theology taught at the Andover Seminary at this time was an evangelical revision of Calvinist orthodoxy.
4. John Keep (1781-1870), abolitionist and supporter of coeducation and the peace movement, was a Congregational minister. In 1833, he came to Oberlin where he served on the board of trustees for thirty-six years.

Andover April 16. 1851.

Dear Lucy

I shall be at home on Monday and right glad to see you here. The notice of your Lectures in the Liberator informed me where you were to be this week and I made up my mind yesterday to meet you at Abington and hear your lecture tomorrow evening at South Abington; but this morning as the storm still continued I began to think I should not go after all and just while we were talking about it your letter came from the post office.

We are all so glad you are coming. I do want to see you *so* much. Stay as long as you can. You ought not to lecture much for you are not strong enough yet, and this will be good place for you to rest so dont make any appointments until the last of the week certainly.

I have many things to say, but will not say them now for there's

a better time coming. Only let me say at present that you and Sarah
were right. I *am in LOVE*. More particulars anon.

Nette

My sister says tell you from her she is very glad indeed you are
coming. So is my brother—little heretic as you are and I promise
you as loving a welcome as though you were a regular blue Presbyterian.

ALS-LC

Abington [*Mass.*] April 28 1851

Dear Lucy

Write you a long letter I certainly will not for you dont deserve
one. Write you a good letter I shall not even if I could. Besides the
very mischief has got into my pen: it is spattering the ink in all
directions as you have the most tangible proof; and you see it makes
a very light hair mark. It got injured in some way and is nearly
spoiled, and I meant to have got it repaired when I came through
Boston, but there was no time.

So here I am comfortably established at Mr. Fords[1] waiting your
arrival. You must know that I have no reason in the world for staying
except the expectation of seeing you at the close of this week. As for
preaching I have graduated from that calling for the present at least,
so far as the town of Abington is concerned and am staying here for
no other mortal reason than merely for the purpose of being your
humble and most obsequious attendant at the meetings next Saturday
and Sunday. I shall sit meekly with folded hands and may be open
mouth listening to the words of wisdom which will fall from your
mouth. *My* lips will be sealed and nothing short of the miraculous
will temp me to open them on these occasions. I thought I would
inform you of this fact before hand in order to save all misappre-
hension and importunity on your part. I say I am going to you[r]
meetings "willy nilly" and shall sit and listen to you all day long.
My pen grows worse and worse and I shall have to borrow another
of Mrs Ford. Well there is no pen to be had so amid the spatters
you must pick out the words for I cant do any better. You ought to
pity me for being obliged to write in this way and no doubt you do
most sincerely. I pity you too for having to read it. So we are even.

Mrs. Ford requests me to invite you here before the last of the week. She wants you to come Thursday if you can and if you cant I say come Friday. You ought to get rested for Saturday and if she must have me here she had rather you would be here too for then it will be less trouble to her, and there will be some body to talk to for I am very silent of course sometimes. O dear me my pen. What shall I do.

Second edition. A new pen! rejoice with me though it is not a remarkably good one. Well I was just going to say that we all wanted you to come here as soon as possible. I am quartered here 'sans ceremony' accepting hospitality as freely as tis freely offered though I cant help thinking they must rather wonder at me for doing so as doubtless they do; but it cant be helped. I want to stay and shall stay no matter what the consequences are. So have the goodness to be forthcoming to this place as soon as it is at all expedient and mind that you do up all your studying and thinking before hand, for you will have no time for that here. If you have any stocken darning, or work of that sort bring it along.

                                                    In much love
                                                    Nette

I forgot to say that I have no belief in such kind of Providences as you talk about. What business had you to wait for the storm. I was twice as disappointed and three times as cross about it as you were and Adams and Skinner called down to see you expressing the greatest regret at the disappointment. My brother looked blue and said he really did want to see you. Mary said she didnt know but she would cry if I would but I would not why should I! I had swept and dusted the whole house over with my own hands while she was washing in the morning for the sake of having every thing very nice for such a particular body as you are and put my room into better order than it has ever been in before since I occupied it. So you see what trouble you occasioned but there was one consolation it has looked very tidy ever since so I have forgiven you with some reluctance and harbor no ill will against you whatever. I had a small audience yesterday during the day but a large one in the evening.

ALS-LC

1. Lewis Ford (b. 1812) was a Garrisonian abolitionist and a supporter of woman's rights. He married Anna Dyer of Braintree, Mass., in 1833.

Dear Lucy

————A lady told me half an hour ago about Mrs. Bloomer's putting on the new costume.[1] She said she sent for a mutual friend of theirs, a gentleman, to call on her; but when he went into the house and saw her in such a dress, he just put up both hands, turned away his head and backed out of her presence making grimaces; and when called back by Mrs. Bloomer and her husband, his only reply was, "Don't speak to me! Oh, don't speak to me!" I suppose this was of course in joke, partly at least; but I fancy "Don't speak to me!" would be the heart language of a great many of our friends if we were to adopt this costume. I find, though, much more prejudice against it among the ladies than the gentlemen. Some of our Henrietta men are anxious to have it adopted, and some of the Misses also, if their mammas will allow them, are willing to try the "new fashion" because it is new, I suppose. My mother seems perfectly willing to have the girls wear those dresses, and if they were not already fitted for the summer I think they would put them on immediately.

Nettie

tf-LC

1. Amelia Bloomer (1818-94), a woman's rights and temperance activist and editor, popularized the knee-length full skirt covering broad pantaloons in her reform periodical the *Lily*.

Henrietta Aug. 7. 1851.

Dearest Lucy

This is letter writing day. I have just finished three sheets that must be writen so now I will commence one that *may* be written. You got my first of June letter doubtless so you see the *feeling* you had about it was a false one, or rather, perhaps, it might be interpreted on the principle of the ancient oracles—it was capable of two interpretations. You had a feeling that there was something wrong about it and so when it came with a five cent postage the presentiment was verified. Well the thing happened on this wise the letter was written and given into my father's charge to be post paid. He laid it where we lay our letters when they are written so any one who goes to the office will take them and my brother seeing it there gave it to a young man who called and was going over to the village—not thinking at all that it was June.[1]

Ill put you in a string of stamps to atone, if you will only be sure to send me an answer to this without delay. What about the Convention at Worcester.[2] Do you expect a full attendance and *who* do you expect. What day does it commence. I have seen no notice of it for we dont take *the* papers and have forgotten when it was to be.

How I wish you were here to day Lucy. My home is as pleasantly situated as yours in this harvest season of the year at least. The wheat is nearly all cut now. there are two huge stacks of it up on what we call the hill. I dont know what you would call it at your home; but you dont have any such smooth gradual elevations that get to be pretty high up at last with almost no aparent rise of ground and then you dont have them covered with such tall heavy waving grain as this was a week ago. You have no such high rich green forests for a back ground and no such grand orchards with ripe harvest apples on some of the trees, no such big horse rakes trailing up and down the wheatfields and doing up poor Ruths work among the gleanings[3] by modern magic and no such overgrown barns running over full of wheat all ready for the threshing. Perhaps you will think I am writing more of utility than beauty but there is something charming beautiful grand even in all this—the landscape is rich rural and picturesk and I do wish you were here to enjoy it with me for we have clouds and skies larger and certainly as beautiful as yours and there is a thunder storm just coming up and the black dark clouds are rooling over us with the multitude of swallows sailing and diving about in them in a perfect glee.

After all Lucy when the storm is over I should like to make a change and go up onto your grand old hill. O dear I am in just the mood for it and I wish people could ride on the telegraph and be carried free. I'd certainly visit you then and be there at sunset and you should come home with me and sleep tonight. O well theres no use in riding these 'beggars horses.' One might as well chase after a Will o'the Wisp in the swamp and yet I often do both. Dont you sometimes. Mother is just ringing the bell that says 'come to dinner.' Please come and you shall have string beans and harvest apple pie.

After dinner—Two or three days ago Charles Foote of Michigan came here to inquire if I had taken the nuns veil. He had two plans for me one that I would go and preach for him at Michigan as he wanted me to last winter I believe I told you, and the other his favorite plan was to get Miss Holly and I to go out together as agents for the *Canadian Refugee Home Society* in behalf of the fugitives to lecture preach &c in behaff of the Refugees and raise funds to buy them houses and lands and schools—etceteras—The fugitive slave

bill[4]—the antislavery topic for the times would of course come up
legitemately for discussion and altogether the field would be a good
one for an antislavery lecturer but this is not my cause in particular.
I shall not go for them for all winter—may possibly go for a month
or two but havnt decided. I *hate* the thought of being an agent for
any thing or any body and I'd rather lecture in the Womans Rights
cause than any other, still I may go for a few weeks how does the
object strike you. I wrote to miss Holly yesterday at their request.
Wouldn't she and I make strange coworkers. I think though she would
be a good person to take of the unpleasant part of the lecturing life
from one. She could elbow her way in the world with all the grace
conceivable and all the majesty of Juno herself and there would be
no necessity of a poor mortals ever talking where she was unless they
felt disposed and there would be always something to talk about. No
body could get the mope in her presence I am sure. Altogether I
fancy she would make a capitol chaperon. I dont know whether we
should loose ourselves in literature or in sympathy for the oppressed.

Perhaps she wont go but I think she will whether I do or not, and
dont much think I shall. We may have several weeks to decide.

I wrote Prof Finney and Pres Mahan about being ordained. President has not answered though it was several weeks ago. Prof Finney
wrote a long fatherly letter called me his dear child, daughter, dearest
sister &c expressed a world of sympathy but said he could not at
present act his wife would if she was a man—but he would examine
the subject pray over and consult with the brethren &c and if he
could assist he would.

Father is just ready for the office so I cant write any more. Im
studying hard these day writing &c. We are all well. Write soon.

Nette

ALS-LC

1. Postal rates changed on June 30, 1851.
2. The second national Woman's Rights Convention was held in Worcester, Mass., October 15-16, 1851.
3. In the Bible, the young widow Ruth followed the harvesters through
the fields collecting the remnants to feed herself and her mother-in-law.
4. A strict fugitive slave law was passed in 1850 in order to appease
Southerners who feared the political imbalance resulting from the admission
of California as a free state. The Compromise of 1850, which included
these measures, also abolished the slave trade in the District of Columbia
and decreed that other territory acquired from Mexico would decide for
itself whether or not to permit slavery. Radicals in both the North and the
South, however, disliked the compromise.

Henrietta Sept. 21. 1851.

My own dear Lucy

It is Sunday. The rain falls pattering upon the attic roof so dreamily, and musically, that I am in just the mood for communing with such a spirit as yours. It is a very rainy day. I had bonnet and shawl all on this morning for church; but took them off again at last, and now have stolen away from the company of cousins, sisters, niece, brother, parents &c; to talk with one who has seemed more dearly dear, and near to me, than many of these—not near in the bonds of the flesh, but of the spirit; and what has been still is, and must be.

Last week was one of interest and excitement. The State Fair was in session through the week. It was a fine affair, never surpassed by the Empire State. I was in on Tuesday before many persons had congregated, and again Friday—heard the address by Senator Douglass,[1] and all the other speeches which were delivered upon the ground—a good off hand one from H. Greely.[2] In the mean time I attended the National Liberty Party Convention at Buffalo.[3] It was a fine meeting. The Fair kept away some from this region, and Eastward yet it was well attended. The citizens filled the hall during the evenings and there was a good attendance most of the time during both days. Prof Hudson and wife were there, and Mr Pelton[4] from Oberlin. *White*[5] in the class behind you at O. was there with his wife. Mrs. *Thomas* and others of your acquaintants. I spoke half an hour or more. F. Douglass is far enough from being a *Free Soiler,* merely;[6] and to me his views are better now than formerly, as they are now nearly with mine upon the constitution. Do you see his paper at all, and do you know what their policy is as a party, their motto all rights for all, and their demand a righteous civil government. If it were not for your views of the Constitution there would be little disagreement between you I am sure; and as it is, according to Gerrits Smith's[7] definition of a Liberty Party man, or rather of a Democratic Leaguer—as that is the name they now take—which is, any man or woman who insists upon an immediately and every way righteous civil government, whether he is a voter or not, and whether, he votes with their party or not, is still one of them in reality—by this definition I recken you, and some of your people are included. And notwithstanding the lamentation that I have heard this summer over Douglass, How are the mighty fallen![8] I dont believe *you* would be narrow minded enough to say that, and I know you would not if you understand his present position.

But enough of this. You are not an antislavery lecturer now by profession, nor I either. So we will not quarrel about men or measures.

I am so glad you are going to lecturing upon Womans Rights this winter and you said you would be glad if I would lecture. Well I will! I had decided before your letter reached me to devote the winter to that subject. So shall be at the Worcester Convention, and shall if not Providentially prevented go on from that place, preaching the gospel of equality for some months to come. Where I shall go will depend upon the movements of the other ladies, who seem to have sprung up so quickly from the seed that has been sown. What a grand company we are getting. I heard *two* of Mrs. Coe's[9] lectures here in Rochester and have heard a great deal about her since. She seems a superior woman with a glorious ambition; but I did not fancy her indoctrinated into a truly reformatory spirit. May be she is though. Shall we all get a chance do you think to open our mouths at W. I am going with the intention of being a most meek listener for there will be so many women there, ready to prophecy that unless we speak two or three at a time, some of us will certainly have to hold our peace. So Stephen Foster was troubled at what I said to you about my ordination. I think perhaps neither he nor you quite understood me; but I can have a talk with him about it at the convention. My brother A. and wife heard Abby speak a week or two ago they liked her very well.

This is a cold, cold rain, and I am getting almost chilled so shall adjourn your letter until by and by, and will go down to have a play with my little niece Ada. She is a sweet, darling little child and the biggest little mimic in the world.

Monday Morning

A cold beautiful day. The cousins departed for their own homes; and the rest of us likely to get warm over the washtub. I wonder whether you will be washing to day, or whether you are just on a return home from some where, where you have been off lecturing.

When you get home give my best love to your friends, especially to *father* and *mother.*—Lettice will be at the convention I suppose! How I do want to hear her speak dont you? I have not heard a word from her this summer—Thank you Lucy for the book you have probably left at the Antislavery office for me. If I should send you one, you would probably enclose it in a letter and send it back. Well that is altogether the most independent way—Be sure to keep all your friends under obligations to you in some way. Do, for that is very philosophical.

I wish you had found time and inclination to say something of your plan of lecturing. For me I have prepared a long series of lectures. So I can give from one to a dozen or more in a place, and can read or extemporize; but shall generally, perhaps always, do the latter. You spoke as though you thought some of coming into this region. How I do wish I could be at home, and you come here, but at any rate N Y is a good field. I have no definite plan at all as to where or how I am to labor, but if I had brains and reputation enough would go to large cities and deliver a course, having two or three lectures a week there, and in the mean time go out as often as I chose into the vicinity and fill up the intervening evenings in that way, but the cause will be too unpopular, & the speaker too unknown, inexperienced, and of the wrong sex. So I shall wait for circumstances to develop for me a course of action.

Sister Agusta is about as she has been—rather stronger than in the hottest weather. H. Cook, sent me a note a week or two ago. She will attend lectures again at Cleveland this winter. Feels very happy over her profession.[10]

> With much love
> your sister
> Nette

ALS-LC

1. Stephen A. Douglas (1813-61), then Democratic senator from Illinois, strongly favored the Compromise of 1850 and promoted the policy of allowing territories to decide for themselves the status of slavery within their boundaries when applying for statehood.

2. Horace Greeley (1811-72) was editor of the *New York Tribune,* the most widely read Republican newspaper on the eve of the Civil War. He was a supporter of the antislavery and woman's rights causes, and became a personal friend of ALB's in the 1850s.

3. The Liberty party, a short-lived effort of political abolitionists to enter serious electoral politics, was established in 1840, but nearly folded in 1848 when many of its members left for the Free Soil party. The remnants of the Liberty party held a convention in Buffalo, September 17-18, 1851.

4. Brewster Pelton, OP (1841-43), a Liberty party supporter, was among the first settlers of Oberlin, where he opened a log hotel in 1833 and later became a merchant. He was a trustee of Oberlin College 1852-72.

5. Orrin Washington White (1821-80), OC 1848, OS 1854, held pastorates in Ohio and Massachusetts before becoming a schoolteacher. He married Lucy Lovejoy, OP (1843-46), in 1848.

6. The Free Soil party was established in 1848 when antislavery forces deserted the Whig presidential nominee, southern-born Zachary Taylor. Many political abolitionists joined it in its early days, including Frederick Douglass. In the 1851 speech that ALB heard, Douglass spoke against colonization and northern racism.

7. Gerrit Smith (1797-1874), a wealthy reformer, supported abolition,

temperance, peace, and woman's rights. He was a founder of the Liberty party in 1840, and its nominee for president in 1848 and again in 1851. His upstate New York district elected him to Congress in 1852.

8. In 1851, Frederick Douglass broke with Garrison and his "come-outer" position to ally instead with abolitionists involved in electoral politics. Garrison's supporters believed this was a betrayal.

9. Emma Robinson Coe was an antislavery and woman's rights activist then living in Ohio. After being denied entrance to law school, she studied privately.

10. Helen Cook was then studying homeopathic medicine in Cleveland.

21 Cornhill [*Boston*] Nov. 3 1851[1]

Dear Nette

I wish you were here. We would compare notes relative to progress in Woman's Rights, and if you have succeeded as well as I have, you may well be proud—and—take courage—

My first lectures just about half paid the expense of Hall, say nothing of travelling expense—then I announced it as free, & had the same result.—I went to the next place, where the meeting was "beautifully less," in numbers, than the first meetings, the vast audience consisting of eleven, (I was going to say *Souls,* and *will* say so—) including myself. I made some *talk* to them and gave notice, that there would be no more lectures—My next meetings are to be at Essex, Dedham and Stoneham.

S.S. Foster says you had not better try to lecture, in the neighborhood of N.Y. City, for they are all Dutch farmers worse than dead.

Please drop me a line *here.* I shall be in again Sat.

Aff—
Lucy

ALS-SL

1. This is the address of the AASS office.

At the Doctors [*Boston*] *Tuesday* eve *March 23d* [*1852*][1]

I did not leave your letter the other day at this office so will add a note. Went to Concord—had a nice time full house pleasant people. Saw Thoreau[2] there got acquainted with him some—heard about him a great deal and so stayed to one of his readings here at the rooms where Mr Alcott[3] meets Monday evenings. Heard a curious, pleasant lecture, unique enough, but conservative in spirit. He looks like a regular back woods genius. Mr Alcott thinks him above Emerson as a writer. Tonight Miss Hunt has Mrs Lesdernia[4] the new reader of Shakespeare & the other poets, here at her rooms to meet friends & critics and get her a start here in Boston. She contemplates reading here Considerably in Boston. Is going to have sacred readings Sunday evenings. I like her have met her here twice saw a great deal of her once, yesterday. I could stay over to meet the friends but had engaged to go to Hopedale.[5] Shall go there in the early train tomorrow morning. Thence Theodore Parker at Millville Tomorrow evening — lecture there through the week & Sunday.

The little Dr. is reading from the newspaper and troubling me so I cant half think. How I wish you would come in now just as you did the other evening. I should kiss harder & throw my arms around you ever so much closer than then. Have you read Uncle Toms Cabin. It is so grand only it was a pity to *Colonize* poor Harry.[6] But do read it its a regular feast. How I wish you were to be here tonight. What a nice time we would have. Mrs. Mowatt[7] is better doing well.

Yours in love & haste
Nette

I forgot to tell you that Saml Brook called here this afternoon in a regular rain storm. Staid only a short time when he found I was not going out of town to night — will be here this evening. He blushed ever so red when I spoke of you. You will see him of course. Somehow I pity you whether you want it or not. These love affaires are real bothers. I have been answering some very *cordial* epistles this very day & it made me think of old times. How I hate love letters & pity lovers.

ALS-SL

1. ALB was staying with Harriot Kezia Hunt (1805-75), a Boston physician, abolitionist, and woman's rights activist. Hunt had studied medicine privately, but on learning of Elizabeth Blackwell's graduation from Geneva Medical College, applied for permission to attend lectures at Harvard Medical School; she was refused entry on several occasions.

2. Henry David Thoreau (1817-62), transcendentalist writer, lived in Concord. He had recently published his first book, *A Week on the Concord and Merrimack Rivers* (Boston, 1849), and had been jailed for refusing to pay his taxes in a protest against the expansion of slavery into territory

acquired in the Mexican War. He was then at work on his most famous book, *Walden* (Boston, 1854).

3. Bronson Alcott (1799-1888), transcendentalist writer, reformer, and educator, father of Louisa May Alcott, was then also living in Concord.

4. Emily Lesdernier was a popular reader and actress.

5. Hopedale, Mass., located about thirty-five miles southwest of Boston, was a cooperative Christian community founded by Adin Ballou, a Universalist minister, and his followers in 1841. The community supported many reform causes, including abolition and woman's rights.

6. *Uncle Tom's Cabin* by Harriet Beecher Stowe (1811-96) was first published in installments in the antislavery newspaper the *National Era*, 1851-52. At the conclusion of the novel the Harris family, reunited after their escape to Canada, migrated to Africa.

7. Anna Cora Ogden Mowatt (1819-70) was an actress and playwright. Her husband died in 1851 while accompanying her on a tour of England, and shortly thereafter, her manager committed suicide. Mowatt returned to the United States shocked and deeply depressed.

Rochester [*N.Y.*] April 14th 1852

Dear Lucy

The convention is over.[1] I have been here most of the time. Some things were good and glorious but they quarreled a good deal *of course*. Douglass and Remond grew painfully personal but you will hear about it! Last evening we had a fugitive slave gathering—the house was full—the impression good—grand so far as one could judge, but I dont think Phil[*l*]ips has been quite himself here—he spoke a great deal but not as he *can* speak in a free atmosphere. News came there were slave catchers in the place after three fugitives—this brought the people together.

How I hate quarrels among those who should be friends. Such scenes teach one wisdom. Some of the people called a part of it nigger wrangling and I kept thinking it was just the way we women should do and be talked of as having womanish jealousies. Heaven save us from it yet it must be that offences must needs come but wo to those by whom they come.

You know the N Y women have been forming a state Temperance Society and they call it the *Womans Society* and have a rule that none but women shall be office holders, though men are members of the society.[2] I am glad they have commenced so in earnest, and think they will do something—have joined the Society, though I had nothing to do in forming it and was not here at the Convention at all. But in the first place the name is a misnomer, for it is not exclusively a Womans Society. If it was so I would have nothing at all to do with it at all. Then in the next place the idea of making it a rule that no men shall be officers is retaliation and womanish at that. It would be a shrewd good joke in a convention (perhaps) to pass such a rule, but a state Society is altogether a graver affair. I shall protest against it zealously. Organizations are rather serious matters if they are really going to affect anything. I am more and more in hopes we shall not organize a National Woman's Rights Society at present—We are not ready for it and if we are ready by fall there ought to be a thorough discussion of the matter during the summer. All this time I have been as mute and mum as a kitten—a looker on and a speculator, ready enough to act independently and allow every one else to do the same while the matter remained at that point, but theres *grit* enough in me and officiousness too upon occasion. None of us will be put in trammels, and do you believe the womans rights advocates are willing & ready to make a broad platform of free speech upon the subject? A Woman's Rights odd fellow clan! Heaven help us! But if we dont organize upon true grounds wont some body get up a narrow minded partial affair of some stamp that will shame the cause and retard its progress. And then there'll have to be a rival organization formed in self defence. If we could start right would n't it be better? But then who is ready to *start* not only, but to stand by the staff and do battle to the end. No society ever did or will prosper, continue and attain its end without there were strong men to stand steadily by it till the conquest was made. We may have a dozen ephemeral Woman's Rights organizations like successive crops of mushrooms springing up & dying one after the other as the temperance parties have done and though the agitation will do good still comparatively little will be accomplished. I am sick to death with this running forward blindfolded without even asking where we are going to. You see I am writing the day after yesterday and some of the burning lessons learned there are still burning into my heart. How I do wish some strong noble minded ~~women~~ men or women would solemnly devote them selves to the cause with the firm earnest intention of making it theirs for life, giving their best energies up to it as the moral reform ladies do to their cause—the Garrisonians to Antislavery, Elihu Burrit to the peace movement, Ministers to their churches &c, then the masses couldnt help being attracted, magnitized, converted & something could be done. Form an organization with such women or men no matter which, having for its constitution the one general principle equality in rights for men and women, and then leave this principle to develop itself in the different directions which it must necessarily take and the society may be permanent and abiding, but it never can be in any other way. But how is it now. In the first place who expects to [give] himself to the cause *Unless* it is yourself. I dont know of any body. They all have some separatte and higher interest.

Much more anon
Nette

There are ever so many things to be said on this subject but not now. Your patience must be well nigh exhausted and I am so tired. Dont lecture on Antislavery because *they* want you to—not unless your own heart impells you. Ive seen Miss Holly. Would like to tell you just how *she & they* all seemed. Mrs Foster says she is "a *glorious creature*," "*a GLORIOUS CREATURE*" but "*peculiar*" & so she is. I could not keep from "laughing inside" all the time & outside some. had a nice visit. Mrs Coe's Husband is dead—they suppose he has left property. Sam'l May[3] praised her & hoped she would study Theology with him.

ALS-SL

1. The Rochester Anti-Slavery Convention met March 20, 1852.
2. Susan B. Anthony and Elizabeth Cady Stanton worked together to organize a Woman's State Temperance Convention in Rochester, April 10, 1852. They hoped to promote an alliance between temperance and woman's rights by having women speak publicly on the legal difficulties of women married to drunkards.
3. Samuel J. May (1797-1871) was a Unitarian clergyman, abolitionist, and woman's rights advocate; he was also active in the peace and temperance causes.

Henrietta April 15th 1852

Dearest Lucy

I say dearest Lucy for I have just written to another Lucy—Lucy D. Fuller,[1] and there should be a superlative adjective attached to your name when the two are put in comparison.

You see I am here at home—my own home and today my own brothers and sisters will all be here. My father has just gone to the city to bring up brother Addison, wife, and the baby. brother W^m came yesterday from Andover, but his wife and child are not with

him. It has been more than 9 years since all of our broken circle
were gathered together, and now when we meet there will be much
of sadness mingled in the cup of enjoyment. Poor Augusta is lying
on a sick bed almost unable to help herself in the least. She was very
low—not able to sit up or bear her weight on her feet, when she
was attacked with the measles, and one night before I came they all
sat up expecting to see her die, but she is now better—has had a
course of Typhoid fever, and we hope she may be more comfortable
than she has been in some time. But we can not tell. This Spring
will be a trying time. Poor dear child how long she has been sick
and how much she has suffered! I shall not leave her again at least
till there is some decided change.

I am disappointed that you do not go to Cincinnatti![2] Why dont
you? Yet you do need rest. You have had a long, long time of lecturing
this winter and I *would* rest, for you need it—you will get worn out
before your time and dont do that, dear Lucy, for you will not do
half the good in the end.

What an experience you must have had in R.I. How glad I am
you stayed and preached down the opposition.[3] You are really quite
a martyr. Miss Holly would open her eyes to you wider than ever,
and bow down to you in real reverence by this time. Has she ever
met any opposition or mobbing do you know?

She spoke in Rochester and it was well received—they said she
was very earnest, as though her whole soul was wrapped up in the
cause, but she seemed timid, embarassed, and her voice trembled,
at first in particular. It was her old home and she must have felt it.

I cant send you the *key* to my states of mind and feelings. It wont
be transmitted by mail, or sealed up in writing paper. Besides it is
misplaced and I have no time to hunt it up. You know I always was
careless about all my things. There is visable improvement however,
and when you will come here I will find it any time in 5 minutes.
The cupboards and drawers of your heart may be *openable,* but they
are not wide enough for me to see in through the almost if not quite
closed doors when there is so little a time for investigation. Never
mind though I do love you dearly and always shall, no matter what
happens. We are having a lovely Spring since the very cold winter
has disappeared; and when the foliage is green on all the trees I
should like then to be in your New England home. The Millville
people have invited me to preach for them the next six months. The
letter came yesterday. I should have been inclined to "accept the
call" if it had not been for Augusta. But they wish me to return there

within the month and I cannot engage to do this. Besides it is probably best I should go to Oberlin.

Sarah P. tries hard to be and do a great deal. I wish she did not care so much for the good opinion of others but she will accomplish something—much in the world I am sure, and she does not seem conscious of the peculiar traits which are so objectionable to you. Indeed she often speaks against caring for what people think of her.

I have been reading E. P. Whipples[4] Lyceum Lectures. Some of them are fine. His Ludicrous Side of Life, Wit and Humor &c I enjoyed exceedingly. I have been reading also some of Washington Irving,[5] since I came home—had read him before but it is better than ever. The Legend of Sleepy Hollow is superfine the style more rich, racy and finished than I supposed. Beside this have done nothing of a study character since I came home. Even these were read at intervals in a sick chamber, I have sat up with Agusta more than half the time since I came home, either half the night or every other night, then I sleep some in the day time to make up. Did not get up to day till nearly noon and my head feels heavy so you need not wonder, Lucy, if this is a stupid letter, but as I sat here alone with Guss who is now asleep, I felt like talking with you, and so began to write. My health is very good—was never better but I feel tired. Write me whenever the Spirit moves you to do so. I love to hear, if it is only a line.

Ever Yours
Nette

ALS-SL

1. Lucy Dale Fuller (1820-1904), OL 1847, a classmate of LS and ALB, taught for several years before marrying Albert Bryant, a Presbyterian clergyman.

2. An antislavery convention was held in Cincinnati, April 27-29, 1852.

3. LS had just completed an antislavery lecture tour of Rhode Island during which she was denounced by the clergy for her radical views.

4. Edwin Percy Whipple (1819-86) was a Boston essayist, literary critic, and lyceum lecturer. The essay to which ALB referred first appeared in his volume *Lectures on Subjects Connected with Literature and Life* (Boston, 1850).

5. Washington Irving (1783-1859) was an editor, essayist, and novelist. "The Legend of Sleepy Hollow" was first published in *The Sketch Book of Geoffrey Crayon* (London, 1819-20).

[*Henrietta*] May 15th [*1852*]

Lucy dear

My sister Augusta has at last gone from a world of so much suffering to a home where pain and sorrow never come.[1] It was hard to have her leave us, but now I would not bring her back again to this sad sinful earth. Your last letter was put into my hand when we came home from the grave, where we had laid the frail form deserted of its living spirit. I was so sad you can not tell how glad I was to get it. You spoke of her and hoped she would be better now the Spring had come, and she is better, well—quite well! We loved her, but she left us. And she was glad to go! It was such a death as one loves to think of. The bright spirit took its flight with such calm joy—such an affectionate farewell. But I will write no more. You have lost loved ones as I have many times.

Yesterday I received a letter inviting me to take the charge of the McGrawville Central College—ladies department. It was mainly on Prof. Hudsons recommendation. He will probably accept the Presidency.[2] Wrote them to day, "If my impressions are correct, you recognize, both theoretically and practically, human equality independent of color or sex. If so, I honor the principle and know of none in which I could more heartily cooperate." This must bring up the real issue. Of course I could give no definite answer till they explained more of the "condition, principles and internal arrangements" of the N.Y.C. College.[3] So they must write again and I am quite curious to know exactly what stand they will take. Then I wrote Prof H. asking if in his recommendation he recognized some prominent *isms* which had come to be very nearly associated with my charact[er] and reputation—told him I was going to be ordained this summer, & asked if they, and he as president, would recognize me as an authorized minister &c. If he would assist in the ordination &c. It all came up naturally and I frankly told him what was most evident that I was acting upon the old Apocryphal text "Improve the opportunity". These issues are fine. There is precious little chance doubtless of my going but let them appoint me with a real practical equality—a privilege of speaking, lecturing, &c like the rest, and Ill go. I have no objections to becoming a *Reverend Professor* when they choose to make me so. Ha ha! The ordination though there is little doubt of.

The "Womens N Y Temperance Society" puts undefined and unlimited power in the hands of what *may* be a *permanent Executive Committee*.[4] It's awkwardly worded. I dont think they meant it so. One article is gramatically & Rhetorically false. They probably wrote it in haste, but on a second reading I withdrew my signature till they got a better Set of articles for a Constitution.

I am going to Oberlin some time in June. Possibly may go arround by Philadelphia & be at the Convention.[5] Think not!—

When I came home started from Millville expecting to meet my trunk which was to be sent from Hopedale. It did not meet me. Went to Charlton where I had an appointment for that evening—spoke there on Temperance waited over 24 hours. Conductors & all said they would bring the trunk there. Mr Crane took it home with him and knowing I could not under the circumstances wait for it— forwarded it to Albany, hoping it would meet me there. It did not. I came on without it & have not heard a word of it since. Many of my cloths, books, & 32 dollars of money were in it, & more than all nearly every thing of value that I have written during the last 10 years. Dont know what in the world to do. All the thoughts & books on the Bible argument were there, & I cant bring myself to begin every thing anew. Think it will come at last, & so am quite thrown out of my summers employment. Brother W$^{m.}$ has been home, he looked for it all the way. Could get no definite trace of it.

This letter is a regular infliction but no matter.

Ever Yours in love
Nette

ALS-SL

1. Augusta Brown died May 2, 1852.
2. Hudson did not leave his Oberlin professorship.
3. The college in McGrawville was also known as New York Central College.
4. At the April 20, 1852, convention in Rochester, which ALB attended, the New York Woman's State Temperance Society was founded.
5. A woman's rights convention was held in West Chester, Pa., on June 2, 1852, although ALB did not attend it. She did, however, travel to Oberlin in July, where she gave a series of talks.

Henrietta Aug. 4. 1852

Dear Lucy

You could not find me mesmerically at Oberlin! Well no wonder for I was not there; but how did you go to work to look for me? Are you yourself a clairvoyant or a mesmerizer, or did you send a neighbor to look after me? Please relate, for as my grandmother used to say, I am all "on a tiptoe" to learn.

I am not ordained yet either, so you may rejoice and welcome; but what a milk sop you must take me to be, if I can be manufactured over in to a "would-be-but-cant-priest" by so simple a ceremony as ordination. It is well that certain grave divines should have drawn back just in time, for they were on the very brink of the fatal spring over the great wall of custom. A little more and I should have been a man acknowledged minister, but somebody happened to think that though a woman might preach she ought not to administer the sacrament, &c. Others thought this and that, so they joined hands and turning round walked backwards together, and I took up my bundle and walked home.

I spent just three weeks at Oberlin—was gone from home something over four, and came back hearty and happy.

So you are at home this summer, but preaching Sundays on anti-slavery. Well that is good. Shall you remain in Massachusetts this winter or come Westward? Come out here do, a little change will be good, and New York is a grand state. Of course I have no *particular* wish that you should make our good Smithsonian abolitionists over into Garrisonians, but if you *can* do this why you may and welcome! And if you can manufacture Come outers out of Whigs and Locoes I shall rejoice over much, so do come in to N.Y. and lecture.[1] Stay here after the Con. at Syracuse[2] whether you lecture on Antislavery or Woman's Rights. But pray dont *quite entirely* give up the latter subject. By the way what time does that Convention come? and when is the call to be out? I shall certainly be there if my intentions are not frustrated. Is Wendell Phillips expecting to be there and will he make his *political report.* I hope so really!

There is one thing which I want and have always wanted in our conventions—that they should be opened with prayer, or at least that there might be some vocal prayer at some time during the sessions. I have not felt at liberty to propose this because the control or management of the matter was not at all in my hands, and most of the members I supposed did not approve of any thing of this kind. Of course I would not insist on it now; but if there are no objections felt on the part of the leaders this would be very satisfactory to me and I doubt not to many others who may be present. Sam'l J. May believes in vocal prayer and he will be present, and you I suppose believe in the freedom of speech both towards God and man. I think I will write Mrs. Davis[3] about it for it really places some members of the Convention in a false position to have no public prayer during the meeting. How sorry I am Mrs. Stanton can not be there.[4] I dont know many N.Y. women, and none who would do well for President.

So you are interested in politics. So am I. I wanted to talk on the political subject you know at Worcester, and if there is an opportunity mean to say a word at Syracuse. Whether there is or not, though, I am determined to have a better meeting for my own feelings than last year, and will have no matter what happens!

What hard work it is to stand alone! I am forever wanting to lean over on to some body, but no body will support me, and I think seriously of swallowing the yard stick or putting on a buckram corset, so as to get a little assistance some how, for I am determined to maintain the perpendicular position. Am expecting to stay in this state most of the winter, but should like to take a short tour to the old Bay State well enough. Dont know about it. Think some of going to Missouri or California or some other out of the way place. Have been invited to go and "take the entire charge of a Seminary as large as any in the West, and to preach every Sunday for a compensation aside from the tuition." but the people there wanted to know my opinion of Psychology, Spiritual Rappings, Fonetics, &C — *"the reforms of the century."*[5] So I'm afraid I would n't suit. A fig for this teaching! I rather fancy McGrawville, though, on account of its principles, and mean to visit them soon. Dont mean to teach there. Shall begin to lecture some in about two weeks. The cholera is now very prevalent in Rochester, and the people are so panic struck, my mother will not let me leave home at present. Am writing some sermons, &C, writing now and then for the papers, sometimes with my own signiture & sometimes without[6] and spend a good deal of spare time in picking raspberries of which there are a great abundance here abouts. How I do wish you were here to go, for I am going to set out on a ramble this afternoon. Do go with me! please do! I should so enjoy it!

Sarah Pellet is quite well but very nervous. She does not know yet whether they will let her graduate and read her own piece or not. She will not graduate unless they let her read.[7]

I stopped some time in Buffalo. Spent the night with Mrs Coe. Her husband left her about a thousand dollars she said. She was intending to study theology with Sam'l J. May. The next day she called with me on Mrs. Williams, the lady with whom I was stopping, a woman's rights lady and a friend to Oberlin. She and another lady advised her to go to O. — She was struck with the thought at once — decided to go — wanted me to write Prof. Finney. Said she would become a member of the institution if they would let her lecture during vacations, &C, and if they would not she would study theology there. I wrote as soon as I got home, stopped a day or two at Rochester

on the way, and had a letter soon after I got here saying Mrs. Coe
had written herself. So she was in quite a hurry. No answer has yet
come to my letter on the subject. Dont know what they will do.
Oberlin is going on famously. Is crowded with students, overflowing
with hope, and almost ready to get intoxicated over the endowment.[8]
I stopped at Prof. Hudsons. Lucy Fuller is now teaching drawing at
O. in the Institution. Wadsworth our classmate[9] has just gone back
there to study, Luman Ingersol & wife were there. His throat troubles
him and he cant preach. Prof. Finney looks ten years younger than
he did when he went to England. Write me soon at Henrietta—that
will for the present be my address. Is your health good, Lucy. You
are doing so much I am expecting to hear you are sick. keep well
do!

> As ever yours affectionately
> Nette

Sarah Pellet expects to go on studying theology this fall. C. Palmella
is in O. thinks some of studying too. Some Oberlin people wont
fancy it over much but let every body do as they are a mind to I
say. We will do the same, wont we? They say the Grimkys are intending to put on the bloomer. I am glad. Will they be at Syracuse?
My love to your father—and mother, and all the family.

ALS-SL

1. Followers of Gerrit Smith believed in the efficacy of political action,
while "come outers" who followed William Lloyd Garrison avoided electoral politics because they believed such activities recognized a political
union with slaveholders. The Whigs were one of the two major political
parties of the time; the other, the Democrats, included a radical or "Loco
Foco" wing.

2. The third national Woman's Rights Convention was held in Syracuse,
September 8-10, 1852.

3. Paulina Kellogg Wright Davis (1813-76), an antislavery, temperance,
and woman's rights lecturer, began her career in 1845 after the death of
her first husband, by speaking on health reform. In 1849 she married
Thomas Davis, and the following year she presided over the first national
Woman's Rights Convention; she also served as president of the third
national Woman's Rights Convention, held in Syracuse in 1852.

4. Elizabeth Cady Stanton (1815-1902), key figure in the woman's rights
movement, first became involved in temperance and antislavery through
her cousin, Gerrit Smith. After her marriage to abolitionist Henry Brewster
Stanton in 1840, she became acquainted with woman's rights advocates

within the antislavery movement and with their help organized the first American Woman's Rights Convention, held at Seneca Falls in 1848. Her fifth child, Margaret, was born October 20, 1852, soon after the Syracuse convention.

5. Some spiritualists believed that the dead communicated by knocking on inanimate objects.

6. ALB wrote anonymously for Frederick Douglass's paper, the *North Star*, during this period.

7. As LS had been, Pellet was prohibited from delivering her own graduation essay before the mixed college class. In 1858 Oberlin's collegiate women students were finally permitted to read their own graduation speeches, and Pellet was belatedly granted her degree.

8. In 1852 over 1,000 students attended Oberlin, making it one of the largest colleges in the country. Two years earlier, it had undertaken a campaign to raise money for an endowment through the sale of scholarships. By commencement 1851 the pledge goal of $100,000 had been reached and collection continued to proceed rapidly.

9. Thomas Arthur Wadsworth (1821-99), OC 1847, OS 1848, later held pastorates in New York, Iowa, Illinois, and Wisconsin.

[*November 1852*]

I stayed until the morning of Election Day in Madison County, held many meetings, had crowded houses always when there were meetings at all, but sometimes there were failures—notices put up and taken down again by politicians who had some kind of nervous fear of an injury to Mr. Smith's election.[1] Well, he is elected in spite of all!

How I should hate to sink so low as to become a common vulgar politician. Let me first be a Garrisonian ten times over. I say, Lucy, I pray you won't get converted to such politics as the world at large advocates and what's more I don't fear it.

* * * * * *[2]

I saw Mr. Smith election morning. Depend upon it he will not even touch the pitch of political corruption and he will not be defiled. He will walk through the fire but there will not be so much as the smell of it upon his garments. But if he does swerve from his own principles I shall give up and say as Sarah Pellet said in the words of the old song,

"There is no faith in man
No not in a brother."
Little girls if you must love
Love one another.

> Lovingly and hastily,
> your friend,
> Nette

tf-SLg

1. ALB worked to secure the election of Gerrit Smith as U.S. congressman from his upstate New York district; he resigned this post in August
1854.
2. Asterisks appear in the typescript from which this letter was transcribed; no original has been located.

West Brookfield Nov. 24—1852

Dear Nettee

You see I am at home again and sooner too than I expected. I
had appointments nearly three weeks in advance, but withdrew them,
on the reception of a letter stating that the wife of my brother Wm.
B. was dangerously sick, hastened home and found her dead and
buried.[1] And today my brother and the little ones, have gone to
spend a sad Thanksgiving with their mothers parents—How like
Autumn leaves we fade, and die!

Did you see Paulina Davis' letter in the Liberator relative to the
Woman's Convention, in reply to Mrs. Dall?[2] I dont know when I
have been so pained—I could not help saying, "Save us from our
friends"—I have not written her, but one of these days I shall—Her
vexation at not having Mrs Smith Prest[3]—made everything seem
wrong side out, to her—and her influence since the Convention, has
been wholly against it. Dont repeat that now Nettee, dear, for the
world. I do wish I could see you, there are so many things that I
rather talk than write relative to this subject. But I find so much
selfishness, instead of real interest in the cause, that I hardly dare
speak freely to any one. Harriot Hunt has made a good protest against
tax paying[4]—A proposal is made to amend our State Constitution,
and if it is within the bounds of possibility, I mean to have the
franchise secured to women.[5] Massachusetts *ought* to do it first.

I just have a letter, put in my hand asking me to go to Beverly,
to hold a discussion at the Mechanics Lyceum, "with a respectable

and gentlemanly antagonist on the question of Woman's Rights" —
How our Cause progresses.

Five years ago, Such a thing would not have been thought of —
Surely, what is *right, WILL* triumph — The women themselves, are
most in the way — Mrs. Oakes Smith has lectured in N.Y. city on
the dignity of Labor, and Womans Rights, & if the Tribune gives
good reports, she has done it nobly — She wrote Sarah Pellet recently,
that she thought she should soon start her paper — I see that she,
and Mrs. Coe, were to be at the Morrow, Co. Convention in Ohio
last week.

I attended the Penn. A. S. Soc. annual meeting[6] — had a grand
time. Gave one Woman's Rights lecture at W. Chester. It paid me
$26. Spent a night with Mrs. Rose. She is doing us good service, by
answering newspaper ridicule.

Have you seen the Rev. Mr. Sunderland's sermon from the text
"A Woman shall not wear any thing that pertaineth unto a man"
&c.[7] The Bloomers have made more impression than I thought, to
be attacked by the pulpit — By the way Mr. Stephen Smith, has made
me a present of a nice broad cloth dress and pants for winter[8] —

So you elected Gerrit Smith — What a place he will have to fill,
and I am afraid he wont be equal to it —

We'll have a Womans Rights Convention at Washington while he
is there wont we? You think he will, be an exception, to the general
rule, that pitch cant be touched, without defilements. I hope he will,
but I cant help feeling, that he wont be, in Washington *just,* what
he is at home. He is a noble good man, but he is in a bad place,
and I cant even pray for him — I am glad that you have learned that
politicians are mean — and more or less compromisers — It is not
best to get in the harness with them. With the *simple truth,* we can
do more alone —

You want I should stay in your State, I certainly never had more
effective meetings in my life, and was urged to more places than I
could possibly go — I may return there, some time this winter — Shall
be at home now only a few days —

Sarah Pellet was selling books on the cars, and Mr. Wilkinson
allowed her to go for nothing[9] — She was most discouraged and
scarcely knew what to do — She did not speak at Seneca Falls, until
after I left. I had to get to Auburn in season for a lecture the same
evening — She has spoken at Verona, and told me she thought she
succeeded very well. I wish the elements of her character were a little
differently proportioned, for her own, and the worlds good —

Do take care of your health Nettee — and to that end, I wish you would wear a bloomer—I had constant, and hard meetings, but I bore it well, from the freedom & comfort of my dress. *IT IS* a *GREAT DEAL* the best for health—Shall you lecture on Woman's Rights?

I shall take both my subjects, and serve the world the best I can with them—Write me at 21 Cornhill Boston.

> Most affectionately
> Lucy

ALS-LC

1. Phebe Williams Robinson Stone, the first wife of William Bowman Stone, died at West Brookfield, November 12, 1852, leaving three young children.
2. Caroline Wells Healy Dall (1822-1912) was active in benevolent reform, transcendentalism, antislavery, and woman's rights. Raised in Boston, at the time of this letter she was living in Toronto with her husband, Charles Henry Appleton Dall, a Unitarian minister.
On October 15, 1852, the *Liberator* published an open letter from Caroline Dall to Paulina Davis in which Dall made several charges, including a criticism that poor transcriptions of the Syracuse Woman's Rights Convention made it appear to have been an antimale gathering. Davis's response, appearing in the *Liberator* October 29, 1852, agreed that better reporting would have been helpful, but defended the basic accuracy of published accounts.
3. Elizabeth Oakes Prince Smith (1806-93), author and reformer, became active in woman's rights after attending the second national Woman's Rights Convention in 1851. With support from her friend Paulina Davis, she hoped to preside at the Syracuse convention, but opponents put off by her extravagant dress blocked her election.
4. For two decades beginning in 1852 physician Harriot Hunt paid her taxes under protest. She cited the injustice of requiring payment from women who had no voice in the government under which they lived. Other suffragists, notably LS and Abby Kelley Foster, later followed her example.
5. A state constitutional convention was held in Massachusetts in 1853 at which petitions for woman suffrage were presented.
6. This meeting was held October 25-27, 1852.
7. Reverend Byron Sunderland, pastor of the Plymouth Congregational Church in Syracuse, attacked the bloomer style of dress worn by some of the women in Syracuse for the Woman's Rights Convention. His sermon, published in the *Syracuse Star,* provoked a response from suffragist Matilda Joslyn Gage, which the *Star* also printed.
8. Stephen Smith (1776-1854) was a businessman and reformer in Syracuse. He gave LS material from which to have new clothes sewn in the bloomer style, with a short dress over pantaloons.
9. John Wilkinson (1798-1862), a Syracuse lawyer, banker, and anti-

slavery supporter, was for several years president of the Syracuse and Utica Railroad, and later president of the Michigan Southern Railroad.

Henrietta Dec. 16 1852

Dear Lucy,

You may be a hundred miles from Cornhill before this time, but at any rate this letter is bound to go there.

I did not see Mrs. Davis' letter in the Liberator, but have heard about it. It was too bad. I wonder that she should have done so. These womanish jealousies are so little! That is a kind of "pitch" I pray never to be defiled with, but who knows? It seems as necessary to keep away from Conventions altogether if one would not be contaminated as it is to keep out of politics for the same reason. This is a wicked world any way, but we can keep good, though it is hard work sometimes.

You will not wonder that you will get some blames with all the praises, and you'll bear it like a hero. I heard that Mrs. Davis and Mrs. Smith are about to commence their paper together[1] — that Mrs. Davis has written to Lizzy Stanton asking her to be a contributor. She said she had a legacy left to her — that she had no child, and could as well spend it in editing a paper as any way.

Take back your kind caution about my health and apply it to yourself. You are more nervous than I, now; and Bloomer dresses and all you cant endure a bit more. I came home two days ago, had spoken 18 times in 19 days, in Wayne Co. Two or three evenings after speaking over an hour liberty was given for others to make remarks, that led to discussions that kept us there till after 9 ock. Two days we had discussion meetings appointed at one ock and held them till dark one day I talked as much as three or four hours. When all that was done came home, stayed all night in Rochester, spent all the next morning running about the streets buying books, engaged the stage to call for me at 2; but it was full and went on and left me. So at 4 I started on foot got a ride of about 2 miles and walked the other 7½ through the snow in the midst of a big snow storm, took a cold water wash when I got home, and the next morning got up as well as ever without even a stiff joint. The only inconvenience felt from the walk which taken all together must have been some 15 miles was, that my toe nails needed trimming and so when I stubbed my toes once or twice it made them sore, but they are quite well again so that I am in sound body and good condition.

The Wayne Co. people want *you* to go there. I was only in 4 towns—intended to go to other places, but got ready to come home, & besides the villages were a good ways apart. I am glad you are coming back here. Come into Monroe Co. wont you? Thomas Wadsworth is preaching in South Butler, Wayne Co.[2] He wants to see you, said he should write you.

You ask what I shall speak about. Woman's Rights generally, but sometimes on the Maine Law,[3] or Antislavery; and preachment meetings sundays. Am going to be at home some weeks now—speaking some in this vicinity. It seems strange to think of your brothers wife being gone so suddenly—gone—yes but if you believe in the spirits you will not think her far off.

What a queer mystery those spirit rappings are? I read Sunderlands sermon & the review. What a dunce he is!—Prof. Finney is in Syracuse preaching.

Yours in love forever
Nette

ALS-SL

1. In February 1853, Paulina Wright Davis began publishing a monthly periodical, the *Una;* her friend Elizabeth Oakes Smith contributed to it regularly.
2. Wadsworth, then a theological student, was welcomed at South Butler, a small community with difficulty attracting pastors.
3. In 1851, the state of Maine enacted a strict antiliquor ordinance that became the prototype for antebellum temperance legislation. Known as the Maine Law, the measure banned the sale of alcoholic beverages, expedited prosecution of violators, levied heavy fines for possession, and mandated imprisonment for repeat offenders.

[*Albany, N.Y. January 24, 1853*][1]

Lucy darling, I want to see you but you are not here.

L Mott[2] wants a woman's rights convention here at Albany right away, thinks there is interest at present which would bring out an overwhelming mass. We had that at the Temperance meeting.[3] What do you think? Will you be here? Will they want an organization? Will Mrs. Smith and Mrs Rose work together, &c, &c?[4] That is what Miss Anthony referred to.

Your meetings in Troy were not advertised. Miss Anthony and I went there Sunday. She spoke on Temperance. I preached & talked

Womans Rights—am to speak there again Thursday nigh[*t*] & also
next Sunday. Mrs E Oaks Smith was there the day before we were
& herself asked the privilege of addressing their L[*y*]ceum—was
refused—but to night I have just written her the friends there will
assist her to lecture in a large hall with an admission fee. They want
you there very much. Say they want a variety and a great blow struck.
Do come back into this state. I cannot visit N. England this winter.
Did not mean to be gone a week from home when I left, but have
been over-persuaded to speak a few times with Miss Anthony on the
Maine Law. She is a driving business woman.

Are you well again. Dont get sick. Am going to stay here at the
Jerry trials.[5] We missed you so much in the Convention. Some of
the faces looked blank as the day wore on. I heard no women speak
at all. Was in the business room half the morning. Sick abed in the
afternoon &c.

Please drop a line at Albany if you get this right away directed
care of A F Dickinson. If not direct N.Y. care of Mrs. L. F. Fowler.[6]
Lydia Mott wants an admission fee & the speakers all paid at the
convention.

Nette

ALS-LC

1. A letter from Susan B. Anthony to LS appears on the same sheet,
preceding this letter from ALB to LS.

2. Lydia Mott (1807-75) of Albany, N.Y., was an outspoken advocate of
temperance, peace, antislavery, and woman's rights. The sister-in-law of
Lucretia Mott, she supported herself and an elder sister by teaching, board-
inghouse keeping, and sewing.

3. ALB, Susan B. Anthony, and others delivered temperance petitions
to the New York State legislature and spoke to supporters in a series of
Albany meetings in January 1853.

4. Ernestine Rose was a controversial figure because of her association
with free-thought reformers; some woman's rights supporters rejected Elizabeth Smith because of her extravagant dress.

5. On October 1, 1851, Jerry McHenry, also known as William Henry,
an alleged fugitive slave, was arrested in Syracuse. Members of the local
black community stormed the jail where McHenry was held and freed him,
but he was shortly recaptured. That same evening, the local Unitarian
minister, Samuel J. May, and Gerrit Smith, in town for the state Liberty
Party Convention, engineered a second and successful rescue attempt, sending McHenry to Canada. The federal government indicted twenty-six people
for aiding the escape of the fugitive, although ultimately only four were
brought to trial.

6. Lydia Folger Fowler (1822-79), a lecturer on female anatomy, physi-

ology, and hygiene, received her medical degree from Central Medical College of Syracuse, and briefly taught there. When the medical college folded Fowler moved to New York City where she practiced medicine and gave occasional lectures.

Buffalo [*N. Y.*] March 29 1853

Lucy Darling

How do you do all this long time. Oh dear if you were only here so I could put my arm close around you and feel your heart beating against mine as in lang syne. Mrs. Bloomer, Miss Anthony and I, are here. We had a crowded house last night—a nice time—are to speak again tonight by request—have the theater tonight so as to get a good room; for half the people could n't get in last evening. This concludes our engagement together and it will seem good to get home again, and to go more on ones own hooks. I like Miss Anthony very much, but poor child she'll never get along smoothly in this world. Its as much her manner as the matter of what she says, and as for Mrs. Bloomer—you know her, so Ill make no comments.[1]

Well, you are going to N.Y.[2] I am so glad. You will make a sensation there and it will be grand. You must speak there several times; and you must be at the Rochester Temperance meeting in June. They'll have warm times I reckon, taking all together. More squirming than we have ever had at any woman's rights meeting, and I fear more meanness.[3] Now dont be frightened over us women for we are, and shall be for the present, a pretty small little set of beings.

Westfield [*N. Y.*] April 1st 1853

Time grows apace. My letter was interrupted the other day and here it is on hand yet. Our last meeting at the Buffalo Theater was a grand good one. Every thing went off well. Miss Anthony & a Miss Wright and I are here in Westfield. How it came about dont know only that without my knowledge or consent was advertised to be here last evening.

Well, when we got here the church which had been granted us was refused for a multiplicity of reasons—we were crowded into a small hall so rickety that they dared not let many people in for fear of a crash—it rained all the evening and yet hundreds who came to meeting were sent home again as wise as they came. The village is

in something of an uproar about us. Miss Wright makes her debut
as a lecturer here this evening, she is a *sensible* girl not over refined
though—a cousin of Jenny Bell, of Oberlin memory. Susan goes to
Rochester at One Ock to day; and I, now the fates so decide it, am
to have a pay lecture here tomorrow night, and preach sunday, though
I've not so much as the scrap of a sermon with me. Hope to recover
from a grim crossness which is over me now, before that time.

Susan says you were very tired when you wrote her. You certainly
will get sick, Lucy dear, if you keep all the time working as you do,
it is wicked, cruel, foolish, outrageous and as many other things as
you please to sit down to the same account. What does make you
do so? My face is as long as the moral law just for what I have done
and yours will get to be as long as the immoral law if you keep up
that suicidal process of all work and no play. Pray do get time to
breath freely once in a while.

It is said you are in favor of divorce on the ground of drunkenness.
So I see is Mrs. Davis. Of course that means you are in favor of
divorce whenever the parties want it. Thats so isnt it? Well I am not
ready for that yet. Let them have legal separation but not the right
of second marriage. Say what you think when you write please.

Most lovingly yours
Nette

Write at Henrietta right off.

ALS-LC

1. At this point in the letter, an addition in the hand of ASB appears:
" 'She [Anthony] was the most angular person I ever had to do with,' said
Aunt Nettie, 'but I always liked her. The papers always pitched into her.
Mrs. Bloomer was pretty and gentle, and was not much pitched into, though
she wore bloomers. I wore long dresses, & was not pitched into. But poor
Susan did not look well in bloomers. She was a sort of scape-goat for all
of us. We travelled together several months.' "
2. LS attended the "Brick Church Meeting" on May 12, 1853, in New
York City; convened to plan a World's Temperance Convention, the assembly accepted the credentials of women delegates, but refused to permit
their participation in designing the forthcoming convention.
3. ALB foresaw problems that surfaced at the first annual meeting of
the Woman's New York State Temperance Society, held in Rochester, June
1-2, 1853. At that gathering, temperance men and conservative women,
disturbed by the positions on divorce and woman's rights that Stanton and
Anthony had taken on behalf of the organization, ousted them from the
leadership.

Henrietta May 4th 1853

Dearest Lucy

Your dear little letter just this moment came. I cannot be at N.Y. at the anniversaries[1] — had engaged to be in Ohio at that time before I knew they wanted any delegates. But do you go, Lucy. Make them admit women to the World's Temperance Convention — then stay here in this state till the first of June — or at any rate do be here at Rochester. Do, do, Lucy! They want you so much! They have advertised you, every body expects it, and you must come.

Do come because I want so much to see you. Both our hearts need warming together.

The blaze goes out you know in two poor sticks of wood placed away from each other, but if you bring them up side by side they burn brightly and pleasantly. So it is with human hearts; but the *friendly* flame in our souls is so pure & holy that it may burn on and the spirit be unconsumed like Moses burning bush.

Well at any rate do come, dear Lucy do! do! do!

The Tribune gave grand good reports of your meetings didn't it? How did you like Horace Greeley? Dont wish him dead for a year or two longer, he seems to be doing *his* work. But isnt he a queer man? Susan Anthony will be at N.Y. the 11th.

I leave here next Monday speak that night at Buffalo on Temperance then go on from there talking on *Woman* every evening till Saturday when I go to Oberlin to see my dear sis Ella & spend a day or two.

Every thing is getting to be so beautiful & Spring like here. Dont your heart sing too now in these times — if it does not you are so tired and *must rest.* You never can get *cold* hearted.

Most Lovingly Yours
Nette

ALS-LC

1. The annual meeting of the AASS was held in New York City, May 11, 1853.

South Butler [*N.Y.*] June 10 '53[1]

Lucy Darling

Mr Goff[2] has just written me again about going to N.Y. He says he is going to write you about lecturing there also, and wants you to meet me there in a week or two. It is utterly impossible for me to go, but I write you by his request and most sincerely hope you will go if you consistently can. He offers me board, washing, &c, & a 1000 dollars a year paid quarterly in advance, 1500 for the second year &c. Well, I cant go! So we'll drop it at once!

I have commited a great sin against you, want to make acknowledgement and if possible atonement. I have stolen your understandings. Now they are drawing heavily around my conscience. You know how it is when we stretch a piece of india rubber and wind it round our fingers. It pulls harder and harder until it becomes painful. Just such is the effect of your lost, stolen property on my mind. Please tell me what I shall do under the circumstances to find forgiveness and relief.

Why didnt you stay at Syracuse to the Christian Union meeting.[3] There was almost every ism in the world represented there except yours. If you had been present we could have had a regular hash of all the religious and antireligious sects enmasse. Have just got home— had a good time.

Have hardly got settled here yet. Have a good boarding place in the village with a firm of doctors. Had an overflowing house Sunday last, have two Sermons to prepare for Sunday next, and its now Friday afternoon.

So good bye
Nette

ALS-LC

1. This was ALB's first letter to LS from South Butler, where ALB was ordained as a Congregational minister September 15, 1853.
2. A note in the hand of ASB has been inserted here between the lines: "(someone in NY—Mr. Goff acted as agent Mr. Dana was supposed to be behind it) & some of the Tribune people."
3. The American and Foreign Christian Union was an anti-Catholic organization.

South Butler June 8 1853[1]

Dearest Lucy

Your letter came in here from the P.O. just this minute. I sat here writing letters when it came and yours shall be the first replied to, still you will not get my answer this week by a good deal for the mail has gone for to day, and this is Friday.

P.O. arrangements are broken up by railroad changes and this has caused the delay.

Put my name to the Call if you choose. I had rather it would be in N.Y. than Cleveland or do you expect one in both places.[2] What has become of the Worlds Temperance Convention Call? I have not seen it.

We had a grand fourth here—a picnic in a grove. Mr May was to have been present; but the cars were thrown off from the train & prevented.

Every body is expecting you here in the fall. Come and make a good long rest here wont you? Do make your plans in that way.

I did not write the N.Y. man again after I got your letter because I thought you had of course given him all necessary answer and I had nothing to write about.

I love you Lucy any way, and if you would only come & take a nap with me here in my bed my head would get rested a great deal faster for it is aching now.

Our Baptist minister wont hear me speak. He went out of the grove twice Monday when I talked. Nice isnt it!

Sisternaly
Nette

ALS-SL

1. ALB misdated this letter; the events to which she referred occurred one month later on July 4, 1853, when woman's rights activists presented addresses in several locations.

2. ALB gave LS permission to list her name on the announcement of a woman's rights convention to be held in New York City, September 6-7, 1853. This meeting followed the Whole World's Temperance Convention, which preceded and protested the conservative World's Temperance Convention planned at the Brick Church meeting and held September 7, 1853.

South Butler Aug. 2. 53

Lucy Darling

Such a scolding! Oh dear! I cant cry, though the skies have been weeping all night. Dont feel a bit like smiling either though the sun is just beginning to coax me into it. Such a big grumble as you can make sometimes! Every word falling on an innocent head too!

"Bless you, child, I am as guiltless as the babe unborn." How should I know that your letters were not to be sent Boston-wise. That *was* your address. I dont take the Liberator, & had seen no counter statements. You didnt tell me at Rochester,[1] though you did say you should be at home resting. But you have said so dozens of times before; & the next I heard of you you were shouting eloquence into the ears of the Man in the Moon a hundred miles away. Then your letter wasnt dated Brookfield but Warren or somewhere else (I forgot where) so I stopped, pen in hand, thought a whole second multiplied I should say as much as 8 times, thought & thought where to direct; & then sent to Corn Hill as the safest course.

"Great people" may be careless, but if this is a symbol of the thing, I am growing beautifully less & less every day; and expect to become before long wonderfully exemplary in all business habits. If you had not known me at Oberlin you would not have dreamed me over careless; but the truth is, one likes old associations so well that whenever I come where you are I fall insensibly into the habits of Lang Syne, if only for the sake of having you scold me as usual. So write as many lectures as you please, only if you *will* take my word about my improvement you will not sigh *so disparingly* about my incoregability.

Well! well! "dear little Lucy, you must let me speak." Of course according to precedent the review has a right to roll out its dull lengths beyond the original article.

Say in your next if you will come here & rest a week, lecturing some in the mean time for us Butlerites. You must come! We expect you!

Where do you stop in N.Y. when you go next, or dont you know?

Why wont you come hence right after, or soon after the Jerry rescue.[2] Susan Anthony says you will come west of Syracuse then.

Remember of all the people in the world somebody has a prior claim over you than all the rest. Of course you must rest somewhere between the many meetings, & Cleveland excitement[3] so come here as your proper place & the quietest ark for a poor tired dove in the whole world. Dont go croaking about, raven like, through the whole season never stopping for a bit of quiet. If you do theres a precious bit of scolding laid up for you somewhere.

Is every thing righted up now for the Worlds Demonstrations.

Why was there not a black man or womans name on the Temperance Call?

Ever
Nette

ALS-LC

1. ALB and LS both attended the first annual meeting of the Woman's State Temperance Society in Rochester, N.Y., June 1-2, 1853.

2. The anniversary of the rescue of the fugitive slave Jerry McHenry, on October 1, 1851, became the occasion for an annual celebration by Syracuse abolitionists.

3. The fourth national Woman's Rights Convention was held in Cleveland, October 6-8, 1853.

Henrietta Aug. 16 1853

Dear Lucy

You are the biggest little goose and granny fuss that I ever did see. So you will not go to South Butler! Then you ought to be giffarooned or gibbeted or something of that sort! They are all expecting you there; & they know besides that you wear bloomers and are an 'infidel.' You told me at Rochester you would go there in the fall, so I told them so.

Now Lucy, dont get into any obstinate fits & do come and see me, O do! What nonsense to think of your injuring in any way my success as a minister by lecturing to them. I know its a little wee village & if you dont wish to speak for them more than once, why dont do so, though of course we should like to have you speak several times. But pray dont get into any such crabbed notions about staying away. If you do we shall quarrel in real earnest; for *I* never will have a friend who is ashamed of me, or I ashamed of her, or *one that must keep away from me to preserve my reputation or ensure my success.* I am still much "more of a (wo)man than a minister." Now dont go to breaking up old associations. *I have still need of YOU whether you have of me or not;* and any congregation I may preach to will not be scared over-much by any thing you will say. They believe in free speech! Besides the two daughters of the very man who was instrumental more than all others in getting me at Butler, (a leading man in the church & congregation) this mans two daughters both wear bloomers. Every body there knows you & your reputation as well almost now as they will after seeing you, for your fame is abroad in the land. They think you of course worse than you are, with the few exceptions of those who have heard you already. Then lots of old grannies like Mrs. P[almeter] are along speaking for us, & I do want a smart one to come once in awhile. In short there are a thousand & one reasons why you must be at Butler this fall. At any rate why you do not pledge yourself to keep away. It made me half mad to know you should think so meanly of me, & to see that you fancied my success to be such an exclusive narrow minded soap bubble. It reminded me of what Stephen Foster said Mr. Finney thought. 'That the Lord run away as soon as two infidels set their feet in Oberlin.' Unless you wish me to become as bigoted as you *think* the church are dont stay away to make me so.

I want to stop with you at N.Y. Mrs. Fowler wrote me some time ago to stop with her & said she *should invite you,* & others. Of course I thought beggars had better not be choosers in a crowded city like that. She wanted an answer immediately so that she could depend upon me, or else invite others, so I wrote her I would stop with her. I wish you would not go to Dr. Wellingtons;[1] but, we'll see! You must be with me some of the time at least. When do you go to the city?

Don't you get *sick* of such humanity as we have extant; & sigh "O for a lodge in some vast wilderness." Of *course* they will quarrel about the presidency, it would be beyond precedent if they did not.[2] But this helping you 'manage'! I dont know what to manage for, I'm sure, since its six for one, & half a dozen for all the others, unless we go to managing for *yourself* or *myself.* On the whole *I* think Ill go to electioneering for no.1. Have been studying parliamentary rules! Have been gathering a world of dignity by presiding over grave church meetings. Think I should make a good president! Think I should grace the meeting exceedingly! Think Ill accept the office! What do you say? ha! ha!

Am at home you see this week, brother Billy & family are here & the other brothers people expected soon. May stay over a sabbath.

Most Lovingly
forever
Nette

Write me a little scrawl again cant you. Direct Henrietta. Shall be here most of the time for two weeks.

There's no time to write better.

ALS-SL

1. Oliver H. Wellington was a New York City physician.
2. After the controversial appointment of fashionably dressed Paulina Davis to chair the 1852 convention, the respected and venerable Quaker Lucretia Mott was chosen to preside at the 1853 New York City Woman's Rights Convention.

South Butler, Feb. 18, 1854.

Lucy darling:

It is a long time since either of us has written one such letter as of lang syne. Have you and I grown strangers? God help us then— this is not a world made up of true friends.

You are sad sometimes. No one was ever ill yet of over mental and physical exertion and excitement without being so. Susan showed me what you said about your dress.[1] Many things sorry and joyous come on the wings of the wind; and one who long ago took a peep into your heart as it beat fast and strongly then can appreciate its heavier throbbings now. God bless you, Lucy! Tonight I could nestle closer to your heart than on that night when I went through the dark and the rain and Tappan Hall[2] and school rules—all to feel your arm around me—and to know that in all this wide world I was not alone. *Alone,* that feeling has come to both of us since. It may be better so! At any rate, don't suffer martyrdom over a short dress or anything else that *can* be prevented. Sorrow enough will come and fate itself cannot prevent. Be strong and brave hearted. There are many years in the distance waiting yet with greater burdens for your spirit. So let every avoidable thing go and good riddance to it.

Now, Lucy, I must go to prayer meeting. It is just time and like to have been forgotten. Do you think me any wickeder for being a minister? John Pierpont[3] says he is more of a man than he is a minister. Write me one letter out of your heart just as you feel. Your soul knows what it is to be hungry for some familiar voice, for one old note of melody that will vibrate some sleeping spirit chord. A cordial good-night.

[*Antoinette Brown*]

tL-SLg

1. LS had worn the bloomer costume since 1850, but wrote to Susan B. Anthony of her decision to include long as well as short skirts in her wardrobe. Anthony disapproved of her decision.

2. The main walk across the campus passed through Tappan Hall, the principal classroom building and men's dormitory at Oberlin during the student days of LS and ALB.

3. John Pierpont (1785-1866), an antislavery activist, writer, and Unitarian minister, had studied law before choosing the ministry; his outspoken temperance and abolitionist sentiments ultimately forced his resignation from his Boston pastorate, after which he moved to West Medford, Mass.

South Butler May 21, 1854

Lucy Darling

It is Sunday evening,—and such a rain! First there came a whirl-wind, then a water spout, the drops hardly separating on their way down from the big black cloud.

Do you know I am very glad of it, for it has broken up the third meeting; and for this once it is pleasanter to write you a letter than go to meeting so tired.

So I shall not see you this spring! Up to the time your letter came we all hoped you would stop here, even if for ever so short a time. Well it must be all for the best; but I scolded first, and then cried about it afterwards.

Miss Parsons paper[1] shall be safely returned. As for the Liberator it has never come. Thank you, though, for the good intention. They doubtless judged rightly about it. I am neither a pauper nor unfriendly to the Liberator; could take it if earnestly enough disposed, and would if there was any probability of getting converted by the means.

Are you intending to be at home most of the time this summer? It seems you were not at N.Y! No account of Boston meetings has reached these benighted regions.[2] The daily Tribune did come here for six months and it is to be reordered this week. It is almost as well to be out of the world as without it.

Dont lecture this summer! You must need rest—heart rest—and mind rest, and some new chapters of thinking, too. Fancy, pictures you going up that wild old hill and nestling down under the shadow of a big rock, whiling away the time in reading and revery. If that old quiet hill was here in Butler there should be one pathway worn up its side, even in the growing time of spring.

And you New Englanders have a Boston Convention! It is a fine idea. The little Woman's Rights ball seems to be pushed ahead, to grow in size and increase in force, instead of unraveling in long and tangled yarns as the people prophesied. Faster and faster let it roll! But *dont* you sometimes get tired of pushing it on?

Have just had a letter from sister Ella at Oberlin. Prof Peck, it seems, offered $900.00 towards an institution Library. The students were to contribute as they felt able, they were to get up a constitution. The whole was to belong to the students, gentlemen and ladies. A constitution was drawn up, making all equals. The Faculty objected to it. Prof Fairchild drew up a new one making two business divisions, one for men one for women, like quaker meetings, though all were to have the Library in common. The students would not accept it. So when Ella wrote it was all excitement, and undecided what should be done. Good isn't it! The poor professors have a hard time of it with their refractory crew.

Write, Lucy dear, if it is not burdensome to you. When you have been for a year in a place where there is not a mortal person for whom you feel a real affinity, and yet, are *a sort of public property for all,* with the delightful anticipation of a twin year to follow, you will realize how welcome a letter or the face of a *friend* would be. This meeting people at wearysome Conventions is not worth a fig. All work and no play makes them all a stupid set of dull boys.

Cordially
Nette

ALS-SL

1. Anna Q.T. Parsons, a Boston woman's rights activist, attended the Worcester convention of 1850.
2. LS did not attend the anniversary meeting of the AASS in New York City, May 10-11, 1854. A New England ASS convention was held in Boston, May 30-June 1, 1854, followed by a woman's rights convention, June 2, 1854.

Henrietta Aug 16 1854

Dearest Lucy

Thank you for the kind invitation to spend the two months with [*you*] at your sisters quiet home! I should so much like to spend some time with you if it might be.

I am at my own quiet home and have been here more than a week am to remain two weeks longer before returning to South Butler. Rest seemed indispensable so I concluded to take it. Susan Anthony was here a day or two since. She said you were nearly sick and could not be at Saratoga as she hoped. She is going there herself whether any one else goes or not, but she still hopes to obtain Mrs. Rose.[1]

Is it not good to rest—to lie still and listen to the crickets and grasshoppers. If they sing in the miner key it is still very pleasant when one is in the mood for listening. If the grasshoppers were men who lived before the time of the Muses and died from neglecting to eat and drink while entranced in listening to these new singers, being afterwards transformed to grasshoppers who have nothing to do but sing, it seems to me it must be quite as acceptable to them to have us wraped in lazy reveries, listening to their music, as it would be to have us forever talking philosophy in their hearing like Plato. They *must* remember how tired they did used to get with all the turmoil of activity, and have an instinctive feeling that we need rest and indolence. I am fully expecting that when they go up to the Muses they will carry our names as persons worthy to receive honor from them, notwithstanding all these "shiftless" moods that I at least indulge in. For you are you really resting or not? or does it seem a sin to you after all to be idle?

My sister Rebecca leaves tomorrow for Oberlin to attend Commencement. Ella will come home next week just when I am ready to leave.[2]

Are you expecting a large Convention at Philadelphia.[3] Shall you be there *without fail?* Does being secretary devolve any duties upon me in the line of sending invitations to any body. It seems to me every one is at liberty to attend and need no inviting. If there are any official duties am quite ignorant of them and am moreover the last person from whom to have expected the discharge of responsibilities.

Most Affectionately
Nette

ALS-SL

1. Rose did not join Anthony in Saratoga, although Sarah Pellet and Matilda Joslyn Gage did.
2. ALB's sister Ella graduated from the Ladies' course, August 22, 1854.
3. The fifth national Woman's Rights Convention was held in Philadelphia, October 18, 1854.

Henrietta Aug. 14 '54[1]

What a busy life you must lead, Lucy darling. It really makes me nervous to think of so much regularity. You must be a perfect little epitome of system! I am the personification of vagabondism. Under favorable circumstances the civil authorities would have me arrested for a vagrant. I should plead guilty and go willingly to jail for six months.

They say there is to be a good Convention at Phi[la.] Success to it! I hope to be there; but am not at all sure about it. Every thing seems uncertain in these days, since I have "taken to idleness." So please choose some better material for a President.[2] After all it is rather unnecessary to decline an honor that has little likelihood of being confered.

I have been reading history also particularly histories of the Dark and Middle Ages—of the Reformation and English War. Have been gathering materials for a cronological analysis and hope to go on with the same course after a short time. Have many serious thoughts of adjourning my relations to South Butler sini die.[3]

Yes this is a beautiful world and life is full of every thing glorious, a tangled inexplicable mystery though it is! How I like to see the sunshine break through the night and roll over every thing in one flood of light and beauty. It should melt the heart of a pagan into genuine spiritual worship; and convert skepticism itself into mysticism. But "living poetry" has not been my forte for the last year, nor is it now.

My sisters are both at home. One sister in law and her little girl are here and we are all having an old fashioned home made visit, eating peaches and grapes and enjoying the good things of to day. What an animal life one can lead, eating, drinking, and being merry. We are not governed though wholly by the expectation of dying tomorrow but are acting in the hope of living till the next day.

So Sarah Pellet has really gone to California![4] Peace be with her. I do most earnestly hope she will stay long enough and be successful enough to come back with a fortune.

Direct your letters for the present to Henrietta.

And now my dearest little cow boy with the utmost affection and the best of good wishes for your future peace.

I remain yours ever
Nette

ALS-SL

1. Internal evidence as well as the correspondence of LS with others suggests that this letter was actually written in September 1854.

2. James and Lucretia Mott suggested that ALB serve as president of the Philadelphia Woman's Rights Convention, but the honor fell to Ernestine Rose.

3. ALB incorrectly spelled the Latin phrase *sine die,* meaning without any definite date for resumption. Official documents date her resignation from her South Butler pastorate July 20, 1854; her resignation was dated retroactively.

4. Pellet departed for California on August 4, 1854; she remained in the West for two years, lecturing primarily on temperance.

West Brookfield Mar. 29 [*1855*]

Nettee dear

I came home last week Friday, and found your little note written in the cars. Thank you for remembering me enough to write in the cars. I saw a little note to Lydia Mott written in the same way.

And so you are to be in N.Y. and I am to be lost in the woods at the West[1] — Well, God bless you, and help you realize your best hopes — your worthiest plans!

"Smiles and tears" follow each other when you think of my "matrimony" — Well Nettee dear, the world is full of both, so you are not alone —

The *day* is not set. I have not been quite well, and so it is delayed. But when it is fixed — I will write you, so that you may think of me, and fancy if you can, what of thought and feeling goes on, under the surface.

If the ceremony is in N.Y. we want you to harden your heart enough to help in so cruel an operation, as putting Lucy Stone to death. But it will be all according to law, so you need feel no punishment. I *expect* however to go to Cincinnati & have the ruin completed there —

Dear Nettee ———

I am tired, my head aches, so excuse, for I must get rested, and strong.

> With love that never dies
> Yours ever
> Lucy

ALS-LC

1. Six months after ALB left her position with the church in South Butler, she moved to New York City where she rented halls in which to hold Sunday services; with the encouragement of Horace Greeley, she toured the slums and wrote for his *New York Tribune*.

LS had recently announced her engagement to HBB, a resident of Cincinnati.

Walnut Hills [*Ohio*] — July 11 [*1855*][1]

Dear Nettee

I got your little bit of a letter written just after Ella's wedding,[2] two or three days ago — So that sad occasion is over and you are resting! I am glad that you do not go back to N.Y. in this dreadful heat—Your "Shadows of Social Life"—can find birth just as well where you are, and it will be much better for you.[3] I expect to be at Saratoga, tho only for one day.[4] But I do not think it is in *any* sense good economy to have a meeting *there*—The people who congregate at Saratoga are not reformers, not workers and will *never* help forward our ideas. I would give more for a patient hearing in some country school-house. The rich and fashionable, move only when the masses that are behind and under them move. So that our real work is with the mass, who have no reputation to lose, no ambition to gratify, and who, as they do not depend upon the Public, need not smother their convictions for its favor—

We mistake, when we try *first* to reach the visitors at Saratoga— They always *follow,* and *never* lead Public opinion—You will of course be *here,* and you must be Prest. In this city of Gen. Carey,[5] the people must see you, and they will get a truer idea of the real war at N.Y. by your presence as Prest. than they can now in any other way, until the history of Woman's Rights is written—So make up your mind for that post of honor—

Paulina Davis has written me, that she wants the marriage question to come up at the National Convention (I hope she wont be here, with her vanity and her jealousy.) It seems to me that we are not ready for it. I saw that at Philadelphia, by private conversations. No two of us think alike about it. And yet it is clear to me, that question underlies, this whole movement and all our little skirmishing for better laws, and the right to vote, will yet be swallowed up, in the real question, viz, has woman, as wife, a right to herself? It is very little to me to have the right to vote, to own property &c. if I may not keep my body, and its uses, in my absolute right. Not one wife in a thousand can do that now, & so long as she suffers this bondage, all other rights will not help her to her true position—This question will *force* itself upon us some day, but it seems to me it is *un*timely now—

Write me what you think about it. I expect to go home next week, and shall stop in Rochester to see Susan A consult with her relative to various matters—I wish you could be there too. I shall have a little 4 year old niece along with me,[6] or I would go out and see you—I cant tell what day I shall be there, as I have not yet decided when I leave here. Ellen[7] will either go on with me or come, a little later. She will find good opportunities to sketch in N.E. and she wishes very much to improve in landscape painting. I wish you would take your sketching materials to the White Mts. with us, for a week. Cant you? We will have good times together.

What do you think of the new abolition plan, started at Syracuse the other day? Mr. *Cune Smith* Prest!!!![8] They certainly have *resolutions* enough. Shall you sail under their flag? I like more and more the Garrisonian platform, which, giving the Slaveholder his due, never dodges, conceals or compromises—How Slavery has debauched the moral sense of this country!

What do you and Susan mean, by such little sentences as, "the world needs you" &c. Do you think I am likely to forget that the *least service* is needed? When you see me listlessly on my oars, heedless of the heavy throbbings of Humanity's tired sick heart, then it will be time to stab with such little insinuations—As yet I *do not deserve them*—

Mrs. Blackwell[9] is gathering raspberries of which we have a rich abundance in the garden—Ellen is at her painting in the barn, where she has a studio. Sam[10] & Harry are at the store—Harry every now and then, nobly helps off a Fugitive—I will leave this open so he can answer your note to him—

Tell me of your plans when you write. I hope you will be able dear Nettee to carry out your highest ideas, and to make your life what it ought to be. I dont hear from Channing[11] only as I saw in the last Standard[12] that the Unitarian Clergy of London had given him a dinner—

ever lovingly
Lucy

ALS-LC

1. LS and HBB resided at his mother's home in Walnut Hills, suburban Cincinnati, immediately after their marriage.

2. ALB's sister Ella married Alexander McCullom, OC 1852, OS 1855, on June 22, 1855. He held pastorates in Massachusetts and Kansas. Ella Brown McCullom died in Kansas in 1862.

3. ALB wrote a series of articles entitled "Shadows of Our Social System" for the *New York Tribune,* reflecting on the poverty and misery she had seen in the New York City slums.

4. For the second consecutive year, Anthony conducted suffrage meetings in Saratoga Springs, N.Y., during the summer season; in 1855, both ALB and LS participated.

5. Samuel Fenton Carey (1814-1900), an Ohio lawyer and paymaster general of Ohio troops during the Mexican War, was active in the antislavery and temperance movements. At the World Temperance Convention in 1853, he was an outspoken opponent of women's participation, arguing that they needed to be protected from the strain of addressing the public.

6. Emma Lawrence (1851-1920) was the daughter of LS's sister Sarah

and her husband, Henry Lawrence; they then lived in Cumminsville, Ohio, near Cincinnati, while Henry Lawrence taught in the local house of refuge.

7. Ellen Blackwell (1828-1901), LS's sister-in-law, was an artist and author.

8. James McCune Smith (1813-65), a black physician, writer, and abolitionist, presided over an antislavery convention in Syracuse, June 27, 1855.

9. Hannah Lane Blackwell (1792-1879) was the mother of nine children including HBB and SCB.

10. SCB was then HBB's partner in the hardware business.

11. William Henry Channing (1810-84), Unitarian clergyman, abolitionist, and supporter of woman's rights, in 1854 left his Rochester, N.Y., pulpit for England, where he spent most of the remainder of his life.

12. The *National Anti-Slavery Standard* was published by the AASS in New York City, 1840-66.

[*Walnut Hills*] Sunday P.M. Jan. 20 [*1856*]

Nettee dear. I have been thinking of you this last Sunday of your unwedded life, and enjoying the holy hopes that I know are blessing your heart today[1] — May they ripen to the *richest fullness* and prove for you, what my love has to me, constantly more beautiful, more *soul-ful,* more necessary.

Harry and I, shall not be here on your arrival but we will leave our heart's cordial greeting and glad welcome to our home, and to the little room which ought to be larger, but which your mutual love will make cosy and comfortable[2] —

I am glad for your sake & Sam's that we are to be absent; for just as when the soul first wakes up to the full consciousness of a love that will last, forever, and color all its future, then, solitude becomes so imperative a necessity, scarcely less does the same need of being alone with the one only loved, exist, when law, and custom first give you to each other—.

You will find our Mother kind and sympathizing—She has not forgotten her own wedding.

You will write your book better dear Nettee, and do everything better when you share the personal presence, and full sympathy & love of Sam—have not *I* a right to affirm, who have been nine months married? Especially when you are both two so really good people!

I congratulate *you* on your rare good fortune, for "Sam is one of the best men in the world and *he* may rejoice in the fact, that he alone of all the men in the world has a *Divine* wife—"

God bless you both and make you more to each other than even your highest anticipations!

Most aff—
Lucy Stone

ALS-LC

1. ALB married SCB January 24, 1856.
2. After their marriage in Henrietta, ALBB and SCB traveled to Cincinnati; when they arrived, LS was away on a lecture tour of Illinois and Indiana, and HBB was traveling for his hardware business.

[Early Summer? 1856][1]

Nettee dear. How much I wish I had you here, where though it is very hot, yet a cool breeze blows through the room, and I am afraid you do not get it there, and you never needed it more. How do you do, with your new experiences, and new hopes & new fears?[2] Dont feel obliged to answer one of these questions, only be sure dear Nettee that I sympathise, with you, and respect the moods, silent or otherwise which these months will give. I am glad that you are so well. Dont blame yourself Nettee, if you find that all the "original sin" seems to try and manifest itself in you, for even Margaret Fuller[3] with all her strength and philosophy says, she was "never so unreasonable and desponding"—Blame the circumstances, though may be the Furies will not haunt you, as they so often do, even the very best. I hope that everything will go pleasantly, and that another new year, will find your heart, made glad & warm & large by a *Mother's* love. For myself, I almost despair. Will you give me one of your seven? I expect some new phases of life this summer and shall try and get the honey from each moment.

Yours in love and trust,
Lucy

ALS-SL

1. HBB and LS traveled around the Midwest combining business and woman's rights lectures from May to July 1856. It is unclear where this letter was written.
2. ALBB was pregnant with her first child, Florence, born November 7, 1856.

3. Margaret Fuller (1810-50), woman's rights advocate, transcendentalist, critic, and author of *Woman in the Nineteenth Century* (New York, 1845), bore her only child in Italy in 1848.

[*Orange, N.J.*] Our New House, June 11th 1858[1]

Dear Lucy

Here we are in our new nursery. Sam is looking for Harrys papers Miss Wright sewing, Bridget just came in with the silver to know where she shall put it, Florey asleep in the bedroom bed, and baby[2] proper asleep by herself up stairs. Florey is shortly coming to her cradle, & we are all going to the land of nod for the clock is just striking 9.

Will you wonder Lucy to learn that we are here; yet so it is. We have brought as many traps with us as we possibly could, & will use as few of yours as may be; & those as carefully as we can. The children shall keep in this room, the 'long one', as mother calls it, & on the porches. & Florence is to eat no bread & butter on the premises. We have brought childrens bedding; & will see that yours is not injured. Our carriage is here also, &c; & every body is directed to be very careful not to do mischief. So I hope nothing will suffer by our being here. We have been having a heavy thunder storm this afternoon. The rain leaked in a good deal through the West windows for it beat down in that direction furiously. When I saw that, I was glad we were here to wipe up the dampness; but I feel a good deal like an interloper. Your man was here with a boy working in the garden to day, & the milkman was mowing grass. Every thing looks well. We did expect to have strawberries for tea, but the rain prevented. You are invited to take tea with us here in our new house tomorrow evening when the first fruit of the season will be produced; & we will entertain you benevolently, & charitably give you a whole saucer of our fine fruit.

When will you pay us a visit? You shall have a cordial welcome, & if you are in need of a house you shall either have possession here or we will make some other kindly arrangements for your comfort. As for Henry if he wishes to visit Orange without you he may come & board with us for a whole month or for the summer if he chooses & we will take the best care of him while you ruralize. But I am too tired to write more. You will understand that we came over to get fresh air & change for the babies &c, & because the house was here unoccupied. I am writing hastily & on a paper on my knee for we only brought two lamps & Sam is afraid to use your style of lamp. So we all sit here at one of the little book cases & enjoy it. You should see how comfortable every thing looks. Mother left this morning.

Write soon. If there is *any thing* you wish attended to let me know. I hope you are having a good visit.

Lovingly
Nette

ALS-LC

1. ALBB and her family lived in Newark, but spent the summer at LS's home in Orange, N.J., while LS and ASB (born September 14, 1857) were in Chicago with HBB, then employed as a salesman of agricultural libraries.
2. ALBB's second daughter, Mabel, was born April 13, 1858.

Newark [*N.J.*] Aug 3 1858

Dear Henry and Lucy

Little Mabel still lives, and now our hearts are vacillating between hope and fear. We have felt that we were past hope; and once we thought and felt that the little eyes which had been looking about with such preternatural brightness and restlessness for so long, were closed at last to open no more. It was only a sleep; but as it was the first she had had we mistook its character. Since then she sleeps a good deal, usually short naps; but over and over again in the dim light at night I have put my hand to the little cheek or listened for the faint breathing with a deadly fear.

Elizabeth[1] says it is now a question of vitality. If she has enough she will overcome the disease—if not——

She takes gum water for a drink; but best of all she now takes mother's milk which a neighbor comes over every two hours to give her, though we have to feed her from the spoon, she is so weak. Kitty[2] says *your* baby is sick once more. Flowey is still unwell and we are dieting her & keeping her carefully. I hope little Sarah[3] is not much ill!

What a world of new emotions and experiences has come with these children! Dr. has just returned from N.Y. Sam has gone to town today. He will return early. We anticipated no immediate result from

the present form of the disease and he thought it best to go in and
return early. Thank you Henry for your kind offer & kind words.

As ever

A.L.B.B.

ALS-LC

1. Dr. Elizabeth Blackwell, ALBB's sister-in-law, was then practicing
medicine in New York City.
2. Catherine (Kitty) Barry Blackwell (1847-1938), an orphan immigrant
assigned to Randall's Island, N.Y., was chosen in 1854 by Elizabeth Blackwell to serve as a domestic helper and companion, and later adopted by
her. After her guardian's death, Barry officially took the name of Blackwell.
3. LS's daughter, ASB, was known in her early months as Sarah.

[*Chicago*] Sunday, Feb. 20, 1859

Dear Nettie:

Today you are preaching for Mr. Higginson.[1] It is the day you were
to have been here. I felt a little chagrined at the result of our plan.
Now if you will come I do think we can get you up some meetings
that will pay you even better than $100, & your expenses.

Fred Douglass had a very large audience paying twenty-five cents,
& you would draw as well as he did. I wish I felt the old impulse &
power to lecture, both for the sake of cherished principles & to help
Harry with the heavy burden he has to bear,—but I am afraid, &
dare not trust Lucy Stone. I went to hear E.P. Whipple lecture on
Joan d'Arc. It was very inspiring, & for the hour I felt as though all
things were possible to me. But when I came home & looked in
Alice's sleeping face & thought of the possible evil that might befall
her if my guardian eye was turned away, I shrank like a snail into
its shell, & saw that for these years I can be only a mother—no
trivial thing either. I hope you gave a good sermon today.

Yours truly,

Lucy

tL-SL

1. Thomas Wentworth Higginson (1823-1911), Unitarian minister, radical abolitionist, colonel for the Union Army during the Civil War, woman's
rights advocate, and author, performed the marriage of LS and HBB; at
this time he held a pastorate in Worcester, Mass. After the split in the
woman suffrage movement he remained a close friend of LS's, and served
as an editor of the *WJ* for many years.

78 South st New York
March 12 1859

Dear Lucy

Your letter was very welcome to me and little Alice's was especially welcome to little Floey who has been desirous to have me reply to it as her amanuensis ever since. Thank you for making an effort about my Chicago meetings.[1] I cannot think of going so far however to try the experiment of whether or not I can get an audiance. Indeed I ought not to leave home though I should have been glad both to have given the sermons and to have received the money even though it were a good deal less than $100.

Miss Wright has gone now; but Florence is a good little thing who amuses herself so well that she seems comparatively little trouble. If we lived in the country I could get along admirably. As it is she must be taken into the streets and that involves a good deal of extra trouble. I am going to get a child across the way to take her out walking every day. Floey improves wonderfully. The growth of children is certainly a miracle.

I wish the spirit would move you to speak a few times this spring; but if it does not never mind! But you must be at the anniversary.[2] There you are needed and could do yourself and the cause great credit. Do you not approve the plan of a few speakers and a single session?

I am trying to decide what to do about preaching. Now is the time for me to be "up and doing." I am in good health and spirits and ready to work if the place to work in would manifest itself. I cannot get Library Hall here for any moderate price. Otherwise I had intended to speak here for the next two or 4 months. Some arrangement can, I suppose, be made to speak for the Spiritualists;[3] but it is very like throwing away time and energy. Some of the Worcester people talked of inviting me there for the next three month. The Free Church[4] is scattered; and I do not expect any thing to come of it; but if they did invite me I should go. It will be a wretched thing, though to break up ones family, to take the baby and leave the husband. I should as soon stay in Newark at a venture.

When do you return to the East? Come to our house of course when you come on at all. Floey is talking of Alice perpetually and thinks she should make her very happy next time. I think they will do better together now both can run about & talk.

Most Affectionately
A.L.B.B.

Dear Lucy.[5] Do you think you could consciencously contribute
something from the Woman's Rights fund[6] towards defraying the
expenses of a Hall for me in New York during six months of next
winter. You would pay a lecturer say $10 dollars per week. Now I
believe that I should really do more good to the cause of woman by
speaking there once every sabbath, *sermons carefully prepared,* than
by 4 lectures up and down the country every week. Hope Chapel[7]
can be obtained for $20 an evening. If you could pledge half the
expense of the Hall I would gladly undertake the rest and would
pledge myself to speak *if necessary* for the whole six months without
compensation if the expenses can only be met. No body would be
more glad to receive a fair compensation for the work; yet I would
cheerfully work for nothing rather than not have a chance to try the
experiment there. I am sure an audance could be obtained but I do
not believe I could cover expenses and take the whole responsability
on myself until my fitness as a speaker for that position could be
made manifest and that cannot be under some months of actual
trial. I dont want to try and fail. Sam cannot meet the expense & I
would not let him if he could. I have no courage to solicit aid from
individuals; but it does seem to me $250 of that fund could not be
better or more legitimately applied. Sam opposes my suggesting it;
but I really cannot see why it is not perfectly proper. Disagreeable
of course it is; but it is like offering myself as an agent. Besides I am
willing if the experiment pays that you should take back the amount
of your pledge and really do not ask the money as a payment to
myself but to aid in carrying out an enterprize which I dare not
undertake without some such support. I have frittered away this
whole winter or nearly so; and cannot bear the thought of spending
another in the same way for time is very precious.

I want to begin next fall and speak at least two years regularly;
and to feel that this is to be my course as soon as may be that I may
be making the right preparation this summer with energy. I shall
write asking Susan what she thinks about it. She has heard me speak
is very desirous to have the new york meeting, commense, and would
feel no hesitation as possibly you might since we are *sisters* now in
presenting the matter to Wendle Phillips. Please write me at once
what you really think. Your Com. would not be expected to take the
responsability of such an undertaking. It would be asking too much;
but surely the contributions in the meetings, and if not, out of the
meetings, would make up the balance. At any rate I will assume all
other expenses and meet them if there is a deficiency.

Ask Henry if he does not think it quite right to appropriate so much of the fund to that purpose. It seems to me it rests with the judgement of the Com. whether the person applying will really do good service to the cause by the course proposed; and that if they decided in the affirmative any woman who proposes to work in any direction might properly receive aid from the fund. At any rate let me hear at once please—and if your judgement is favorable and the others will agree to it, it will relieve me from an immense anxiety.

I have just read the letter to Sam. He laughs and says send it, and in his heart admits it would be right; & is forced to acknowledge it, though he dislikes seeming to be a beggar.

ALS-LC

1. After the death of her three-month-old daughter, Mabel, in August 1858, ALBB desired to return to work either as a lecturer or as a minister. LS tried to arrange some speaking engagements in Chicago where she and her family then lived.

2. The ninth national Woman's Rights Convention or "anniversary" was held in New York City, May 12, 1859.

3. Spiritualism, the belief that the living could communicate with the dead, was extremely popular at this time. Many spiritualist lecturers were women.

4. A later hand has added "Troy" after the reference to Free Church in the text, but its meaning is unclear. In the early months of 1859 Susan B. Anthony attempted to establish a Free Church in Rochester, similar to that of Theodore Parker in Boston, but she abandoned the project for lack of funds.

5. After a sheet on which ALBB penned for her daughter Florence a note to ASB, she continued her own letter to LS.

6. In 1858, Francis Jackson (1798-1861), successful railroad promoter and investor, abolitionist, and woman's rights supporter, secretly established a $5,000 fund administered jointly by Wendell Phillips, LS, and Susan B. Anthony for the support of woman's rights. Only Phillips knew the source of the monies.

7. Located in New York City at 691 Broadway, Hope Chapel was often used by religious liberals for lectures and sermons. In April 1859 it served as the meeting place for a Free Church.

                                        Home April 14th [*1859*]
Dear Lucy

I have been intending to write you for a week. First. Thank you for suggesting to Francis Jackson to invite me to Parkers' pulpit.[1] I go there next Sunday. They are probably wearied out with much coming. Susan & Higginson had both suggested the same thing.

Before this you see the result of the application to Phillips. It is well. I expected so much from the tenor of Susans letter to him and from his utter want of faith in me combined.[2] There is time enough to decide what I shall do next winter—at present I do not know. To take a $20 hall upon uncertainties is out of the question while we owe more than $7000 dollars of depts, and have nothing to pay with but real estate which is eating us up with taxes instead of being of any service at present.

By the way *if* that Walnut Hills house does sell as we *hope* strongly, Sam will pay *you* at once. That will be some comfort all round.

I am glad you are going into the country for the summer. It will be so much better than Chicago. It is a pity you cannot be at New York if the mood for working then is upon you; but if not I should not care a fig if I were you. When you are *strong* again *the energy will come with it!* Then you will feel courage & eloquence and can do any thing you like. For me you say you are glad I can satisfy in the world, &c. Ah me! The world has voted me dead long ago I have been coolly told over & over again that the time was when I stood first as a preacher but now a host of other women mostly spiritualists have "gone ahead" of me. That I ought to have accepted the invitation to preach in N.Y. when it came; but that now there is no way but to commence & see if any one will take an interest in me again. Pleasant is'nt it. They could secure Hope Chapel to a green girl, offer her $1200, & board & get up a world of enthusiasm over it, but they can do no more than wonder that a married woman can expect to succeed, in the midst of such brilliant mediums too!!! Such is life & I accept it!

You see I am a little cross; but it will go away tomorrow. That's a comfort!

But in all soberness I often doubt whether I can ever do any thing worth while publicly. I am not a popular speaker. My subjects are metaphysical & not well adapted to the masses; and no one has faith enough in me to lend a fingers worth of help while I am too poor to attempt anything and also too much oppressed with a consciousness of my own deficiencies to dare to strike out boldly.

Good bye
Nette

ALS-LC

1. Theodore Parker, seriously ill with tuberculosis, left Boston in February 1859 for a year of travel and rest abroad. Visiting preachers filled

his pulpit at the Boston Music Hall in his absence. He died in Italy in 1860.

2. Anthony wrote to Phillips proposing that ALBB be given $260 from the Woman's Rights Fund to cover half the cost of renting Hope Chapel once a week for six months, but noted that she disapproved of the plan.

Seneca Falls [*N.Y.*] Friday July 22 [*1859*]

Dear Lucy

Here Susan and I are at Mrs Stantons. We had a meeting yesterday at Clifton Springs a good gathering in the grove and rather a grand time altogether. The Niagara Falls meeting was a rather small one. I doubt whether we shall have great success at this season of the year in drawing out the people; but we can try.[1]

We are to hold a Convention at Saratoga on the 16th & 17th of Aug. Lucy do please see if you cannot come East a few weeks earlier & take that on the visit! Judge Hay[2] is in desperate anxiety to have you present. He says he can think of no other lady who wil[*l*] do at all, & we all say amen. How I should like to meet you there! *If* there is no new baby in the question why can you not come?[3] Susan as general manager would gladly write you herself, but she is afraid you will think she *teases* you to come, & she dont like to do that though she wants you badly and will willingly pay whatever you think right, if that will be any inducement to you to come. Bring little Alice & we will take care of her while you go to the meetings. I am sure we can make her very comfortable.

I go tomorrow morning to my brother Addisons. W*ᵐ* and his family are there. Next Tuesday we have an all day meeting at Trenton Falls. Then a meeting at Holland Patent then on Sunday I speak for Mayo of Albany,[4] &c. Write me at Albany. We shall be in that neighborhood & on the river for some time.

I am too tired & they are all talking too much to enable me to write you this evening; but I have a long letter in my heart for you. I am out on this tour almost for the sole purpose of making the poor 12 or 15 dollars per week that I may have some thing to begin the N.Y. experiment with this winter. Of course the subject, political rights for woman is a grand one & has my fullest sympathies; & the change is for me a good one after being so long at home. I try to throw my whole soul into the movement & have certainly not lost in power as a speaker by the years of comparative rest. I shall accompany Susan only two or three months. Am to take a week for visiting home next month with Sam. Little Floey is doing nicely at Fathers. I went home after being out a few days, the dear little soul was delighted, & it made my heart ache to leave her again, though my reason tells me she will be as well off there as with me. Wm's family will spend most of Aug. in Henrietta & Florence & Aggie[5] now play very well together.

Of course I shall be homesick long before the time of return & it only takes a little thinking to make me feel so at any time for a minute; but on the whole I enjoy or shall enjoy the work & the change when I once get again into the harness. This will say that I am alive again; & *may* bring some Lyceum invitations; but I wish most to begin my proper work & to be able to carry it on while I still have the home & its goods also.

Much love to Henry! Thank him for offering to be one of the Deacons of my church. He may have a chance yet.

Very Affectionately
Nett

ALS-LC

1. In the summer of 1859, supported by money from the Woman's Rights Fund, Susan B. Anthony organized a lecture tour of upstate New York that began with a speech by ALBB at Niagara Falls on July 13.
2. William Hay (1793-1870), a lawyer and poet from Saratoga Springs, was an outspoken temperance advocate and woman's right supporter.
3. In June 1859, LS miscarried a male fetus.
4. Amory Dwight Mayo (1823-1907), a Unitarian clergyman then serving in Albany, wrote and spoke on education and the public schools.
5. Agnes Brown (1851-62) was the daughter of ALBB's brother William.

Westport N.Y. Tuesday Aug. 29 '59[1]

Dear Lucy

For a month I have intended writing you; but your letter received last night at Albany makes me ashamed to delay longer. We are having a pleasant and in some repects rather successful tour. About half our meetings have been free. In the evenings we generally have 10 cts admission. At Saratoga & Niagara it was 25 cts. The audiances have never been large—in some cases they are decidedly small; but no where so small as at Niagara in the beginning when Blondin[2] was the great attraction. We have hardly paid expenses to say nothing of a compensation to either of us. Mrs Rose was advertised for three meetings including Saratoga but she fell down stairs, sprained her

wrist, bruised her forehead &c. and was not able to be present, and
we waded through the *4 sessions* as best we could without her, in
each place. I have never known so cordial an earnestness on the part
of the people before. It is the thinking earnest people who come to
hear. The rest stay away. The fashionables do their best to ignore us;
but the people are awake & eager to hear. Susan[3] has sold *quantities*
of books—the money going into the general fund. I think I speak
better than I have ever done before. I know I do and so write the
fact for your comfort & encouragement. A long quiet rest at home
is a real blessing & of value; but the people will not believe it till we
prove it. Theres time enough for that!

I think Phillips did get your letter but cannot say with certainty.
The matter of employing Mrs Jones[4] has been spoken of I know.
Susan feels that if Mrs Jones will not extemporize that she is hardly
the person at any rate to travel with her which is of course true. The
thing, as I understand it, is in about this light. Phillips has no time
or thinks so to manage agents or assume responsability for them.
Susan proposes to do what she can in N.Y. state. Phillips has thrown
the whole responsability upon her telling her to employ whoever she
pleases—to work as her judgement dictates, & that the fund to the
amount of $1,000 shall be at her control for this state campaign,
though he hopes she will not need it all. Susan could not employ
agents till she had tested the matter herself. Mrs Rose is sick could
not at present undertake continued meetings. Aunt Fannie[5] has been
invited to join us by the middle of next month. We planned to hold
a few meetings together then I was to drop out & they two go on.
Mrs Gage is still uncertain about it—writes that she has been invited
or perhaps that it has been suggested rather that she & Mrs Jones
should travel together in Ohio. Of course therefore Susan is doubtful
what to decide upon. *I think* she would about as soon travel alone
after I leave her. Besides she is about as much interested in antislavery
as in this cause wants to do something with the Personal Liberty bill[6]
& to get Parker Pillsbury to preach & lecture in the vicinity of
Rochester. So with so many desires & aims her plans are not altogether
fixed but she will work. Her desire is to have a meeting held in each
county of the state before January. I dont think it will be done
however; but she will work towards it. In short the movement in
this state originates with herself, & she bears all the responsability.
It is as every thing has always been & must always be in our movement
a personal matter & individual action. Can we have any form of
organization now do you think? I want to talk that matter over
during this year again but will not write about it.

If Mrs Jones & Mrs Gage would plan & execute a work for Ohio probably Phillip[s] & the rest of you committee people would pledge then a support from the fund at least I see no other way of getting the thing started. There is no body to assume the general agency or any thing of that sort & never has been & with the Com. scattered as you three are it is impossible for persons so absorbed as you all are to cooperate. Phillip[s] never write letters. Susan finds it impossible to get any opinion or even answer from him until it is too late & she has sent half a dozen letters pleading for some reply.

It is not singular that he does not write you. It is the same to every one. He told Mrs Dall he would write me about my New York preaching some months ago but no line has come from him. I dare say he will never write unless I write him direct as I shall when I receive pay from the fund, which as it comes at second hand from him will make an opening & I wish to state the matter as I wished him to have it at first.

Dear Lucy we shall all be glad to see you again & so glad to have you in Orange or Bloomfield.[7] I have missed you & wanted you back again often & often; but in these days I am not demonstrative over much & so have not said so; but now that the time approaches I very much rejoice. You must know that I have heard of the poor premature little baby & that I sympathize with you deeply. I have not spoken of it; but the temptation to do so has been great; but I did not know how you would feel about it & so was silent but at Saratoga Mrs. Hopper, Lucretia Motts daughter[8] asked me if you had another child. I said no, — with a world of pain, — & she looked so surprised; said Mr. Somebody had seen you not long before; & they all were expecting we had heard something so evidently, that I did not know what to say, & so said nothing at all. Perhaps that is best, & yet I think every body who is so anxious to have Lucy speak again would feel better if they knew how impossible that has been & still must be for the present. I confess I should like to tell Susan. She does not blame you or feel hard towards you for not talking but she often says that *if* you are not *disabled* again she should be so glad to have you speak now & then, &c & in her heart I think cant quite understand ~~you~~ why you dont. Shall I still be silent on that point—I know how it has made your heart ache to lose so many new hopes. It is almost like losing something of ones own life, but Lucy dear when one had held a little living thing in ones arms for almost 4 months till its little face began to brighten with smiles when you looked in it that is sadder still. Sam was with me at intervals for two weeks. We had a grand time three days at lake George. I shall be at home by the end of the month perhaps before some few days. You will see the report of Eastern meetings in papers.

I am too tired to write more. Write me at 78 South street & Sam will forward immediately.

Nette

ALS-LC

1. August 29, 1859, was actually a Monday.
2. Emile Gravele (1824-97), better known as Charles Blondin, an acrobat and tightrope walker, was most famous for crossing Niagara Falls on a wire.
3. Susan B. Anthony.
4. A later hand has added "J. Elizabeth" between the words "Mrs" and "Jones."
5. Frances Dana Barker Gage (1808-84), known as "Aunt Fanny," abolitionist, author, temperance advocate, and woman's rights lecturer, was active before the Civil War primarily in Ohio. After the war she worked with ex-slaves, and later lectured throughout the North to raise money for their relief.
6. Anthony spent six weeks in Albany beginning in late January 1859 lobbying for woman's rights and a personal liberty bill to impede the return of runaway slaves.
7. LS owned a home in Orange, N.J., although shortly after her family's return from Chicago, they moved to a farm in West Bloomfield (now Montclair), N.J.
8. Anna Mott Hopper (1813-74), the oldest child of abolitionists James and Lucretia Mott, was herself active in the antislavery movement, and later in social work in Philadelphia; she also raised money to establish Swarthmore College.

Jan. 19, 1861

——Mrs. Stanton, Susan & Co. are giving Anti-Slavery lectures in New York. They have been mobbed in Buffalo, Utica, and Rochester.[1] Won't Susan enjoy it? ——

Lucy Stone

tf-LC

1. With feelings running high after the election of Abraham Lincoln to the presidency, mobs attacked abolitionist lecturers touring upstate New York. At Buffalo on January 3, 1861, a mob crowded onto the platform and extinguished the lights, causing chaos in the hall. Soon after this, at

Utica, the mob that gathered in anticipation of the arrival of the speakers so frightened the managers of the hall that they refused to open its doors. In Rochester, the speakers were hissed and their words drowned out by the rowdy behavior of the crowd.

The Young Women

Antoinette Brown, Oberlin College Institute
graduate (Oberlin College Archives).

Lucy Stone, antislavery lecturer (Sophia
Smith Collection).

New Mothers

Antoinette Brown Blackwell and Florence, 1857 (Schlesinger Library).

Lucy Stone and Alice Stone Blackwell at three months (Library of Congress).

Husbands

Samuel C. Blackwell (Schlesinger Library).

Henry B. Blackwell (Schlesinger Library).

Mature Daughters

Antoinette Brown Blackwell's daughters, Agnes, Grace, Edith, Florence, and Ethel (Schlesinger Library).

Lucy Stone's daughter, Alice Stone Blackwell (Schlesinger Library).

Abolitionist Reunion at Pope's Hill, Home of Lucy Stone and Henry B. Blackwell

In front of porch: Samuel May, Harriet W. Sewall, Samuel Sewall, Henry B. Blackwell, Theodore D. Weld. *Seated on porch:* William Lloyd Garrison, Jr., Elizabeth B. Chace, Sarah H. Southwick, Abby Kelley Foster, Lucy Stone, Zilpha Spooner, Wendell P. Garrison. *Standing on porch:* Francis J. Garrison, Alla Foster, George T. Garrison (Sophia Smith Collection).

Antoinette Brown Blackwell, circa 1890 (Schlesinger Library).

Distinguished Women

Lucy Stone in 1893 (Sophia Smith Collection).

Part 3

"Full to Overflowing"

1862-81

I feel full to overflowing of enough to talk about that I
care for intensely; but prefer a few months longer at home.

— Antoinette Brown Blackwell to Lucy Stone,
February 9, 1879

No letters between Lucy Stone and Antoinette Brown Blackwell
survive for the years between 1861 and 1869 when the friends lived
near each other in and around New York City. Despite the absence
of correspondence, this period was especially significant for both
because of the events in the world in which they lived. The Civil
War ultimately decided questions debated by individuals and the
nation for many years. All abolitionists, including Lucy Stone and
Antoinette Brown Blackwell, applauded the emancipation of the
slaves, but some expressed disappointment when the reconstruction
of the Union brought with it retreat from the political victories of
radicals during the war years. Stone was the more outspoken of the
pair, prodding the party of Lincoln to fulfill its pledges of equality
for both the races and the sexes.

By 1869, when the correspondence between Stone and Brown
Blackwell resumed, the growing social conservatism of the nation
manifested itself in political retrenchment, even within the woman's
rights movement. Woman's rights advocates increasingly emphasized
the specific goal of woman suffrage, although some sought to maintain
the broader focus that had formerly characterized the antebellum
movement. Tensions over strategic differences in representing the
woman suffrage cause to a wider audience continued to rise until in
1869 they split the movement into two factions, with Lucy Stone
emerging as the leader of one of them. Antoinette Brown Blackwell
expressed basic sympathy for her friend's strategies and positions,
although she never broke as decisively with Stone's rivals Susan B.
Anthony and Elizabeth Cady Stanton.

Family as well as politics provided an ongoing bond between the
two women. As the letters after 1869 demonstrate, the visits of nieces,
cousins, aunts, and uncles wove together the Blackwell clan even as
geographical distance drew them apart. Public appearances often
provided the occasions for private visits, and family letters integrated
household and career news. While Stone and Brown Blackwell shared
their hopes and their more personal thoughts, they nonetheless remained contrasting personalities. Stone emerged as a disciplined organizational leader with a developed sense of politics, while Brown

Blackwell concentrated on more independent intellectual work pursued in the interstices of her bustling family life. The letters in this section thus detail years important to the special friendship and to the larger political world.

When the long-awaited Civil War commenced, Stone and Brown Blackwell thought carefully about what actions to take to secure the freedom of black Americans and the reunification of the nation. Scheduled to speak at the annual Woman's Rights Convention held in New York City in May 1861, Brown Blackwell wrote to Susan B. Anthony that she could not complete her talk "The Home and the Workshop," for "in these times of present interest and peril I am preparing now upon 'The Relation of the Woman Question to our National Crisis.' "[1] She never delivered the speech, for woman's rights activists canceled the 1861 convention, and to show their patriotism, forsook agitation on their own behalf until after the war ended.

In early 1863, however, Stone and Brown Blackwell joined with Anthony, Stanton, and other supporters of both racial and sexual equality to press for full black emancipation through a new organization, the Woman's National Loyal League (WNLL). At the founding meeting, Brown Blackwell spoke passionately on the need to incorporate former slaves into the republican tradition; but her involvement with the WNLL was short-lived, for two months later a new daughter, Grace, was born.[2] Now, with three small children to care for, Brown Blackwell spent the following years close to home. Only at the end of the decade did she reemerge to again involve herself in the organizational debates, gender analysis, and theological questions that framed her mature commitments.

For Stone, on the other hand, participation in the WNLL marked her reentry into the world of politics. With ample savings from his wise investments and remunerative employment, her husband, Henry Blackwell, left his salaried position as a bookkeeper to devote himself to a career in social and political reform; and Stone abandoned full-time domesticity and steady residence in her New Jersey home to join him, first in laboring with old abolitionist allies to secure full freedom for former slaves and then in pursuing a strategy and organization for woman suffrage.

At the end of the war, Stone and Henry Blackwell devoted themselves to the fight to establish full rights of citizenship, especially the vote, for ex-slaves. They hoped this broadening of the electorate would be accompanied by the attainment of woman suffrage. To this end, in May 1866 they joined in the founding of the American Equal

Rights Association (AERA), with its commitment to universal suffrage. The next month, Congress approved what would become the Fourteenth Amendment, which because of its wording proved controversial among the coalition of woman's rights advocates and former abolitionists. The measure mandated black citizenship, but it also introduced the first explicit gender reference into the Constitution when it specified that male citizens could not be denied the right to vote without bringing penalties upon the states in which they resided. By implication, then, women would remain second-class citizens in postwar America.[3]

To some woman's rights supporters, the new constitutional provision appeared to be an unjust and unjustifiable abandonment of their cause by Radical Republican politicians who formerly, as abolitionists, had been their allies. Others, however, argued that the measure was a necessary compromise undertaken in order to distance the fragile gains of the ex-slaves from the controversial "woman question." Stone herself wavered on the issue, at first accusing Abby Kelley Foster of deserting her female allies, but later chiding Stanton and Anthony for their willingness to forsake the cause of black Americans.[4]

Factions began to solidify when the state of Kansas prepared to vote separately on the questions of black and female enfranchisement in November 1867. While the state Republican party endorsed the black suffrage referendum, it was silent on the woman suffrage measure. The AERA supported both state issues and in the spring before the election sent Stone and Henry Blackwell to campaign, especially on behalf of women. By September when Stanton and Anthony arrived, desperation drove them to accept the financial and oratorical aid of George Francis Train, a Democrat who had opposed the Civil War and who now spoke out against black enfranchisement. With others, Stone and her husband reacted strongly against what they saw as abandonment of both the moral principles of racial equality and the political alliance with the Republican party. In addition, Stone charged that Stanton and Anthony had undertaken the dubious alliance before properly consulting the elected leadership of the AERA. But Stanton and Anthony maintained their relationship with Train and, shortly after the defeat of both Kansas referenda, accepted from him funds for the establishment of their own newspaper, the *Revolution*. Ever more openly critical of the Republican party for its subordination of the cause of woman suffrage to political exigencies, Stanton and Anthony increasingly distanced themselves from their old friends and former coworkers, including Stone.

By April 1868 New England woman's rights supporters, suspicious of the New York–based AERA and especially the power of Stanton and Anthony within it, met in Boston and constituted themselves the New England Woman Suffrage Association (NEWSA). They re-affirmed their support for universal suffrage and their loyalty to the Republican party. While Stone and Henry Blackwell were at this time still residents of New Jersey, they felt close ties to Massachusetts, Stone's home state, and to the fledgling NEWSA. Having spoken before the Massachusetts State House on woman suffrage in 1867 and again in 1868, Stone attended the founding convention of the NEWSA and supported its first president, Julia Ward Howe.

The formation of the NEWSA foreshadowed the split in the woman suffrage movement that took place at the May 1869 meeting of the AERA. After expressing disapproval of AERA backing for black enfranchisement proposals when unaccompanied by woman suffrage measures, Stanton and Anthony invited their followers to meet. This gathering founded the National Woman Suffrage Association (NWSA). Six months later, in November, Stone, Henry Blackwell, and others including Antoinette Brown Blackwell, gathered in Cleveland, where they instituted the American Woman Suffrage Association (AWSA), reaching beyond New England to join together their own network of supporters. Despite some early efforts to heal the breach, the suffrage movement remained officially divided between two national organizations until 1890.[5]

While the factions had originally split on the issue of the relation of woman suffrage to black suffrage and the Republican party, other differences soon became apparent. The NWSA accepted as voting members all interested, dues-paying individuals, while the AWSA was organized on the basis of recognized state and local chapters, and allowed only representatives of these affiliates to vote at the annual meetings. The AWSA emphasized campaigns for woman suffrage at the state and local level, while the NWSA focused on passage of an amendment to the federal Constitution. In addition, the NWSA viewed male supporters with skepticism, while the AWSA welcomed them and even encouraged them to hold office. Moreover, as the groups developed in the 1870s, the AWSA attempted to eschew po-tentially controversial discussions of marriage and sexuality, while the NWSA explored the significance for women of divorce, adultery, free love, and infanticide. Both organizations manifested concern with broadening opportunities for women, but the AWSA sought new roles within the more conventional boundaries, while the NWSA experimented with more radical, and often less popular, changes.

To publicize the advances of the suffrage movement in general and the AWSA in particular, Stone and Henry Blackwell organized the *Woman's Journal*. With capital raised through the sale of stock (of which Henry Blackwell was the major purchaser) and the profits from specially staged bazaars, they arranged to buy the *Agitator*, a Chicago-based woman suffrage paper edited by Mary Livermore. They then moved the paper and its editor to Boston, where they also enlisted their old abolitionist allies William Lloyd Garrison and Thomas Wentworth Higginson and woman's club organizer Julia Ward Howe to join Livermore and themselves as editors. As the first issue rolled off the press on January 8, 1870, the *Woman's Journal* took its central place in Lucy Stone's life. For the next twenty-three years, Stone held primary reponsibility for the paper, gathering and reporting news, analyzing turning points and trends, and recruiting editors, contributors, writers, and subscribers. "Devoted to the interests of woman, to her educational, industrial, legal and political equality, and especially to her right of suffrage,"[6] the *Woman's Journal* followed closely the openings of colleges and universities to women, the entrance of women into law, medicine, and the clergy, the formation of women's organizations, and all the state and local political campaigns for woman suffrage. Stone's pen informed her readers of both historical and recent developments, while encouraging them to work for the achievement of women's equality.

Although Brown Blackwell attended the Cleveland convention that founded the new organization, other matters took precedence in her life. Her last child, Ethel, was born in September 1869, completing her household of five daughters; and the same year, her first book, *Studies in General Science,* was published. With these two key events, Brown Blackwell began to establish a new balance between home duties and intellectual work. Stating in this first book, "Family love is the broad stepping-stone to universal good-will,"[7] Brown Blackwell strove to live the maxim, seeking reinforcement and support from her maturing family. *Studies* constructed a "scientific" case for the immortality of the human soul, arguing that human perception, like all other "forces," could be neither created nor destroyed; *The Physical Basis of Immortality* (1876) returned to this theme. Her only novel, *The Island Neighbors* (1871), grew out of family vacation experiences on Martha's Vineyard in this period and suggested issues she subsequently explored in the nonfiction work *The Sexes throughout Nature* (1876). This collection of essays exposed as artificial the differential rewards for male and female achievements, while defending the innate differences between the sexes that allowed women to excel in "sharp-sightedness . . . direct insight . . . [and] quick perception." Brown Blackwell's work argued for equality based on the division of labor between men and women. She demonstrated her familiarity with contemporary scientific thinking, including the works of Darwin and Spencer, and she challenged the scientific community to apply its standards for pure, unbiased research to the study of sex differences, noting, "Current physiology seems to be grounded on the assumption that woman is undersized man." Urging reevaluation of this view, she countered, "Men are the real inferiors of woman . . . they never can develop the highest sympathies of sex, those broadest and most impersonal of special social instincts."[8]

Stone appreciated Brown Blackwell's intellectual interests and printed in the *Woman's Journal* many of her lectures. Yet while participating in the AWSA conventions and contributing occasionally to Stone's newspaper, Brown Blackwell did not share her sister-in-law's passion for practical politics. Brown Blackwell always supported the cause of suffrage, but she regretted the sectarian controversy between former friends. Although she had attended the founding meeting of the AWSA in 1870, four years later she addressed the annual meeting of the rival NWSA, and the next year she abstained from discussing with Stone the merits of women's participation in the United States Centennial Exhibition to be held in Philadelphia in 1876.

Although Brown Blackwell never found the details of political organization compelling, she did participate actively in the founding of the Association for the Advancement of Women (AAW) in 1873. The organization reflected the growing popularity of social science methods to investigate aspects of the "woman question," including eugenics, social purity, enlightened motherhood, and the institution of marriage. Members of the AAW ranged from popular reformers like Catharine Beecher to scholars like Vassar's professor of astronomy Maria Mitchell. Brown Blackwell regularly presented papers at the annual congresses of the AAW, and enlisted the aid of the *Woman's Journal* to cover its meetings and publish its reports.

Brown Blackwell's growing interest in social science accompanied her renewed interest in organized religion, albeit Unitarianism, not the orthodox Congregationalism she had left in the 1850s. In 1878, the same year that Oberlin finally recognized her seminary education by granting her an honorary A.M., Brown Blackwell opened a dialogue with leading Unitarian thinkers. Finding herself drawn to its liberal theology, she officially joined the denomination and then entertained hopes of taking charge of a congregation. But at this point in her life, it was still difficult to locate a position that did not conflict with her family responsibilities.

As the letters from this period reveal, family concerns predominated in the correspondence between the old friends even as each blossomed in her public capacities. Brown Blackwell detailed the shifts in her household precipitated by financial, geographic, and emotional changes. In contrast, Stone's home became increasingly stable after 1870, although Stone maintained its openness to visitors and especially to family.

During the early 1860s, Brown Blackwell lived in New Jersey with her husband and daughters near members of her husband's extended family, including his mother, sisters, brother Henry, and Lucy Stone. When Samuel Blackwell became ill in 1865, the household broke up, with the daughters staying at the homes of various relatives, and husband and wife temporarily joining her parents in Henrietta; but as soon as his health and financial circumstances permitted, the family reestablished itself in the Roseville section of Newark, where the couple shared the duties of operating a real estate business. Although the purchase and sale of houses, including those in which they resided, kept Brown Blackwell moving from one home to another, she nonetheless continued to invite members of the ever more widely scattered network of Blackwell relatives to visit, particularly during the holiday season. This proved an essential ongoing link between the old friends, since it allowed Stone's only daughter to maintain close ties with her cousins, aunts, and uncles.

Brown Blackwell's household also met shifting needs by sending off daughters to reside with other relatives. Educational, social, and financial concerns prompted their extended visits to the homes of aunts, including that of Dr. Elizabeth Blackwell (who had moved to England in 1869), the pleasant seaside home of Ellen and Emily Blackwell in Rockaway, New York, and especially the Dorcester, Massachusetts, residence of Lucy Stone and Henry Blackwell. These trips also enabled all to maintain close ties with the children adopted by Samuel and Henry Blackwell's unmarried sisters, including Dr. Elizabeth Blackwell's ward, Kitty Barry, and the various children for whom Dr. Emily Blackwell and her sister Ellen shared responsibility.

In 1870, Stone's family moved into a rambling, seventeen-room "old-fashioned" house on Pope's Hill in Dorchester, overlooking Boston Harbor. Here, for the rest of her life, Stone practiced the skills of New England housewifery first learned as a child in West Brookfield, while directing one of the key nineteenth-century woman's rights organizations and editing its paper. For all her radicalism on the suffrage issue, Stone still valued her domestic proficiency, raising her own chickens, canning her own fruit and vegetables, and doing much of her own sewing. Indeed, Brown Blackwell had always held her friend's household skills in highest esteem, and now regularly sent her daughters to Boston to learn from their aunt, offering their assistance while they enjoyed the schooling and cultural opportunities Boston provided.

While neither her nieces nor her own daughter appeared to inherit Stone's aptitude for household management, Stone did impart to Alice a drive for education and a sense of the struggle for woman's rights. Stone carefully supervised Alice's schooling at coeducational Chauncy Hall in Boston, and then Boston University, which had accepted both male and female students since its founding in 1869. Stone always assumed her daughter would take her place in the suffrage movement, and began grooming her early for her role. In 1872, when Alice was only fourteen, her aunt Antoinette Brown Blackwell wrote to her inquiring about her efforts for the *Woman's Journal;* Stone herself called the young girl "the daughter of the regiment."[9]

Stone also watched and planned the education of her nieces, hoping some would show an interest in or aptitude for the politics of the woman suffrage movement. But Brown Blackwell's daughters displayed other inclinations. Florence, the eldest, at first shied away from any plans for a public career; only in her mid-twenties did she begin training for public speaking, although her interest in men and marriage still took precedence. Edith, the second daughter, preferred the patterns of her aunts Elizabeth and Emily Blackwell to those of her mother and her aunt Lucy Stone. She chose to study and eventually to practice medicine. Ethel Blackwell, the youngest of Brown Blackwell's daughters, also took this path, while Agnes, the next to youngest, later took art lessons from her aunt Marian Blackwell. Except for Grace, the middle child, who was too emotionally troubled to undertake a career, Brown Blackwell's daughters participated more in the social than the political advancement of women.

Stone's strongest supporter and greatest political ally remained her husband, Henry Blackwell. For him, woman's rights was a noble cause, and he reveled in speaking, writing, and lobbying on its behalf. Henry Blackwell did, however, pursue some separate interests. In 1870 he accompanied a commission appointed by President Grant to Santo Domingo to investigate the possibility of annexation. Although the plan was never realized, Henry Blackwell did return to the island several times to investigate business opportunities, particularly possibilities for sugar production, for he had never abandoned his father's dream of manufacturing sugar from free labor. Later in the 1870s with his brother Samuel, Henry Blackwell undertook a project in Maine to produce sugar from beets. For Henry Blackwell, it provided the rationale for the European voyage he undertook with his daughter, Alice, in 1879. But the failure of the short-lived enterprise more seriously inconvenienced Samuel Blackwell and his financially strapped family. Despite the difficulties the experiment had caused, Lucy Stone and Antoinette Brown Blackwell viewed their husbands indulgently, and found that the fiasco provided another experience they could share.

All in all, the long stretch of years between 1861 and 1882 saw the two old friends renew their political and intellectual interests while reinforcing in new ways the family ties that bound them together. Their shared concern for the advance of women took different forms in the two lives. Lucy Stone applied herself in her work as the key officer in the AWSA and the editor of its paper. Hers was a full-time career involving the daily details of politics and publishing. Antoinette Brown Blackwell became a prolific free-lance author and lecturer. Amidst the care of her tumultuous household, she carved out the time to read and write on metaphysics, theology, and social science, and their relation to the woman question. Meanwhile, the circulation of ideas and daughters between the two households gave to all great pleasure and a secure sense of continuity as Lucy Stone and Antoinette Brown Blackwell balanced and rebalanced domestic responsibilities and public work. Stone's rededication to speaking and writing on woman suffrage, and Brown Blackwell's reentry into the world of organized religion, the lecture circuit, and the publishing world enriched the women individually, their friendship, and the woman's rights movement. Together, they guided the next generation of Blackwell women to maturity.

NOTES

1. ALBB to Susan B. Anthony, Apr. 30, 1861, BFP-SL.
2. *HWS* 2:50-89; for ALBB's speech, see ibid., pp. 69-73.
3. For a detailed discussion of the debacle, see Ellen Carol DuBois, *Feminism and Suffrage: The Emergence of an Independent Women's Movement in America* (Ithaca, N.Y.: Cornell University Press, 1978), pp. 53-78.
4. LS to Abby Kelley Foster, Jan. 24, 1867, BFP-LC; for Stone's disgust with Stanton and Anthony, see ASB, *Lucy Stone,* pp. 212-13.

5. Many participants wrote partisan accounts of the split in the woman's movement and the formation of the NWSA and AWSA. For the AWSA position, see, for example, ALBB, "Woman Suffrage Organizations," *WJ*, Feb. 2, 1870. The official NWSA view appeared in *HWS* 2:400-406.

6. This logo appeared regularly just below the *WJ* masthead.

7. ALBB, *Studies in General Science* (New York, 1869), p. 170.

8. ALBB, *The Sexes throughout Nature*, pp. 131-32, 233, 204.

9. ALBB to ASB, Jan. 1872, BFP-SL; Mary Livermore recalled this comment at LS's funeral service; see *WJ*, Oct. 28, 1893.

Newark, Feb. 10 1869

Dear Nettie

I have just come back from Providence where I yesterday addressed the Judiciary Committee of their Legislature, on Woman Suffrage.

——Our petitions in Massachusetts are referred to an excellent special committee, and with a little help, I do believe Massachusetts will submit the word "male."[1] You know I belong there, body, soul, and estate. At any rate the field is the world, and *my* field is that part where the gurgling brooks, old moss-covered rocks and stunted trees make New England forever beautiful, and all my own.

Did you know I had been to Oberlin? And Walnut Hills? At both places a great many kind enquiries were made for you, but especially at Oberlin—dear, old place! I wandered round and round, with my heart in my throat, trying in vain to find our Oberlin. I should not have known the place. Every change had been for the better, and yet a nameless sadness tugged at my heart for the something that is gone forever. I was fortunate in seeing a good many of the old pupils. Eliza Fairchild, Charles Penfield, King, Martha Rawson, Miss Blanchard,[2] Miss Wright, Miss Thompson, and the children of the old students who are there to be educated. James Monroe's daughter— a fine, tall, comely girl, with her father's dark eyes and her mother's features, gave me a pleasant greeting. Charles Penfield's daughters said they never knew their father had any lady classmates but you and me, till to-day. They had never heard him speak of any others. It seemed to me that the intellectual life they live there is very good for them. They all looked so cheerful. Prof. Morgan does not look a day older than he did twenty years ago. Prof. Fairchild, always good-looking, is now decidedly handsome. He has grown much stouter, just enough to give dignity to his person and he seemed so comfortable and jolly! Mrs. Fairchild too, seemed not older, but much more of a person than she used to. I went to church on Sunday. Prof. Morgan preached a sermon which seemed to belong to the dead ages, and I longed for something living to be spoken to the young men and women who sat without one sign or look of interest. Miss Adams has one daughter. I saw Dolson Cox at Cincinnati. May Atkins[3] sent much love to you and Sam. What has become of your book?

Love to you all
Lucy Stone.

tf-LC

1. The Massachusetts legislature began annual hearings on woman suffrage in 1869 when a special joint standing committee was established for

173

this purpose. Woman suffrage supporters hoped the committee would draft an amendment to the state constitution striking the requirement that voters be male.

2. Harriet Blanchard (1820-98), OL 1847, taught school after her graduation and before her marriage to Nathaniel Gerrish, an Oberlin mechanic, in 1861.

3. When transcribing this letter, ASB's amanuensis Ida Porter-Boyer wrote "May" instead of "Mary" for the first name here.

[Somerville, N.J.] Monday *[April 1869]*

Dear Lucy

Alice came safely and is evidently happy. For the present we will keep her! She may as well remain till she begins to think of home. It must do her good on such a day as this. They are all out at least half the time.

I will send the Revolution.[1] Please keep the *book notice* for me.[2] Any thing *SO* complimentary should be preserved.

Does mother hunger for the country on a day like [*this*]?[3] When she does her room shall be made ready for her on the briefest notice and she will be affectionately welcomed to enjoy it.

Affectionately
A.L.B.B.

ALS-LC

1. The *Revolution,* a newspaper with a radical perspective on woman's rights, existed between 1868 and 1870. Edited by Stanton and Anthony, it was financed by the maverick Democrat George Francis Train.

2. A review of ALBB's *Studies in General Science* (New York, 1869) appearing in the *Revolution* April 15, 1869, noted that the book did not contain "any new discoveries or explorations," but called the volume nonetheless "a valuable addition to the class of literature to which it belongs."

3. Hannah Lane Blackwell, the mother of HBB and SCB, then lived with LS, HBB, and ASB in Newark.

Eastport Maine Oct. 31 — 69

Dear Nettee

The point from which I write is 18 hours by Steamboat, beyond all rail roads. New Brunswick is in plain sight, apparently as near as Squibnocket is to Mrs. Stewarts,[1] so you see how far away I am. I came down here to lecture for Woman Suffrage, and have had two meetings, as I had to wait over Sunday—The boat not returning till Monday.

I write especially to ask if the N. Jersey State Soc. will make you a delegate, to the Cleveland Convention.[2] Will you not go? I am afraid we shall not get rid of the N. York host[3] unless those who know the real need of doing so are there.

Col. Higginson, either influenced by Theodore Tilton,[4] or from a feeling (what shall I say,) mistaken magnanimity, perhaps, told Mrs. Stanton, and Susan, that he expected to see them at Cleveland.

They neither of them intended to go—I do not know that they will—But it will be so dreadful an incubus, to take them up again! tho' perhaps there will be no help for it if they go. But I do very much wish you could plan to be there, so that we may counsel.

I saw Wm. H. Channing, in Boston. He called on me, with the same look and manner, & the same earnest interest in our cause. We talked of you, and your children, and I gave him your address. He will go to Washington by and bye and wants to stop and see you. He will drop you a line, that you may meet him at the Station. His daughter has just been confined, Dr. Garrett attended her, with eminent success.[5] He seemed delighted—Did not see Elizabeth in London, tho' he had tried to find her. I enjoyed the little interview very much. I find this place, is the home of Mary & Hannah Bartlett, one sister lives here still, & she seems to know more, even of the Blackwell family, than I do.

You know Alice goes to Newburyport this week.[6] I think it the best thing for her, but I feel crushed, and torn and homeless—But I shall make myself very busy—Harry will join me at Newburyport, and we shall set to, to raise $10,000 to start a paper. I suppose you know the N.E. Woman Suffrage Association propose to take the "Agitator"—call it the "Woman's Journal," with Mrs. Livermore[7] Mrs. Howe[8] T.W. Higginson & Mr. Garrison as Editors—*If we can raise the money.* If we do I shall try and work through the paper, for the future, and quit this lecturing field nearly altogether.

It is not consistent with any home life, or any proper care of my family. I feel it more and more, and shall certainly not continue this mode of work—tho' it is my natural way.

But I long for a snug home, by myself, from which I can send out, what I think, in some shape not so effective for me perhaps, but on the whole better, under the circumstances—If I were only a ready writer, I should be so glad!—

I hope you are nicely settled for the winter, but you will miss Sam, so much more than before he gave his time to the family as the last year.

With much love,
Lucy

Write to me at 3 Tremont Place Boston.[9]

ALS-LC

1. LS used references to the geography of Martha's Vineyard, where both families spent summer vacations.

2. After the formation of the National Woman Suffrage Association (NWSA) in New York City, May 15, 1869, LS, HBB, and Julia Ward Howe, among others, held a convention in Cleveland at which the American Woman Suffrage Association (AWSA) was established.

3. The NWSA was founded in New York City; Elizabeth Cady Stanton resided in nearby Tenafly, N.J.; and Susan B. Anthony lived in New York City.

4. Theodore Tilton (1835-1907), editor, abolitionist, and woman's rights supporter, was prominent in the American Equal Rights Association (AERA) and sympathetic toward Stanton and Anthony during the split in the woman suffrage movement. His career later collapsed in a debacle over the alleged affair between his wife and Henry Ward Beecher.

5. Elizabeth Garrett (1836-1917), pioneer British woman physician, was inspired by Elizabeth Blackwell to become a doctor. Excluded from regular medical schools, she studied privately and in 1866 began to practice. In 1871 she married James George Skelton, a steamship entrepreneur.
Channing and his family had, by this time, settled in England.

6. ASB attended the Newburyport school conducted by Jane Andrews (1833-87), a progressive educator and author of children's books.

7. Mary Ashton Rice Livermore (1820-1905), woman's rights and temperance activist, lecturer, editor, and author, worked for the U.S. Sanitary Commission during the Civil War and then became active in the woman suffrage movement. In 1869 she established in Chicago the woman's rights newspaper the *Agitator,* which merged with the *WJ* when Livermore moved to Boston later that year to continue editing the publication. She was active in the Massachusetts WSA and New England WSA (NEWSA), and served as president of the AWSA 1875-78.

8. Julia Ward Howe (1819-1910), author, club woman, and suffragist, was a founding editor of the *WJ*. She was active in establishing the Association for the Advancement of Women (AAW) and the General Federation of Women's Clubs. Howe also held leadership positions in the NEWSA, the Massachusetts WSA, and the AWSA.

9. The address of the NEWSA.

Boston, Mar. 22 1870

Dear Nettee

Theodore Tilton is making a great effort to "Consolidate[']] the Equal rights, National and American Woman Suffrage Associations.[1]

There is an *executive Com. meeting of the American Equal* rights soc. on Thursday, next (Mar. 24.) to vote the Equal rights soc. into this plot. — Now, since the 15th amendment is adopted and two National societies for woman are in existence, *we* think it much better to *drop* the Equal rights soc. If *all* the members of the Committee meet next Thursday, at 76 Columbia St. Brooklyn — we can carry this, and save our good old Equal rights soc. from being smirched, by an Alliance with the National soc. which will be done, if we are not there. Now can you not come up, even at some inconvenience, to the meeting on Thursday, to give a last vote?

It will give a good chance too, to talk over many other things of family, and friendly interest — Do come Nettee.

Mr. Tilton has also sent out a circular, asking a "conference meeting" — Three from Mrs. Stantons soc. Three from our soc. and three, whom the Signers of the Call, for a conference will chose, to unite all the old friends and to unite the National and Cleveland societies.

We have private advices, that the object is, to make Mrs. Mott Prest. of the soc. which unites both, and Mr. Beecher Vice Prest.[2] Of course Mrs. Mott, to resign, and nominate Mrs. Stanton as her successor—

Strain a point Nettee, and come on to N. York — Thursday Mar. 24 —

With much love
Lucy Stone

P.S. You know, you are one of the Executive Com. of the Equal Rights Association.[3] Come so as to meet us at No. 136 Hicks St Brooklyn at 2 o'clock for Conference.

The meeting is at 4. P.M.

ALS-SL
Written on the stationery of the *WJ.*

1. Both the AWSA and the NWSA split off from the AERA.
2. Henry Ward Beecher (1813-87), Presbyterian clergyman and supporter of abolition, temperance, and woman's rights, was then at the height of his popularity, preaching regularly to enthusiastic crowds at his Brooklyn church. His reputation suffered greatly when in 1871 he was accused of committing adultery with his parishioner Elizabeth Tilton, wife of his protégé Theodore Tilton.

3. Another hand added in pencil here: "and your vote may turn the scale."

[*Somerville December 14, 1871*][1]

Dear Lucy and Henry

We are so sorry it is done and so glad it is no worse![2] There is doubtless a Providence in it all saying "turn back again to the neighborhood of New York!["] and we echo turn! Come to Jersey! Well, come and see at any rate. Alice, Henry, and now that there is no house to look after, of course Lucy also. There is room enough here and a welcome; and if Christmas is to be merry then the more the merrier and merry it must be in spite of fire and worry.

Marian went in to New York a day or two ago and has not yet returned—will probably be here this evening. I fancy Henry will wish to take Mary Hooper[3] home at once and then will bring Alice to us. It will not be worth while to find a boarding place for her until after Christmas in any case. We are all very well now and as Edie is away Alice will only make up to us the lawful number in any case and all the young ones in great consequent delight. I have heard nothing yet from the Washington meeting except that Sam saw it noticed in the Herald. Alas for the Tribune!

With love sympathy and haste that we may not lose a mail.

Yours affectionately
A.L.B.B.

ALS-SL

1. ALBB's letter to LS and HBB follows a letter by SCB to them.
2. In early December 1871, while LS and HBB held suffrage meetings in Pennsylvania, Maryland, Delaware, and Washington, D.C., their Dorchester home suffered a major fire. Although damage to the house and its contents was extensive, no one was injured in the blaze.
3. The Hoopers were friends and neighbors of ALBB's in New Jersey.

[*Somerville September 6, 1872*][1]

Yes all honor to Republicanism in the old Bay State! If I lived there I would vote for their candidate for *Governer* with right good will.[2] Why do you talk of giving up the paper *just now?* That would be a miscalculation surely. Beg or borrow but do push on through the

year somehow. We feel as poor as church mice, but I pledge 25 dollars
and think scores would do likewise rather than see it thrown up just
as it is getting started. Wait till our houses sell!!

Yours,
Nette

Af S-SL

1. This note appeared as a postscript by ALBB to a letter written by
SCB to LS and HBB.
2. In 1872 HBB and LS supported Massachusetts Republican gubernatorial candidate William Washburn, an advocate of woman suffrage, in
his campaign against Francis Bird, a Liberal Republican then running as
a Democrat and a personal friend of many woman suffrage supporters. LS
and HBB also backed the Republican presidential candidate Ulysses S.
Grant, but ALBB probably supported her old friend Horace Greeley, formerly a Liberal Republican, but then running as the Democratic party
presidential nominee.

Somerville Dec. 1st 1872

Dear Lucy, Henry, and Alice,
    One and all, you are here by invited to spend a week with us at
Christmas; or if not the whole, then any fraction of a week which
you can make convenient. We have rooms, beds, bedding and po-
tatoes enough and to spare for all of the Blackwell name and relationship, real, by birth, marriage, or adoption, and dwellers upon
this side of the Atlantic Ocean, to spend with us the twelve days of
Christmas and two or three of those preceeding. Will you come?
    In all seriousness it does seem wrong to allow ourselves to be so
much separated that even a yearly festival cannot bring us all together.
What is life without some sociability?—And who is there for closer
friendships than ought to continue among ourselves? Yet as the years
go by we shall inevitably draw a little farther apart unless we can
meet often enough to share some thing of mutual family life. For
the sake of all *the children* you certainly ought to come. Christmas
can be only half Christmas with out you all. It is the time to take
Emily's little strays[1] into the family fold, but how can that be done
properly with the Boston Branch represented only by Alice? Then
Alice's Christmas memories will be all the brighter twenty years hence
for having a father and mother as central figures. Of course we shall
expect *you*.
    You know we have furniture for two houses. You have only to say

you will be here and if necessary we will fill the attic so full of beds that it will be jolly and sociable for as many children as need to go up there, but we can make three spare rooms without that—quite as many as we shall need unless nurses come with the New York tinies and I dont think that is expected.

I have very good women for helpers, both staid, reliable and willing and shall make a holiday week of it, whether there is a houseful or not but it is always stupid to enjoy things half alone.

Say yes at once and stay for three days at least.

A.L.B.B.

ALS-SL

1. In 1871 Emily Blackwell, sister of HBB and SCB, adopted a daughter, Hannah, or "Nannie." At the same time, her sister Ellen adopted a daughter, Cornelia Howard, or "Neenie," but proved unable to support her financially, so Emily soon began to supply maintenance for this child as well. The sisters with both babies kept house together in New York City. Despite her straightened circumstances, Ellen soon adopted another baby, Susan, and in 1876 took on yet another child, adopting a boy, Paul Winthrop.

Somerville Feb. 17 1873

Dear Lucy

I have waited for a few days before replying to you because it has been a little doubtful whether or not I might not turn up bodily in Boston some week or two hence—in which case I could have saved you any trouble about Edies wardrobe. I sent, in her trunk: pieces of the red dress and of the school plaid. She will find them either in a little bag or a box. The *blue plaid* I intended for a spring school dress, though it is rather light in color; and the calico with the overskirt ought to look respectably with white aprons. The other old calico was intended for a summer working dress. If it was expected that the child would return in July to remain with us I thought in that case I thought that the *brown dress* could be made a school dress on occasions, and still, with the silk basque[1] and the white one to help it out, be made to do service for best*ish* also—until that time. When I came, I proposed to bring on a brown skirt for the silk; and to get such dresses as then seemed necessary: for I have not wished to trouble you with looking after the making of clothes.

But if you think it best, get her such dresses or any thing else, as you think she needs for convenience, respectability, or for a feeling of comfort to herself. The brown looks well now; but does not wear well, & I should prefer to keep it nice as long as may be, and would *rather* she had some such school dresses as you think she most needs. My coming at all this spring now seems to be problematical. The two women we have are better than most others we are likely to get; but Mrs. Phillips has intended all winter to leave in the spring to keep house for her sailor son; and I have planned to visit home and you before she left, supposing that would not be till about May. Now she seems likely to go in March—a fact which might have started me off on my travels almost at once; but Lizzie, the cook, more than a week ago got a telegram that her child was very low, not supposed to live; and she went to her at once. We have heard nothing from her yet, nor are we sure when she will come. So you see I am bound here, and Edie may see papa first after all; and if so possibly Agnes will be with him. Gracie was going with me because it is her turn to visit grandpapas, and I hoped to make one journey answer for both places; as Harry has always insisted that Boston was on the direct road to Henrietta. Our cook is sure to come back some time. We like her and she us; but she is an English woman with the fault of her kind, a love of beer, or something stronger; and after all her sorrows, I must probably allow some days even after she is safely here before the kitchen department will quite run itself again. Such is housekeeping life; and I have now quite given up an early spring journey. Grace and Agnes are to be nurse and chamber-maid after Mrs. Phillips leaves, for a while; and we shall see how we shall all get along. It will do them good and give me a little sense of change, and Lizzie is really very efficient when she is here.

You know, Lucy, that I have sent Edie to you to suit your convenience, as well as my own and her good. You may send her to us at any time; but if she proves a comfort, you may keep her as long as it seems best to you—at least for the present; but in that case she might make a summer visit at home. So arrange the wardrobe as you like. I will send money for the purpose. Her summer dresses, such as she has, were all lengthened ready for wear at the time; and I would make new ones about to the top of the boots—plainly, but some thing in the way that Boston children wear them.

Will Harry go to Santo Domingo with George.[2] I rather like the plan. Ask him to look out a fair little shantee somewhere which we can take next winter; for we are all going there to spend two or three months; or else I intend to go with the children. We want change and warmer weather for the young ones, Agnes in particular who is a little deaf each winter. There is many a slip though twixt cup &

lip — I need not express thanks, need I though I fail there! But *must* you give up the Journal? I send a 10 dollar bill for Edie and check for Journal. I will quadruple it; but cannot now. Mr. Alofsen[3] has taken 30 acres of our land; but we shall put it into more buildings and after a while when a few newer sales are made, we shall get out all we have put in the place and then shall have enough left to make us feel that it would be possible to die without leaving our children "land poor," and nothing besides. The third house is expected to be finished in April — the second is almost done — both really attractive and decidedly helping the value of the rest. The front of the farm begins to look quite village-like, and will be the prettier part of Somerville in a little while longer. Come and see for yourself or send Henry when he takes some of those trips to N.[Y].

Love to all.
Aff.
Nette

I shall write Alice & Edie sometime.

ALS-SL

1. A close-fitting bodice.
2. HBB advocated the annexation of Santo Domingo by the U.S. government, arguing that it would lend stability to the island and promote the "moral and material" interests of the United States. When annexation failed to occur, he became involved instead in an investment firm granted special privileges to establish a territorial base on the island. In conjunction with these interests, he made several trips to Santo Domingo.
   George Washington Blackwell (1832-1912), the youngest brother of SCB and HBB, was a prosperous real estate developer. In 1875 he married LS's niece Emma Lawrence.
3. Members of the Alofsen family were old friends of Hannah Blackwell and her children. Marian Blackwell had instructed the Alofsen children, and was especially close to the daughter Frances.

Boston, July 12, 1873

Dear Nettee

Emily is coming to us before long, and will go with us to the White Mts. Will you not let Floey come with her? We have a place engaged, and have paid for it by advertising in the Woman's Journal, so it will not be a money cost, and Floey is welcome to share it with us —

It will do the child good, and the two girls will be company for each other.

Alice goes today up to my old home for a week.

Tell Edie that I fully intended to send her music, and stocking and scrap book by Geo. but I forgot it. I had just come back from Anna Lawrence's funeral,[1] and other things were out of my mind. She died on the 4th, and though they all expected it, it was a sad blow, for all of us.

I was ever so sorry not to see you Nettee dear. Could you not come on with Floey? I wish you could, even if you did not go to the White Mts. take a week or so here with us.

Love to all of you, including the little girls who have come on since we left N.J. and not forgetting Edie who is in some sense one of us—Tell her, that Annie Coe,[2] wishes she were here, as she would play. The dry weather, has spoilt nearly all the flowers, few seeds came up—But we have abundance of cherries & raspberries which are just now in their prime.

We have canned a lot.

Ever aff
L.S.

ALS-LC
Written on the stationery of the *WJ*.

1. Anna Lawrence (1860-73) was a daughter of LS's sister Sarah and Henry Lawrence. She died in Gardner, Mass.
2. Annie Coe was a young playmate of ASB's.

[*Somerville late Winter 1874*][1]

Dear Lucy

Will you publish this as No 1 on *Sex and Work* and take a dozen or so of others one a week,[2] if I wont go over the ground already too much beaten, will be short and to the point, on Woman's Methods of Working in general. I have not sent any thing yet to Youmans[3]— the subject grows and wont get into compass and for him I must stick to the Psychology of the Sexes.

I am to prepare a paper for the N. E. Woman's Club for April 20[4] so you will be likely to get a visit if nothing unforseen prevent. Too much in haste to write decently but with hosts of love to all I am

Yours forever
Nette

If you dont want the whole string then publish this alone or with another.

ALS-SL

1. ASB dated this letter "1873?" but references to ALBB's paper for the New England Woman's Club and her articles for the *WJ* clearly indicate the letter was written in late winter 1874.

2. "Sex and Work," a series of seven articles by ALBB on women and work, appeared in the *WJ*, March-June 1874; later the articles were published together in *The Sexes throughout Nature* (New York, 1875).

3. Edward Livingston Youmans (1821-87), lecturer, journalist, and proponent of the work of Herbert Spencer, founded and edited the *Popular Science Monthly.*

4. ALBB delivered a paper, "Work in Relation to the Home," at the New England Woman's Club, April 1874.

Somerville May 21 1874

Dear Bostonians

I have had it on my heart to write you ever since we parted— now the purpose just begins to drip from the pen-point. We are all well and busy: Sam getting up a sale of lots for the *15th of June;* three children going to school, and Florence and Ethel the busiest of all in doing nothing. I wrote the N. York speech on "Evolution applied to the Woman Question," and gave it in Susan's Convention;[1] first because I had something to say, 2nd because they are anxious now to be respectable and proper, and I am desirous they should; and would like to help them. Some of their elbows were apparently quite ready to give me a poke; but if they did, it was not hard enough to hurt; and it was really a good meeting. The press of 2nd day exhausted all their energies in reporting Frothingham. His speech *was good.*[2] The Tribune has made "a rather careful abstract" of mine and will publish it soon—provided it doesn't get pushed out at last.

Prof. Youman's has—not the series of articles first-offered, on "Comparitive Physiology and Psychology;" but a short one on, "The alleged Antagonism between growth and Reproduction" which he may or may not publish (months hence if at all, I suppose);[3] but he writes a kindly letter offering to *call attention* to whatever I may publish on these Points, etc.

On the whole one couldn't well be much busier and that must go on all summer if I get up the Woman's Book in the Fall or early winter. The house is not rented, and the houses not sold. My father, 90 now tomorrow is tried by each return of the hot weather. Sam and I may both go there next week; taking the two youngest. If so I shall stay a fortnight.

Tell Alice to get Goldsmiths Essays and fiction. Flo has been reading it with satisfaction, & all of us. The essay on the squirrels chasing the men, brought Alice and her Graham theories to mind.[4] We all mean to write a special letter to welcome Kittie. If we fail, I send a welcoming greeting in this. Keep my *duds* Lucy till some one comes for them. Miss Eastman is not the only absent minded woman![5] That visit to Boston was very enjoyable. I wish we lived nearer. Another "Sex and Work" will be on hand in time.

Always affectionately
A.L.B.B.

ALS-SL

1. The NWSA met in New York City May 14-16, 1874.

2. Octavius Brooks Frothingham (1822-95) began his ministerial career as a Unitarian but later helped found the even more unorthodox Free Religious Association. He spoke and wrote on theological and contemporary topics, including women's rights. His speech to the sixth NWSA convention in New York City on May 16, 1874, explained that "while women and men were different in mind, morals and affections, suffrage was a question of humanity and humanity is not masculine or feminine."

3. In 1874 Youmans's *Popular Science Monthly* published ALBB's essay "The Alleged Antagonism between Growth and Reproduction." The essay was later reprinted in ALBB's *The Sexes throughout Nature.*

4. Oliver Goldsmith (1728-74), English author, essayist, and historian, satirized sentimental vegetarianism in his essay "Ansem The Man-Hater: An Eastern Tale."

Sylvester Graham (1794-1851), temperance and health reformer, urged a diet of raw fruits and vegetables, pure drinking water, and coarsely ground grain; he linked good health to proper nutrition, exercise, fresh air, and chastity.

5. Mary F. Eastman, of Lowell, Mass., a lecturer and writer, was active in the New England Women's Club and the AWSA; she also assisted in the *WJ* offices.

Somerville Sept 13th 1875

Dear Lucy

Will it trouble you too much to put two or three Woman's Journals in your satchel and bring them to me in New York. Or if you have no room for them, then will you mail to me four numbers containing the first and second No's of Congress Papers, two of each.[1] As we send our copy to the library, I have no paper with my own essay, and would like also to send one away elsewhere.

If you will consider me a member of the Suffrage Association from this time on (I forget what the terms of admission are) I will pay you the admission fee in N. York. Then if I remember right, I can be a speaking member, though perhaps that is a mistake, and if so I must either get appointed as delegate or speak by courtesy.[2]

I never withdrew through intention; but simply from neglect to pay the annual dues at a time when I was not present at an annual meeting; and if any one had dunned me for the fee, as they did in the Congress, I should have paid it. But finding myself out and dropped, I simply staid there. Now let me in again, as I *have* no desire to be counted out from the suffrage movement when the papers are saying that the women of the Congress are giving up suffrage.

I hate the machinery of both the A. Association and the Congress; but have concluded that those who run societies must have their own way about that. I shall work with them "under protest," not public protest, only to you privately.

I should really like to make a 15 minutes suffrage speech if my voice will make itself heard, and if I can speak when fresh from home, it ought to be as loud as in the old days.[3] It was at Henrietta apparently; but at Syracuse I was tired from visiting and over excitement. If you can sandwich me in on the first evening, I will try, and if my voice will not make itself heard, I will stop in 8 minutes. Will that do?

The Centennial sparring can come on next day, as I have not much to say on that subject and can reply easily enough on the spur of the moment.[4]

Affectionately always,
or till we meet in N York
Antoinette

ALS-LC

1. The proceedings of the Congress of Women, the annual meeting sponsored by the AAW, were published in the *WJ;* ALBB helped found the

AAW in 1873 and frequently presented papers at its congresses. The third congress was held in Syracuse, October 13-15, 1875.

2. ALBB's AWSA dues had lapsed; in reactivating her membership, ALBB regained the right to speak at the annual meeting, but not to vote, since only delegates of the recognized state organizations had voting privileges.

The seventh annual meeting of the AWSA was held in New York City, November 17, 1875.

3. At the 1875 AWSA meetings, ALBB spoke on the differences between the political perspectives of men and women.

4. LS differed from most contemporary woman suffrage workers on the issue of women's participation in the Centennial Exposition held in Philadelphia in 1876; originally LS urged women to take no part in the celebration marking the one-hundredth anniversary of national independence, since women still could not claim self-government. ALBB took a more moderate position, favoring participation under protest because, she argued, a display that emphasized women's achievements would further the cause of woman's rights. LS ultimately relented and helped organize an exhibition of tax protests by women and held one day of AWSA meetings in Philadelphia during the exposition.

Somerville Oct. 20 1875

Dear Henry and Lucy

Sam must speak for himself, but I cannot go on to the marriage of George and Emma.[1] I *should* like to though, much more than you will think. It is not half so much time as means which must prevent; but both are at rather a low ebb.

But I will be in New York at your suffrage meetings—ready to pick a quill with Lucy if that seems best to be done, to speak or not to speak there if that seems desirable. But not being a member of your organization how can I be a delegate or ask to be sent as one. No I will be there ready for whatever turns up. New York is a hateful place to speak in for me at present with my deficient voice and the disuse of extemporanious speaking. But in our smallish church at home I spoke wholly without notes and with as much ease as ever before in my life. At Syracuse once trying to make extemporanious remarks I couldnt get the hang of it and once I could fairly well. So in that line I am at present very unreliable. If you have an ample fare I dont care to speak. But Miss Eastman has probably told that Mrs Livermore, will not be present and there will be many counter currents to meet in N York. So get all the force you can. I like Mrs.

Churchill![2] Mrs Howe of course will be present etc. Jane O. Deforest[3] writes asking me to have her a meeting here, enroute to your Convention. Well *make* it a success.

I want to have a long talk with you when we meet. You know that there is a yet incoate project for getting up a woman's daily paper in N York, Mrs Croly[4] a practical Journalist as principal Editor. That is what has taken Mrs Livermore off but dont quote me as authority for it is with me one surmise.

Most affectionately
Nette

[*I*] have never seen my Syracuse paper since it was published and dont know if it was printed correctly.[5] You must judge, if I do not get a paper with it. It was to be sent me but has not yet come. I was too busy at the time and the papers were all sold before I could get one; but understand they would all be sent to the Journal and published there.

ALS-LC

1. LS's niece Emma Lawrence married George Washington Blackwell in Gardner, Mass., October 28, 1875.
2. Elizabeth K. Churchill (1821-81) from Providence, R.I., was active in the suffrage movement and the New England Women's Club.
3. Jane O. DeForest (1839-76), OL 1860, taught school until in 1871 she turned to lecturing on woman's rights to support herself.
4. Jane Cunningham Croly (1829-1901), known as "Jennie June," a journalist, edited the woman's department of the *New York World*, 1862-72. In 1868 with others she founded Sorosis, which claimed to be the first organization in the nineteenth-century woman's club movement; she served as its president for over a decade while also assisting in founding the General Federation of Women's Clubs in 1889.
5. The *WJ* published "Marriage and Work," an address ALBB delivered at the Congress of Women held in Syracuse, October 13-15, 1875.

[Dorchester, Mass.]
At Home, Sunday May 21 [1876]

Dear Nettee

Your letter is here. In reply let me say, our Philadelphia meeting is to pay special honor to the establishment of woman suffrage in New Jersey.[1] It will continue only one day. Those who are there will be very likely to stay over the 4th, or longer. I shall ask for hospitality

for some of our speakers and among them, I will ask for you—I
dont know how Susan comes to have a meeting.² We do not expect
to have any clash, i.e. we shall not go to their meeting, and hope
they will not come to our. Susan is in this city today, speaking for
the Parker Fraternity on "Woman and Purity"!³

Geo is here today and Emma also. She came on Thursday, and
has been to a dentist. Geo. came this morning. Harry and Geo.
carried Emma and Ada, to hear Mr. Murray⁴ and Alice to hear Charles
G. Ames,⁵ preach. The two gentlemen then went on to ride. The
world is so lovely with the fresh green, and with the blossoms of
cherry and pear, and the pink peeping of the apple buds, which will
soon be in full flower, that a ride is as good as a sermon. Geo. looks
so proud and satisfied and happy, beside of Emma, to whom he gives
a loving pat or stroke with eyes full of affection! His marriage has
done him good, and Emma says, he is more and more to her all the
time. She liked *all* the kith and kin on the other side, especially
Elizabeth, who advised her in her time of need in the most friendly
way.⁶

We all thought Florence much improved. A year at her age, makes
a great difference, and the entire change added a good deal beside.⁷
I advised her to take your house keeping this year. It would be an
invaluable experience for her, before she has her own housekeeping.
Alice was vexed at her sudden departure. She "had not had half visit
enough" she said.

We have nearly finished housecleaning. But the dress question is
a constant horror—The spring and summer clothes of Alice are
begun, but as one dress has been taken apart five times, and is still
unwearable, it seems as if there would never be an end. Ada can cut
and make her clothes, and always looks well dressed. But poor Alice,
who now, would like to look well, [*several words blacked out*] finds
it very hard. She does however keep up well at school, and takes no
end of comfort with the students and teachers—We have not had a
single application for our house. If we do not have, we cant go to
Europe, as the money from the rent, would be essential. I am sorry
both on account of Alice, and because the Presidential year, gives
much less chance to go on with our work. Besides we all need rest,
and change.

We shall try to run out to see you, when we go to Philadelphia.
We have been looking for Sam, and Ethel. He wrote us that he
thought he should come. We hope he will—If you could both leave
the nest, you might come with him. I am glad you could be with

Rebecca, and your father. It must have been a comfort to them and to you.

We have not had a copy of your book to my knowledge.[8] I do not at all under stand about your Woman's Journal and the Nursery. Last year and this, I sent Mr. Shorey a notice of the Nursery which he *said* should pay,[9] for the No. sent to you and for your *Journal,* your articles, and Sam's poetry pay. There is no money *ever* to be sent for it. We are all well, hard at work, I with stiff joints and Alice with troubled eyes. But we all send love.

Ever aff.

L.S.

There is a letter from Marian to Ellen, which is to go the rounds.

If you see Miss Lindsley please say to her, that I fully intended to have had her to tea. But some thing always crowded out the opportunity.[10]

I had her twice, to the N.E. Womans Club, and to the State House hearings—I called twice to see her at Mr. Lindsleys, but she was out each time.

Two days before she went home she sent to tell me, and to ask if she could take a package or anything to you. I called, but she was out. It was a series of misses. She seemed very nice and pleasant. I am glad you have so sensible and cheery a neighbor.

ALS-LC

1. Some New Jersey women claimed their right to vote under the state constitution in effect 1797-1807. The AWSA celebrated these early women voters at their meeting in Philadelphia, July 2, 1876.

2. Susan B. Anthony called for a meeting of the NWSA in Philadelphia July 3-4, 1876.

3. In 1858 Theodore Parker opened a series called "Fraternity Lectures" in the Music Hall in Boston to provide a platform for speakers too radical for other sponsors; the series continued after Parker's death.

4. James Ormsbee Murray (1827-99), Presbyterian clergyman and educator, held pulpits in Massachusetts and New York before joining the faculty of Princeton University, where he became dean of the faculty.

5. Charles G. Ames (1828-1912), a liberal Unitarian minister, supported suffrage. After organizing churches in Minnesota and on the Pacific coast, he held pastorates in Philadelphia and later at Boston's liberal Church of the Disciples.

6. George and Emma Lawrence Blackwell took a wedding trip to Europe, where they visited Dr. Elizabeth Blackwell at her home in Hastings, England. Their first child, Howard Lane Blackwell, was born in July 1876.

7. ALBB's daughter Florence had spent the previous year with her Aunt Elizabeth in England. She returned to the United States with George and Emma Lawrence Blackwell.

8. *The Physical Basis of Immortality* (New York, 1876).

9. J.L. Shorey was an editor of the *Nursery,* a children's periodical.

10. The final three paragraphs appear on a separate sheet and are presumed to conclude this letter.

[*Dorchester*] July 20—1876

Dear Nettee

Sam's chronicles of his trip to Cincinnati came yesterday. They have been duly read by me. Alice would read but she is flat with her usual summer attack of dysentery. It came last night. Harry had a severe attack too, which began in Philadelphia but he is well now though not quite strong.

I am glad "our boys" took the Cincinnati trip.[1] It will be a pleasant thing for them to remember always.

Mrs. Hallowell's address is Mrs. Sarah C. Hallowell No. 2017 De Lancey Place.[2] I utterly despise being written about Nettee. But Harry thinks I ought to give you dates, and trust your good sense.

So I was born Aug. 13 1818. I went to Oberlin Aug. 1843 graduated 1847—married May 1 1855.

There is nothing particular about me [*word blotted out*]. My father was a farmer—My mother made cheese. I helped, and worked hard—and played hard, and studied hard—At Oberlin I worked for 3 cts an hour and boarded myself—Had 12½ cts an hour for teaching—Earned my education as I went. Taught a Select School after I graduated in North Brookfield and paid a debt incurred in my education, and then began to lecture[3]

[*Lucy Stone*]

Af-SL

1. SCB and HBB attended the Republican National Convention held in Cincinnati in June 1876 to lobby for a woman suffrage plank in the party platform.

2. Sarah C. Hallowell of Philadelphia, a woman's rights supporter and author, was president of the Woman's Commission of the United States Centennial; during the celebration, she edited the *New Century for Women,* a weekly newspaper entirely written and printed by women.

3. The rest of this letter is missing.

Boston, Jan. 21 1876[1]

Dear Nettee

I have sent the "Wide Awake" and "Baby Land" to your chidren. I have paid for both, with a friendly notice, so that no money is to be sent, or for the "Nursery," which has always been paid for in the same way.[2] I have also had "C." put to your Woman's Journal, which means, "paid by contributions." This should have been done long ago, as what you have written for the Journal each year has more than paid for it.

I always wish that your family lived near mine—both to keep up the acquaintance and that you and Florence might enjoy the N.E. Woman's Club, and all of you have the benefit of the bracing air of N.E. Harry has been for the last few days pottering with beet sugar,— Litmus paper—bone black, lime, white of egg, and a mashed mass of beets ornament the kitchen at this moment. Did I tell you that he is seriously thinking of going to Santo Domingo[3]—and that we both really expect to go to Colorado, to help there next Fall, when the question of Woman Suffrage is to be voted on?[4]

I suppose you are busy, reading and writing—and that all the children but Florence go to school—

We never hear from Emily, rarely from Geo. Never from Elizabeth direct. But now and then from Kitty. At last accts. they were in Italy, expecting Marian to join them—Elizabeth much better—and Kitty studying Italian.[5]

Alice's eyes give her trouble. I shall take her to an occulist as soon as her exhibition is over. And I am not sure but she will have to stop studying. But this must not reach Alice, who need not grieve in advance. We are all well, and all send love.

L. Stone

ALS-LC
Written on the stationery of the *WJ.*

1. Internal evidence indicates this letter was written in January 1877.

2. *Wide Awake, Babyland,* and the *Nursery* were children's periodicals that received favorable reviews in the *WJ.*

3. HBB did go to Santo Domingo and Cuba in March 1877 to investigate the cultivation of sugar beets in preparation for opening a sugar beet business in Maine.

4. Colorado, which achieved statehood in 1876, held a referendum on the enfranchisement of women in the fall of 1877. Despite the efforts of LS and HBB, who toured the state the summer before the election, the referendum did not pass.

5. To conserve her threatened health, Dr. Elizabeth Blackwell and her adopted daughter, Kitty, spent winters in Italy in the 1870s.

Boston, July 15 1877

Dear Nette

I wrote to Mr. Magill,[1] at once, on receipt of yours saying that if it could be arranged, Edie could go.

Day after day, no answer came. So last week I wrote again, and hope for better luck—I write now to know what days the Woman's Congress will take in Cleveland[2]—It may be that we can have the Annual meeting of the American Association in the same week and city!—so that ladies can attend both who wish—

Alice is in Gardner boarding with Geo. and reciting Greek to a Harvard student who lives there—I was very glad that Harry met Florence and Edie at Rockaway.[3] We hardly keep up our acquaintance with them—We are trying to settle everything, before we go to Colorado.[4]

Poor Hayes finds himself in hot water[5]—I reckon there are rough times a head—

Is the prize paper done and gone? If you win, let us know.

One of the calico wrappers which Harry took to Rockaway was so dismantled, that it is fit only for a nightgown, *but it will do for that,* and so I sent it.

Alice is in long clothes now, and will have no more outgrown ones.

Harry has had a very hard cold, and cough, and so has Geo. and both cough still. But H's is better—We expect to start for Colorado in about a month. I dread it ever so much—I enclose a postal card, on which please send as soon as you can, the *time* of the Congress.

Did I tell you that Martha Rawson's daughter[6] invited herself here, and staid a week? She is just such a person, as one might suppose Martha would have.

Love to all
L.S.

ALS-LC
Written on the stationery of the *WJ.*

1. Edward H. Magill (1825-1907), educator, served as president of Swarthmore College 1871-89.
2. The fifth Woman's Congress, at which ALBB delivered the lead paper entitled "The Work Adapted to the Workers," was held in Cleveland, October 10-12, 1877.

3. By 1876 Ellen Blackwell owned two houses in Rockaway on Long Island.

4. In September 1877 LS and HBB campaigned for suffrage in Colorado.

5. Radical Republicans and former abolitionists attacked President Rutherford B. Hayes for ending Reconstruction by removing federal troops from Louisiana and South Carolina in April 1877.

6. Lenore Congdon Schutze, OC (1866-68), the daughter of ALBB's and LS's classmate Martha Rawson, received an honorary A.M. from Oberlin College in 1882.

                                                    Somerville July 18 '77

Dear Lucy

I enclose you a Congress programme. Did you *join* or not?

Thanks for your kind trouble about Edies matters. We are and shall be obliged to you: yet I wish and have wished ever since it was done that we had not made the application. I dont believe, on reflection, that any one except *friends* can get the gratuity.[1] Possibly they may: but it is humiliating to apply at all, and to get refused will be far from agreeable. Still it seemed best at the time. The girls are or were still at Rockaway. Edie is probably now on her way home— is expected here this afternoon. The rest all well. What will you do with your house and with Ada while you are gone?

My writing was finished the last day of June as it had to be: and was sent to the authority. Of course I desire the prize, but *dont* expect it. There may be a number of competitors who had leisure to do themselves justice; but more than that, we know almost nothing of what they want,—or on what grounds they would award the prize. One of the Company is a rather outlawed Scientific Methodist who has been *dealt with* for heresies. That is all we know of any of the Set. —I rather *hope* they may be induced to *publish the book,* however.

I have been suffering from a series of boils or something like them and ought not to use my arm much and am idle.

                                                    Love to you all
                                                    Nette

ALS-SL

1. LS's intervention with Swarthmore President Magill insured the acceptance of her niece Edith Blackwell and allowed her to compete for financial aid, which ALBB feared could be awarded only to Quakers.

Somerville Sept. 24. [*1877*]

Dear Lucy

We hope you are planning to be at the Congress at Cleveland. Miss May[1] has especially asked me if you can be stop there on return from Col.[2]

Your Mass. suffrage meeting I see is to be on the 9th.[3] Why was it put just then? However, Harry can go home to that and you remain at Cleveland can you not?

There is to be a good deal of discussion, etc. Mrs. Livermore has many reasons for staying away and will be at Boston doubtless, so you can be excused I am sure and help us.

We have some *good* papers but must depend much more than last year on the *Speakers.* And we wish to hear about Colorado!

Will you give, or send the enclosed card to Miss P.

I hope you are having a glorious time. It is hard of course; but there are many compensations. We have read your and Harrys letters and pronounced them capital.

Edie is studying with her father and me till January, when she will go to Swarthmore if all is well.[4] The younger children are all in school. If I did not thank you for your kind invitation to Edith, then I do so now very cordially. She is so silent and shy she would not be a very pleasant inmate of your home I fear. She is a nice girl; but peculiar what in the green uncompromising age. She had better go quite among strangers for a time.

Sam is still trying to sell or rent, and we are all working at the scores of things which occupy people overmuch.

Florence has quite given up her Scotchman.

Sam wrote and received some letters praising him extremely: but one quite unsatisfactory and Florence felt it, as we all did, to be best to know a man thoroughly for good before accepting him as a husband. She was not very much enlisted in him I think, and to some of us he never could have been satisfactory. So it is for the best. The child is just now spending a few days at Plainfield with some young friends.

Send me a line or a postal if very busy, to say you will be at Cleveland.

Affectionately
A.B.B.

ALS-LC

1. Abigail Williams May (1829-88), known as Abby, was the daughter of abolitionists and feminists Samuel and Mary May. A member of the

AAW, she was active in charity work, suffrage, women's education, and the women's club movement. In 1874 she was among the first five women to serve on the Boston School Board.

2. LS and HBB worked for the Colorado woman suffrage campaign in September 1877.

3. The Massachusetts WSA annual meetings began on October 9, 1877.

4. Edith entered Swarthmore as a freshman in January 1878.

Somerville Oct. 25 / 77

Dear Lucy

Florence is steadily getting better—thinks she shall be able to sit up all day to day. I sent you a card the other day; but directed it to 101 Milk St. thinking the Journal had moved there.

Possibly you will not get it, or it may be only delayed. Flo, has been quite sick. She was threadened with inflamation of the bowels and had a low lingering fever with it and afterwards; but is now all right again or nearly so, yet it will take a few weeks to bring her back to usual health. She was to read Miss Malory on the Chinese question for the benefit of the Library and though she felt sick when the evening came, she went with the rest to the entertainment and read—next day she was in bed and the next had the Dr. who came several times. They sent me a telegram which missed me, but a letter previously forwarded reached me, and I hastened home. This will delay Flo's visit to Boston; and I think if you need some one to do the little care taking things which she will do for you as well as she can, that you might best make other arrangements for the present. Later on, if you still desire it, we will send you the child and you can see how she fits into your household. I should like her to take lessons in elecution in Boston. We used to think of Kindergartening; but there are so many teachers in that line it would be a doubtful profession. But reading is in place every where.

Now about a matter of business. A Mrs. *W^m* or *Louisa* Southworth *521 Euclid Ave Cleveland*[1]—I forget which name she gave—subscribed through me for the Womans Journal $2.50. I gave the same to Mrs. Churchill who doubtless sent it on correctly. But afterwards Mrs. S. thought she would add 60 cts which would give the Journal to the end of the year and would let the first sum carry it through next year.

I did not see Mrs C. again and have been too busy to straighten it before—enclosed are the 60 cts.

Please see that it is made right. She is a nice woman, my hostess at C—about whom I shall write in Journal when there is time.

My Mss. were shabby—not copied—but I could not help that. The Congress was not a failure—under the circumstances was a success.[2]

With much love
A.B. Blackwell

ALS-LC

1. Louisa Southworth, a suffrage activist from Cleveland, held leadership positions in the Ohio WSA, the AWSA, and later the NAWSA.

2. The AAW's 1877 meetings may have been controversial because they included a speech by Frances Ellen Watkins Harper (1825-1911), black abolitionist, reformer, and poet who often addressed white audiences on racial themes.

Somerville March 18 [*1878*]

Dear Lucy

For some time I have intended writing you but so many things have occurred to prevent. Now that Hillside[1] is sold, or rather exchanged, if I do not sit down in the midst of pressure it will never be done at all. The prospect of moving is not agreeable, especially when one leaves *home* to go elsewhere. But we are both relieved, Sam and I, that the sale adds something more to the income and so relieves us to that extent.

Now about Flo. Of course she has not done you much service and has earned little or nothing for herself. If it must go on in that way of course it would be best that she should come home soon. But now that spring has come and the child is stronger is there any thing that she could do for a month or two Such as soliciting for Journal etc. If she could now try in earnest we should like it. She might give up the elocution if necessary and try really to work her way. Here though we are in the village there will be nothing for her to do or be which will be satisfactory. Still when she has tried helping herself if she does not succeed then she should come home at once.

As for her "young men," all that seems to be premature. She does right to be friendly and not too much interested in any one before there is something more definite than seems likely to be for the present. The child has faults and virtues. I wish I knew whether or not she has troubled you or whether she and Alice have done each other good. I am a very little blue today so will wait for a brighter mood and then send you a good friendly letter—The love and friendliness is all there whether it is expressed or not. It is already looking lovely here. Grass quite green and buds starting. I am beginning slowly to put things in order for the flitting being intent on working up and fixing over all the old things.

                                                        A.B.B.

ALS-SL

1. ALBB's and SCB's Somerville home was known as "Hillside."

                                            Somerville Apr. 10 '78
Dear Lucy

This is Agnes 11th birthday. I stand almost appalled at the flight of time. And Florence will be 22 in Nov. Still the child is younger than many girls at 18. None of my children, though large in size, develop early. Grace is nearly as high as I am, yet in figure, and in all traits physical and mental, she is still a child. It is the nature of the Browns, who were made to live long and to develop slowly; but they do become grown up after a while. If Florence were either settled that she was not to marry, or if she were happily married, she would begin to unfold naturally in new directions. She has mother-wit enough; but it is, as you suggest,—her mind is elsewhere; and to increase the evil her surroundings have led her to the belief that too much wisdom does not generally contribute to the kind of future which she most desires.

I believe she is right in thinking that she is best adapted to a home of her own; and that she would learn to be a good wife, mother, and housekeeper; with a good deal of energy to spare for wider outside interests.

Be that as it may, and whatever her future, household skill in all directions will do her good and be to her a real and lasting service. So you have our full approbation in "putting her through" the whole routine as effectively as you can. If she is rather awkward in handiwork, please consider it in part constitutional. I suppose she will come in, in that line, somewhere between Alice and Ida, Alice who never expects to learn much of such things, and Ida who never remembers when she did learn—being to the manor born, as many New England girls are. I will write Florence most seriously on the subject of taking hold resolutely.

As to C.S. we think well of him for his father's sake and from all we have heard about the young man from his childhood up. G.W. is also a nice bright youngster; but he seems to us just enough wanting in "~~common sense~~" discretion to find that his row in life ~~has been~~ will be an easy and pleasant one to hoe.[1] Flo has, I think, no serious disposition for flirting or for trifling with any one; and as far as one can judge from what she says, she gets on with Charley as well as might be expected. She must make acquaintance before there is any thing serious of course. But if C. *should learn* his own mind and desired a closer relation, she should of course at once let me say as much to Washburn. He can not be seriously interested, and knows that he has two years of studying to do yet; though he is evidently rather attracted to the child. Well, you will easily understand all that.

For the rest, I am glad Alice finds Florence a home comfort; for I fear you have not been used to exactly such a girl and must have found her ways often rather trying. Ah, well! She will be grateful some time. But if she does become a trial let us know at once, — please. She says she "likes Boston and the Boston people" and does not like Somerville. Neither do I, and now that Hillside is sold, nothing but the land will hold us here very firmly. That may not. My Brother has been offered a Secretaryship for the Church Building Ass. He is considering it.[2] I very much hope he will take it for his own sake and a little for our own; for he then may need more or less *help* from Sam. The compensation will be small but Sam would be glad of it at least for a time, while the hard times continue. However, the matter is still too unsettled for me even to speak of it. Yet it came into my mind and some business engagement as a last resort was one of the inducements towards leaving Hillside. One could go into N.Y from the Village. Or if a permanent opening came, we could leave here altogether and go nearer town.

We are all busy making gardens in two places etc. I have entirely stopped all attempt at writing for just at present.

Write us now and then.

Affectionately
A.B.B.

Please give my message on the subject of work to Flo. I have not time now but will write her in a few days. Much love to the University student![3]

ALS-SL

1. The initials refer to two of Florence's suitors.
2. After the death of his first wife, William Brown became severely

depressed; he recovered when he immersed himself in work for the American Congregational Union, which collected statistics on churches and building-fund monies.

3. ASB enrolled in Boston University as a freshman in Fall 1877.

Hillside [*Somerville*] May 25 [*1878*]

Dear Lucy

Flo tells us that she will now soon be at home. This is probably for the best, for I fear she has not been able, or perhaps sufficiently desirous, to adapt herself to your methods of work and to your ways in general.

Do you know how very sincerely we thank you for your real care and kindness to the child. If she could have stayed long enough to have learned to do all kinds of work thoroughly well, I should have been rejoiced; but we will do what we can for her in that line here. I was expecting her return this summer, especially when I found she was still going on with the elecution instead of taking hold of housework. Once more, we thank you most sincerely for what has been a pleasant long change, which in many ways has been not only pleasant, but profitable to Florence.

But you must not actively expend for the child any thing in the money line. Does the writing she speaks of come from the Journal, so that you do not have to pay it yourself. If so, very well; if not do not give her any thing more. You have already done quite enough for us and her.

You see we are still at Hillside but since F. and E. will both be at home soon, we think, on the whole, since we are so nearly moved, we will finish up and be settled in the new home early in June—possibly even before Flo returns. Do you know how I dread to leave here as the time approaches. So to we all; though the new house is pleasant enough and the neighborhood a cheerful one. Financially we are just a little more comfortable than last year, but not able yet to quite live on one income as the new home will involve some extra expenses.

I suppose you find the Journal suffers with every thing else in these depressed days. I do hope it can struggle on till better times. To stop that, would be a national calamity. I have had an article half written for it for some time—one that I must finish as it is now seasonable.

Henry seems to be staying a long time in Maine. Does he succeed with his experiments?[1] How relieved Alice must be to have a good

genuine rest. Edith says "I *wish* it was the 19th of June!" She is
doing well for the circumstances went not well prepared, but stands
mid way in a class of over 30. She must study, however, a good deal
in *vacation* that she may have it easier the next year. I helped her
on a year beyond what she thought she could do, and on the whole
it was for the best. The young ones are all still at s[c]hool; but when
we move we shall have to have home studying till next fall. We are
measurably settled at the new house, but still there is much to be
done. Housekeeping is a trial and I have turned painter, stainer,
varnisher and many other th[in]gs being—about as busy one could
well be for a month—past, yet I am very well and rather thrive on
work. I am very stout. Love to you all.

> Affectionately
> Nette

You are in the midst of May meetings.[2] Wish I could be there.

ALS-SL

1. In 1878, HBB founded the Maine Sugar Beet Company, hoping to
demonstrate that sugar could be manufactured without relying on sugar
cane grown by slave labor. Although he developed a successful process to
make sugar from beets and sorghum, it never proved commercially profitable.
2. The NEWSA held annual meetings in Boston each May; the 1878
meetings took place May 27-28.

> [*Somerville September 8, 1878*][1]

Dear Bostonians

There is time for only a line. Of course just now I am occupied
with getting Edie refitted for Swarthmore. The poor child rather
dreads and at the same time desires to go. In a day or two we shall
give her a long drive to New Brunswick to make last purchases. We
shall miss Agnes[2] but perhaps she will get much good from the change.
Emily[3] I suppose is still with you.

> Love to all
> A.B.B.

ALS-SL

1. ALBB appended this note to a letter written by SCB to HBB, LS, and
ASB.

2. Agnes, the next to youngest daughter of ALBB and SCB, resided with HBB and LS at Pope's Hill for the fall and winter of 1878.
3. Dr. Emily Blackwell.

[*Somerville September 18, 1878*][1]

Dear Lucy

I have in part over looked the winter wardrobe of the absent child in your care and am afraid that a good many things will have to be provided in Boston. There is a dress half made, flannels and other underclothing which shall go forward soon; & possibly a warm school cloak. But I may have to ask you to get her a ready made cloak and other things. You should not be troubled with these details if it could be avoided; and I will make what despatch is possible to supply a warmer wardrobe before it will be greatly needed.

Love to the little chicken who ought to write home once a week if only on a postal. Nor should she attend too many meetings in the evening, I think, as you also do you doubtless. So does papa, Agnes.

With love to all
Nette

ALS-SL

1. ALBB appended this letter to a letter written by SCB to HBB and LS.

Somerville Sept 27. 78

Dear Lucy

Agnes has outgrown her thin sack and her winter cloak is too shabby to send. She has outgrown her flannel drawers also; but the cantons[1] I send will probably be warm enough just for a time.

Will you buy for her just what you think she needs, to be made both comfortable and respectable, and we will, at any time, send on another check to defray expenses.

The old plaid was already fitted to her, or I would not have posted that off to Boston; but plaids are worn again and I hope it will look respectable for school.

It is quite cold here this morning. Yesterday in the morning it was really hot.

There is some thought of Flow's teaching a small elocution class;

but we are not quite decided whether or not it will be for the best. She ought to have a few terms more to make her feel self confident, especially with the young ladies, her old school mates, who might wish to take lessons.

I cannot go to Providence this year.[2] Wish I could! and to you!

Graceanna Lewis[3] is coming to give us four scientific lectures in Oct. and will stop with us here. Prof. Mitchell[4] writes; "How gladly would I have had you for our Prest at Vassar!" which of course may mean very little, yet it is rather pleasant to have her say it (not for the public of course).

My paper on the "Ice Closet" was sent to you and was with a letter *about Florence,* before she left. You received it as she told me on returning. Could you look five minutes among your own private papers; and if it is not found I must reproduce it, as I am under pledge to do so, but my paper of dimensions etc. is mislaid in moving[5] & will take trouble if it is found. Otherwise, to redeem my pledge, I must write to Cleveland.[6] But dont trouble if it is really lost, Ill manage. I am so much obliged that you make my chick so happy, and give her in change & novelty advantages which we cannot provide here.

Yours always,
Nette

ALS-SL

1. Canton is a variety of cotton flannel, napped on one side and twilled on the other.

2. The sixth Congress of Women met in Providence, R.I., October 9-11, 1878; ALBB did not attend.

3. Graceanna Lewis (1821-1907), author, lecturer, and artist, particularly on topics in the natural sciences, had been an abolitionist and was a lifelong advocate of woman's rights and temperance.

4. Maria Mitchell (1818-89), astronomer and Vassar College professor, was a founder and the first president of the AAW, and a supporter of the development of women's scientific abilities.

5. In the summer of 1878, ALBB and SCB moved from Hillside to another home in Somerville.

6. The previous October, ALBB had attended the fifth Congress of Women, held in Cleveland.

[*Dorchester*] Monday Sept. 30—1878

Dear Nettee

I wrote on Agnes sheet yesterday, when I thought I should not ·have time to write more. But I wanted to tell you how widely, and with how much good will, I saw the recommendation of you for Vassar. The Oberlin review had it and a good many other papers.[1] It *is* pleasant to be so held in the good will of the people.

I meant to send Flo my thanks for the mat but somehow when Sam gave it to me I only considered it as something I already had I was so used to it last winter. Will you tell this, and give her my thanks—

I am glad she will teach a class in Elocution. She ought to be competent, she had one whole term of private lessons last winter with no other pupil in the class—all winter with a class. This with her natural aptitude for it, and her experience before, ought to give her confidence and make her a good teacher. If she could have a class of little fellows too, it would be good for both.

I will look through all my last winter's files to find your article, but I dont think it ever came. Flo must heard it said that you *would* send it. I think this, because there could have been no reason why we should not have put it in then, if we had had it—I am very sorry about it, and trust it will appear somewhere.

Agnes does very well indeed both here and at school. She is a bright, sensible, active little thing and does with apparent pleasure the little chores that are assigned to her—she enters with real spirit into the family interests, and plays with the best children. They come here for croquet, and she goes to play the same at their houses. I will attend at once to her Fall sack. But any cloak that would do at Somerville will do here.

Agnes is plumper and fresher, than when she came. Has a good appetite and enjoys herself. Harry was sorry not to slip off to Somerville when he [*went*] to N.Y last week, but he had too much to do. He has a dreadful cold and cough now, and has had for two weeks, and does not seem to get over it—

The rest are well & Nell Hooper[2] is here with Lizze, but she leaves for N. York tomorrow. [Clara?] has her green house nearly done.

With remembrance of Ethel's birthday and love to all.

In haste
L. Stone

ALS-LC

1. On September 25, 1878, the *Oberlin Review* quoted a report from the *Orange* [N.J.] *Journal* endorsing ALBB as an outstanding candidate for the Vassar College presidency should the college decide to hire a woman for this post.

2. The Hooper family lived close to ALBB and SCB in New Jersey; Nell Hooper was also a friend of ASB's.

[Dorchester] at Home
Sunday Oct. 20 1878

Dear Nettee—

I will put in a line with Agnes. The child is always cheery, always makes the best of everything, helps in many ways, does not seem in the least homesick, likes her school, and is evidently taking a good rank—she looks plumper and stronger, than when she came—Alice and Lizzie both like her, and she reciprocates particularly with Lizzie who has more time, to talk, or rather they talk as they work together— she is in high favor all around—she makes the butter, salts it, and puts it away. She dusts and brushes, and is prompt and ready. She is a nice child, with a fine promise.

Now about your article. If Florence really read it, I suppose it must have come here. Wont you ask Florence what she did with it after she had read it. I will certainly look for it. But until after the annual meeting at Indianapolis,[1] I fear I cant even look—The fall work out doors, and the looking after fall and winter clothing, and arranging for that meeting, besides the Journal, and the family care, quite crowd me to the wall—

They begin to make sugar tomorrow in Portland. Harry has gone on to see, and if possible, to arrange for next year. They dont expect to make anything this year. They will be glad if they clear themselves.

I suppose you have had Miss Lewis and her lectures. Miss Lewis is in danger of speaking over the heads of her audience—she assumes that they know too much—

We have had no frost yet, but it is getting cold early—We have a fire on the hearth all the time.

Love to all
L.S.

The Woman's Congress was regarded as a great success. But they mean to publish a pamphlet report, and so did not want to put it in the Journal as usual. Tomorrow we make an occasion of the 43d anniversary of the mobbing of Mr. Garrison.[2] We will be at the N.E. Woman's Club rooms.

ALS-LC
Written on the stationery of the *WJ*.

1. The ninth annual meeting of the AWSA was held in Indianapolis, November 13-14, 1878.
2. On October 21, 1835, a hostile crowd dragged abolitionist William Lloyd Garrison through the Boston streets, nearly killing him. Over a hundred abolitionists gathered on October 19, 1878, to mark the anniversary of the event.

[*Somerville November 10, 1878*] 9 am[1]

Yes Lucy dear we do congratulate you very sincerely![2] Why cannot you and Henry stop over here for a day or two on your return from the West?[3] You will pass very near us and possibly might even take this road from the Ohio connections without additional expense. We should be *very* glad to see you both. Success to your Convention!

What a lovely fall we are having are we not?

With love to all — to Alice in particular.

A.B.B.

ALS-SL

1. This note by ALBB concluded a letter written by SCB to LS.
2. ALBB rejoiced at HBB's recent report of the success of his sugar-making experiments in Maine.
3. LS and HBB traveled west to attend the AWSA convention in Indianapolis.

[*Somerville*] Monday 9. A.M. [*December 1878*]

Dear Lucy

Dr. Clarke,[1] Higginson, Mrs. Love, and Ames were the four people whom, for one reason and another, I wrote to about Unitarianism, etc. All replied very kindly. If nothing turns up before, my plan now is to go on to Boston May meetings,[2] and from there begin actively to push my way into pulpits and other places; and see if I can get an opening after a while which shall have more of permanence. Sam and George, you probably know, are to begin actively to advertize and keep open a N Y office for the next 3 month at least.[3] The experiment may succeed fairly, or it may not. But I shall stay at home till that is over, unless something new occurs. It is very well to repost myself sermonwise at any rate, for about that length of time, though Flo could be housekeeper, or so could Grace at a pinch. It would do them good, especially if Ann gets well again to take the heavy burdens. She has been failing for months; and has done almost nothing outside her kitchen. She is getting old, and has only half wages when she is here. We hope she *will* return; but it may be otherwise. She preferred going away rather than trying to rest here.

Mr. Ames kindly offered to speak for me to the public in his paper.[4] I said yes; and left the time of doing so to him, as well as the method, telling him my plans about as was told to you. Whether he will do it judiciously or not, I dont know. It was he who suggested the May meetings—

When he speaks, then the Journal would confer a favor by doing so also.

With love and haste this washing day morning! I keep the run of you and Harry, and always read what you write for Journal! One half wishes to be 60, if that will bring so many friends to the front.[5]

With love always & *to all*
Nette

ALS-LC

1. James Freeman Clarke (1810-88), transcendentalist, Unitarian clergyman, and later pastor of the radical Church of the Disciples in Boston, supported temperance, antislavery, and woman's rights.

2. The NEWSA held its annual meetings in Boston, May 26-27, 1879. ALBB, who had just announced her availability as a Unitarian minister, spoke to the gathering on the role of women as guardians of the moral education of future citizens.

3. For a time, SCB worked with his brother George Washington Blackwell in the real estate business.

4. Charles G. Ames edited the Unitarian paper the *Christian Register,* 1878-80.

5. LS turned sixty years old on August 13, 1878; the New England Women's Club gave a reception in her honor to mark the event, on which the *WJ* reported December 21, 1878.

[*Dorchester*] Sunday evening Feb. 2—1879

Dear Nette

If you will write what you would like to have said about your
~~entering~~ reentering the ministry, we will put it in the Woman's Journal
as from ourselves.[1]

The Parker Fraternity are tired of, and dont like Mr. Dudley, their
present minister.

May be you could be settled there. The fares between Boston and
N.Y. now being only $1.56 each way would make it possible for you
to live at home, and still serve here.

We all hope the N.Y. Deal, will prove the right door to let off, a
great deal of real estate.

Agnes *does* enjoy the school, and gets high marks. She is looking
forward in triumph to the time when she will send you her card,
with its high per cent. But the day she staid at home, it was the
"Little Women"[2] so interesting! that tempted her. She is very well,
very active and apparently not in the least homesick, though she did
say when she read in your last that you should be here in May that
she should go home with you.

You are here by invited to come to us in May—and to make the
most of your opportunity to use the neighboring pulpits.

Washington Gladden[3] speaks at Meeting House Hill, next Wednesday. Agnes had a delightful time at the theater yesterday, with the
little Beals. They all went together.

It is late Nette dear so good night.

Did you see that Prof. Morgan's son[4] has lately died in California?

L.S.

Agnes wrote her letter this week to Flo, and now it cant be found,
but she is well and gay.

ALS-LC

1. On March 15, 1879, the *WJ* announced ALBB's intention to reenter
the ministry.

2. Louisa May Alcott, *Little Women* (Boston, 1868).

3. Washington Gladden (1836-1918), a liberal Congregational minister,
advocated municipal reform, labor organization, and government owner-
ship of public utilities as part of his program of Applied Christianity.

4. John Paul Morgan (1841-79), OP (1851-58), son of ALBB's Oberlin
theology professor John Morgan, was an organist, teacher, and cofounder
of the Oberlin Conservatory in 1865. He died in Oakland, Calif., January
5, 1879.

Somerville Feb 9 [*1879*]¹

Dear Lucy

Many thanks for your kind offer, invitation, and suggestions. There is time enough to advertize my speaking before the time for beginning. Mr. Ames, may or may not say anything at present. But we will wait till he does. I said wait unless he thought it might help to speak to the Public in advance.

If the invitation could come from the Parker Society I should be *very* glad to speak for them once or more and see what would be the result. I feel full to overflowing of enough to talk about that I care for intensely; but prefer a few months longer at home.

Ann has not yet returned though she fixed the day for doing so and we have not heard from her since. She may be sick again or may need a longer rest. My hands are full, and Flo is busy with her elocution both teaching and the necessary practice in order to keep in advance of her girls and also prepare for one and another social or public gathering.

You seem to have had a very good Annual meeting!²

Love to all, Agnes included for I will not especially write her today except to suggest that if she was at home she would have plenty of work to do, so she must save steps and do ever so many nice little helpful things for the other home and Aunt Lucy.

Affectionately
Nette

ALS-LC

1. The year on this letter was added in a later hand.
2. The annual meeting of the Massachusetts WSA was held in Lowell, January 30, 1879.

[*Somerville March 30, 1879*]¹

Dear L.   Harry's absence must add cares to your burdened shoulders; but the hope of success and the necessity for work itself is wholesome sometimes.

I hear that "the Channing Gathering" is on the last of April. Is this the denominational annual? I am to speak in Providence, May 5th, for Mrs. Churchill² — the same lecture given at Poughkeepsie; also sometime at Cambridgeport. Probably Mr. Slacks(?) church committee either *do not invite me,* or will wait till I am in Boston. When and what are your meetings?³ I shall soon know that, however, from the paper. So never mind to answer by letter.

Till we meet, Thanks!
A.B.B.

tL-BMS⁴

1. ALBB appended this note to a letter written by SCB to LS.
2. ALBB spoke at a Unitarian conference named for William Henry Channing held in Providence, R.I., May 1879; on the same visit she spoke to the Providence Woman's Club at the request of Elizabeth Churchill.
3. The NEWSA held its annual meeting in Boston, May 26, 1879.
4. This transcription was taken from a typescript copy in the possession of Barbara Miller Solomon, Cambridge, Mass.; the original has not been located.

Somerville July 10 1879

Dear Bostonians

Congratulations to Harry and Alice and both congratulations and condolences to Lucy! I did not quite believe that you would be off for Europe this summer, especially that our Junior would.¹ But it is better so. It will be a good time for an ocean sail—just the ideal weather for that.

Lucy will have a quiet good time with Agnes Read,² and I hope not find the paper a dreadful nightmare since she can keep it well in hand and quietly ahead of time in preparation.

For ourselves, we are still doing our own work—washing and all; and find life busy enough in these dog days. Grace is still at Rockaway. Both Florence and Edie are dressmaking, Agnes says lessons with Sam, Ethel goes to school, and I read stories now and then for recreation and write sermons for variety. Sam is rather tried this last few days with the hot weather, but we are all fairly well for the season.

Good wishes are sent out from all to the outward bound! Love to them on the other side! But the burden of all our sympathy is with the one stay at home and her work, and worries, and rest.

Very affectionately
A.B.B.

ALS-LC

1. HBB and ASB traveled to Europe in the summer of 1879. They met Blackwell relatives in England, and HBB went to Germany where he purchased machinery for his sugar refinery.

2. Agnes Reid was a classmate of ASB's at the Harris Grammar School in Dorchester; the families of the two were on friendly terms.

Somerville Aug 1 1879

Dear Lucy

I wonder whether the great quiet still continues to be "very good" or whether it already leans a little towards total depravity! You and Agnes Read must have a rather nice time in the quiet house. Much good will to you both and good wishes many and various!

The travellers will soon be heard from now I suppose. Send us word when you hear, please.

As for ourselves, we are all here now. Grace came home on Monday last. But poor Sam has another such hand as last year—a gathering in exactly the corresponding part of the other hand. It is however apparently doing well, was lanced yesterday and discharges freely. If we can keep it open long enough to quite cure the evil at once, I hope it will be less serious than last year. It is a week now since it began to inflame. It must have come from a bruise, probably, though Sam has not used his hand excessively this year. But he evidently cannot work in such ways as other men can; cutting a little hay for the cow or some such trifle did the evil, it would appear. He must have the predisposition to such troubles.

Emily came out and spent a night. She was rather unsettled about her next movements. I hope all will settle itself about little Paul, who isnt wanted anywhere by most of the Blackwells I suppose and is not wanted either by the people who have him—at this time it seems.[1]

Sam copied the Mss. I was very busy with the housekeeping; as we did our own washing while Ann was away. She returned the day before Sams hand trouble came—a very fortunate thing for the heat here has been intense and the children all feel it greatly.

Besides the sewing for a family of women is a great bore; and that we chiefly do ourselves.

I hear nothing from Mr. Weld.[2] Probably they will not send for me then what next after the heat is over will be a problem.

Sams general health seems better so far than last year. I hope he will get over this easily in comparison. S. could not do any better with the Mss. He left out some things, transposed some, and added a few closing sentences. I hope the lady will not be disappointed about a publisher; but the whole article is too long.

Grace was 16 yesterday. Is it not astonishing! She is the tallest

person in the house, I think—at any rate about as tall as her father
and quite up to me. So they grow.

Yours ever in love
Antoinette

ALS-LC

1. In 1876, Ellen Blackwell adopted Paul Winthrop, but found it difficult
to care for the child both because of her precarious financial position and
the boy's energetic nature. Many members of the Blackwell clan suggested
to her that she part with him, but she proved reluctant to do so.
2. Theodore Dwight Weld (1803-85), outspoken abolitionist and author
before the Civil War, later operated a school with his wife, Angelina Grimké
Weld, and her sister, Sarah Grimké. By 1879, the family had moved to
Hyde Park, Mass., where Weld was active in founding the local Unitarian
society.

Somerville Aug 7 1879
Dear Lucy
We are very glad to hear of the safe arrival of the travellers. They
will get much good out of the visit—even Harry will do that—and
Alice will have unmixed good in her cup I hope.

Sams hand is doing very well—all things considered. It is not to
be so severe as last year—at least unless something new supervenes.
It begins to mend already—is not so deeply seated as the other, and
not so painful; then we understand better what to do. Practice leads
towards perfection. Sam has, I think, done the best he could about
the article, but from the first he wished me to say to you that we
owed the work to you, not to ourselves, which is true! There is some
hope that Sam may be engaged to go to Nevada for six months, as
a good salary—he is rather gray headed and went in to the needy
firm with hand bound up and looking thin. If they reject the idea,
it will be in favor of a younger, stronger man. Mr Minturn[1] rec-
ommended him. We shall see in a week or so. The *journey* should
be of real value.

Florence is going to a camp meeting near Boston week after next.
She will be there about a week, then proposes to join the Methodist
church at Harrison Square;[2] and come home again soon after. I would
rather she stopped over Sunday or so with you, if convenient. Mr

Bragg[3] spent a day here not long ago. We are well but busy, like yourself.

With much love ever
Nette

ALS-LC

1. Samuel Minturn, a businessman for whom Samuel Blackwell had once worked as a bookkeeper, was a longstanding friend of the Blackwell family.
2. The Pope's Hill home of LS and HBB was near Harrison Square.
3. Mr. Bragg was a Methodist minister in Woburn, Mass., who probably knew Florence Blackwell through her denominational interests.

Somerville Aug. 14 '79

Dear Lucy

It is very pleasant to know that your voyagers had so very, positively, good a crossing. It will give Alice courage on the return trip alone. Henry will soon be back again!

Sams hand is rapidly getting well; yet, at the best, it will cost the entire month in time, and will be tender still for a good while longer. Still the worst of all is that Nevada matter. I think he would have been engaged if he had been in usual health—The Minturns fully expected it and felt a little chagrinned. They may find something else.

Florence will start on Monday next for the Hamilton camp meeting[1] and will spend about a week there—perhaps a little more. Then she will go to Harrison Square. If any of the ladies invite her, she might stop with them chiefly, though I fear they are all people with small accomodations and may not give the invitation. Still, as you are alone and enjoy the quiet, I dont want her to trouble you. If you would rather she did so, she might get some place to board for [a] week. It would not be of large expense and the change would do her as much good as any other way. She is very thin and needs something. We can devise nothing better considering the desire she has to complete the uniting with that church.

Mr Braggs visit was nothing in particular. He had been at Ocean Grove. Florence had decided to go to the camp meeting before he came. He seems a gentle and good young fellow and friendly. He may rather like Florence than otherwise.

We have all felt the extreme heat here. Agnes has lost her plump cheeks again and so have they all but now it is cool again. We are taking little drives and picnics which will do them all good.

I have done almost no studying but much sewing and some daw-dling, some easy reading and any amount of waiting, waiting for whatever may come, which seems to be nothing for any of us as yet. If only we can sell the Elizabeth house to the people who are living there. They like it, and talk about it, just now, a little.

Let us hear now and then if only a card. While you are alone we think of you the oftener. Love to Agnes Reid.

Affectionately
Nette

ALS-LC

1. Hamilton, Mass., is on the Atlantic Ocean north of Boston.

[*Dorchester*] Aug. 25 1879

Dear Nettee

I had a letter from Miss Andrews this morning which I enclose. You will see that Grace must be at Newburyport next week Wednes-day—I have written Miss Andrews that she could consider Grace as a pupil, and arrange accordingly.[1] I felt so sure of this that, as she needed to decide, I did not wait to hear further from you, but if Grace cannot go, you should telegraph at once—But nothing *ought* to hinder her.

I wrote Miss Andrews that Grace would be benefitted by a share in the daily work, which might be credited towards her expenses— you see what she says. It will be worth a great deal to the child to get the orderly ways of Miss Andrews by actually doing some daily duty under her direction.

Now this week from last Friday was to have been my little "outing." But Friday Ada Watson came here ill with her bowels, and as she had no home, she staid—and a dear old lady died, and I was sent for to speak at the funeral, on Sunday. Today Mr. Buckpitt[2] says the camp meeting breaks up, and Flo may be here tonight, but as I have heard nothing from her I do not know—Mr. Buckpitt said their house was too small to take in another. So I went to get Agnes Reid's mother to take her, but Mrs. Reid is over driven, with preparation for her daughter to go to St. Louis. I have therefore brought Agnes Reid home with me, that she and Flo may take care of themselves. Agnes broke her collar bone (I think I wrote you that) and she is not much help, but she will be company, and the two will get along some how. I do not mean to be cheated out of my small holiday— since last August, I have not had a day of respite, and I have sore need of it.

Sam had better bring Grace on Tuesday, and take her to New-buryport Wednesday and be back in time to greet Harry who expects to be here that day. If Grace needs things made, it will be easy to send to her or Flo can make them while she stays here—But Grace ought not to be absent from the opening of the school, i.e. it will be better to begin with the others.

In haste
but truly
L.S.

I had a letter to day from both Harry and Alice dated London Aug 14. Harry was not very well. The bad wine and German drink had disagreed with him. He had breakfasted with Elizabeth in London that day. Alice and Kitty were to join them, Anna had not arrived was detained by "important business." Harry is shocked to find that all Germans say he *must* keep his beets buried till they are ready to use. And the Maine beet Sugar Co. has no place to bury them. L.S.

ALS-LC

1. LS and HBB helped finance the education of ALBB's and SCB's middle daughter, Grace, at Jane Andrews's school in Newburyport, Mass.
2. The Buckpitt family was active in the Methodist Church in Harrison Square.

Somerville Dec. 9 1879

Dear Lucy

I hear that you had a fine convention at Cincinnati.[1] I would have joined you gladly but engagements prevented. Is it true that you are to meet next year at Washington. If you do, I should like to be there. It is time I should see the Capitol of my country for once; and to go on there for nothing is not to be thought of; besides I should *like* to be a little more identified with your wing of Suffrage now that I begin to speak again.

Do you think Sam will keep on with the sugar business in Port-land?[2] If he does, I think the family, or at any rate part of it, had best join him there. The children would all vote to go, I suspect, unless it be Edie.

For me, my Western trip must on the whole be counted as a success.[3] I can undoubtedly find a small half-dead society somewhere Westward if I choose—with about half pay. But it is so far away, especially from Portland, I shant think of it for a moment. If I could get a *good* Society, I could go for a year or two even if Sam did go to Portland. That would pay off debts and then we could be together again. Flo and Agnes could keep house for Sam; and the others be either with me or in School. That I dont expect, however, and in my heart I dont want it; though *if* the chance offered, I should feel bound to accept.

But I must speak more or less somewhere. My gifts, such as they are, evidently lie more in that direction than any other. If I can get back into the lecture field and also preach as opportunity offers, that will, under the circumstances, be really best of all because I can be a good deal at home and look after the children and see to the general running of affairs; as well as give and take some home comfort. My ABCs; or Does Science prove Immortality? the plain and popular expression of the gist of *my* book, is certain to take well.[4] I must get it a little more into shape for a short series of two or three lectures; and begin here about. But in Sams absence there will be so little time. Still, I'll do my best as soon as I am rested. Flo is going, after Christmas, to visit her aunt Emma. Edie will be here in a week or two. Dont think that I am not steadily appreciating all you are doing for me and mine, Lucy dear. Somebody quotes me as saying that Sams pay is a poor little sum for so great a separation. So it is; but every thing is relative. Half the sum, we should have accepted just then.

I see you notice *one* meeting. Ill send a general notice. It may help me somewhat.

Love to Alice and much to yourself. I must write hastily, if at all, you see.

always yours
Nette

The children are all the better for being left alone a while.

ALS-LC

1. The tenth annual AWSA Convention was held in Cincinnati, November 4, 1879.

2. SCB joined HBB in the Maine Beet Sugar Company in the fall of 1879 when the business was prospering.

3. After she attended the seventh Congress of Women, held in Madison, Wis., October 8-10, 1879, ALBB preached and lectured on immortality throughout the Midwest.

ˈ 4. ALBB's *The Physical Basis of Immortality* argued a "scientific" basis for immortality. As ALBB explained, forces as well as matter can be neither created nor destroyed; thus human perception, a force, can be neither created nor destroyed; hence the soul, the seat of human perception, is immortal, although its form and manifestation may change.

Somerville April 18/80

Dear Lucy

We all sympathized very much in your illness and now rejoice in the amendment.[1] I have hesitated to write you thinking you would be overwhelmed with correspondence. Since Sam left, have been too busy to write under the treble pressure of dressmaking, gardening, and writing to get a few [*Je*]rsey women appointed as Enumerators of the coming Census. We hope to succeed!

Cant you and Alice spend a little time here with us when you return. This is a really pleasant house with an outlook towards the mountain—a large yard, and windows in superabundance. Ethel would hardly know "cousin Alice" I think and A. would not know Ethel. Do stop if you can.

You had an article some time ago about the 30th anniversary of the Woman's Convention at Worcester.[2] You mentioned the dates, which I think came in the first week of Oct. or possibly the 2nd week. It cannot be as late as the third week, can it. If so we have put the Boston Congress in the third week also and that must be changed.[3] I should have a report of the Worcester meeting; but it is not to be found and I have no way of fixing the date.

Sam has been gone over two weeks now. He writes cheerily and hopes to return early in May or possibly this month. He seems to be having a pleasant trip and rather to enjoy it I think. Letters have just come from Edith and Grace. Both seem well and happy. Grace reports that Boston has just ordered 1200 copies of "The Seven Little Sisters." That will be very good for Miss A., will it not?[4] It is to be made a school book for the small Bostonians.

Does Alice enjoy Wilmington is she almost pining for the Boston University? Flo seems to be getting very fond of Emma's baby[5] and indeed of both of the children.

It seems as though Harry ought to be a little more hopeful about the beet sugar business as the beets get pledged at least for this year. I do hope he will succeed! Poor fellow he has had a long hard pull. And so have you, Lucy dear but I hope the worst is over now for you both.

We are still almost in the midst of winter though some of the earliest trees are in leaf enough to look pretty and green. But we have fires feel rather chilly at that.

Get well as fast as you can. The people of old Kennett, when they heard you were in Wilmington wished you could speak for them but feared as you were there for recr[ea]ting you could not be obtained.[6]

Love to Alice

Affectionately

A.B.B.

The two home children send love. They are preparing for an examination tomorrow and studying.

ALS-SL

1. In the spring of 1880, LS traveled first to New York City for treatment by her sister-in-law Dr. Emily Blackwell, then to Delaware for further recuperation from an illness brought on by overwork; ASB left Boston University to join her mother in Delaware.

2. To commemorate the thirtieth anniversary of the first national Woman's Rights Convention, held in Worcester, October 23, 1850, the AWSA held a convention October 27-28, 1880. LS, HBB, and ALBB all attended.

3. The eighth Congress of Women was held in Boston, October 13-15, 1880.

4. *The Seven Little Sisters Who Lived on a Round Ball that Floats in the Air* (Boston, 1861) was a popular children's book written by Jane Andrews, proprietor of the progressive school to which ALBB and LS sent their daughters.

5. George Lawrence Blackwell (1879-86), or "Laurie," was the second son of George and Emma Lawrence Blackwell. He was a sickly child who developed a hunchback.

6. Over the years, both ALBB and LS spoke to meetings of the Progressive Friends in Kennett Square, Pa.

Somerville July 5/80

Dear Lucy

I hope you have waked this morning after as grand a rain as we had here yesterday. After the extreme dryness, we have a cistern *overflowing* which is an immense luxury.

Gracie may be here today; but if not she will come, doubtless, next Monday night from Boston. My brother will go on Eastward next Friday night; and will take Agnes so far on her way to Marthas Vineyard as Boston where she can meet Emily. We have not positively decided to send the child. But she looks thin and tall and in need of a bracing air, and the temptation to accept Emilys suggestion and invitation is very great. If we do send her, she will make her appearance at the Journal Office Saturday morning. But she knows Boston and can get a horse car, if needful, ride out to Fields Corner[1] and walk up to you.

You see Lucy we do not hesitate to send you child after child on extemporized visits. I hope you will give them so many little things to do while they stay with you that they will at least save you as much trouble as they make. Agnes is our dishwasher now. We shall miss her here, & shall have to install Gracie in her place. — Sam, just now and probably for some time to come, is examining the old Democratic Somerville Bank accounts. Whether they will think best to continue what must be a long slow work, if finished, remains to be seen. They (accounts and men also[)] have been kept both most carelessly and dishonestly.

What about the Worcester 3d decade? Are you going to let it slip by at the risk of having the National women summarizing it at the last moment. Can you and shall you work with them? I would under all the circumstances; but you and others must decide. If any thing is settled, let me know, I mean to be at the Congress and may plan other meetings about that time so that it becomes important to know how to plan to the best advantage. Where will Alice spend her vacation principally? Love to all Dr E included and G. if there.

ABB

ALS-LC

1. Fields Corner was close to the home of LS and HBB in Dorcester.

Somerville Aug 16/80

Dear Lucy

We all feel the kindness that prompts you to return Gracie to Miss Andrews. The child is glad to go and yet she rather shrinks from leaving home again so soon. She says she is lazy and likes to stay just where she is. That when she is in Newburyport she will like best to stay there she supposes. Rather a good frame of mind on the whole.

Yes, it will do the child great good to have another year there, and to have some drill in teaching little children. We will all remember it as a long white mark in your callender forever.

Of course we are overwhelmingly busy. I have been half sick all summer and cannot tell what the trouble is, but suppose it will cure itself after a while. Sam is now away all day. He may possibly be busy with bank affairs so long as to interfere with his going to Portland; but it is quite as likely they will decide to discontinue at almost any time. So I suppose he will join Henry. Edith goes about the middle of Sept.

Grace thinks she cannot return alone. She has a horror of the boat. There may be some one going on. If not, as she is so nervous, and as Flo rather needs and has earned a little change, she *may* go to Boston with Grace. G might go directly on to Miss A. and F go out to your house and see her church people and get her church letter and take a final farewell of Harrison churchites. She is eager for that plan; but could not be long away as it will be about time of Ediths going, and I suppose I shall have to take her on and help settle her. Then she must travel alone.

I hope you are getting strong!

Hastily
Nette

We are expecting my brother, & the new wife.[1]
Love to all at Gardner & Boston if you have returned.[2]

ALS-SL

1. In June 1880, William Brown married Charlotte Emerson Brown (1838-95) who was active in missionary support work and the women's club movement; she was a founder of the General Federation of Women's Clubs and its first president.
2. LS visited her sister Sarah Stone Lawrence and her family in Gardner, Mass., in August 1880.

Somerville Sept 1/80

Dear Lucy

Florence and Grace propose to leave here Friday to reach Boston Saturday the 4th, and Grace has written Miss Andrews she will go

on Saturday to Newburyport. She would spend Sunday at your house
if she could meet Agnes there, as Emily proposes; but I think there
is not time to get word to Emily. It would hardly do for Grace to
lose several days, I think, and it is making your house too full for
them all to be there! Florence will wish to visit her friends of the
Methodist persuasion a good deal, and Washburn[1] invites her to some
little days excursion; so she will not return here till about a week,
more or less; but not *much* more at any rate. Dont have Harry stay
at home for the Sunday. Flo will go to church and be full of her
people and she will see H. on his return. Perhaps Alice may be at
home before F. comes home. Her college must begin later though,
I think. — Alice says you have seen 'Robert of '47.'[2] Was it a good
visit? I suppose he is a portly bald man!

Did I thank you for the clothes. Edith fitted the dress for Grace
and one of the skirts went without fitting, matching one of her dresses.

We have dressmaker, washrwoman & are getting house ready for
company.

So excuse this hasty scrawl with love to you and Alice & Henry.

Yours
Antoinette

Grace has company and I am needed in 4 places at once.

ALS-SL

1. Probably the same suitor of Florence Blackwell's mentioned in ALBB's
letter to LS April 10, 1878.
2. Robert Kedzie.

Somerville Oct. 8 1880

Dear Lucy

I shall take the Monday evening boat for Boston reaching there
Tuesday morning. Probably I may go directly out to Harrison Square
but I can walk up if I do. Whether I shall stay with you during the
Congress or not I dont know. They have evening sessions of officers
which would trouble you, and me also. So *If* a good home in Boston
offers, Ill stay in Town till that is over, then spend the time between
that and Worcester with you. I am half sick and cannot get over it.

Nerves I think, and dullnes too dense for ordinary humanity.—!
Hope that will fly away under excitement.

Till we meet, with ever so much love!

Nette

ALS-SL

[*Somerville January 23, 1881*][1]

Dear Lucy

. I send on the children's letters though Agnes has not finished hers.
She was stopped when writing it and now she is off to school and
as I know she has some history writing to night of an extra kind, it
may as well go at once. Both the children are writing for the prize
and on the whole are doing very well in the little stories. Ethel dashes
off rapidly but will have a good deal of revising to do. Agnes writes
more slowly and it is more nearly done when first written. As Agnes
is 13 she must send hers before her next birth day. They may not
go on, though I think they will. Could you send the Christmas number
of the Wide Awake which has *directions about the prize stories.* We
would return it if you cared to have it. We are all well here.

I send you my last little ~~poem~~ rhyme as it is fitted for Journal
readers. Sam has some prospect of being needed by some other Bank
in trouble: one that appreciates his work and his clear admirable
report of the bank here. It will not be a long work but will take him
away from home—not just yet though.

A.L.B.B.

ALS-SL

1. This letter was accompanied by letters of ALBB's daughters Ethel and
Agnes to LS.

[*Somerville, late Fall, 1881*][1]

[. . .] and we shall find it easy and pleasant to entertain a part or *all
four of you* here. It is so long since Alice has been here at Christmas.
It would seem like old times if she would come, and that would *fully*
content and delight our young tribe. Edith *may* not return to Xmas.
She thinks they will not have a long vacation, and that her class will
probably graduate in May instead of June as the hotels are only

engaged for May and the new building cannot probably be ready for the remainder of the year.[2] She has a good deal to do and would not mind *very much* if she does not come home for holidays. She would regret not seeing Kitty and Grace off, and meeting Alice, etc.[3] We will not decide till we know just what programme is expected to be carried out and how long her vacation will be. Edith did not know where to address K. and sent thanks and good wishes, especially for the photograph. She asked *where* K. was. We shall report to her.

Yes; Grace would *prefer* a stateroom with K. She is very social in feeling; but not a great talker, in general.

Mrs. Browning sent me a postal to say she should write and remit something soon — a fortnight ago. Nothing heard since from her.

A merry Christmas to all, here or there. Why not all come on for holidays?

A.B.B.

ALf-SL

1. This fragment appears on the same sheet as a short letter from SCB to LS, HBB, and ASB. The beginning of ALBB's letter has not been located.

2. Edith Blackwell was to graduate from Swarthmore College in late June 1882.

3. In the fall of 1881, Kitty Barry, then living in England with her guardian, Elizabeth Blackwell, visited Blackwell relatives in the United States. When she returned to England she was accompanied by ALBB's daughter Grace, who spent several months there.

Part 4

"Fruitage-Weighted"

1882-93

Snows adrift above our foreheads!
    Pearly blooms wreathe every brow
Quaintly furrowed! Yes, with thinking,
    not with time or care, I trow;
Life is brimming yet with promise;
    Summers, full-leaved elbow Spring!
True but autumns, fruitage-weighted;
    Far off coming, slowly wing.

—Antoinette L. Brown Blackwell,
"The Class of '47"

The 1880s brought to Stone and Brown Blackwell awareness of their own aging and increased sensitivity to the progression of generations within their extended family and within the political world. As they relinquished their roles as managers of their children they felt more strongly the need to regulate the ways in which their personal histories would be written and their public achievements judged. Each self-consciously strove to maintain her commitments and to insure their recognition. Stone continued to lecture, edit the *Woman's Journal,* and fight for woman suffrage, while Brown Blackwell pursued the topics that had long been her primary interests: the relationship between science and religion, and the equality of men and women. In the final years of their relationship, their shared concern for the recognition of their rightful place in the record added a new dimension to their individual lives and to their friendship, now long secured by the ongoing bonds of family and personal affection.

For the country as a whole, the 1880s were years in which popular organizations made known the discontent of farmers and industrial workers. The rise of the Grange, the Populist party, the Knights of Labor and the Socialist Labor party all aided the organization of rural and urban working-class women. In addition, some newly college-educated women entered the slums in order to aid immigrant women and children in their struggle for survival and dignity. Yet despite their earlier concerns for the social justice of abolitionism, neither Stone nor Brown Blackwell expressed much sympathy with these mass movements. Even among the next generation of woman's rights leaders, only a very few were able to build alliances between the cause of women on the one hand, and organizing efforts among farmers, immigrants, and the working class on the other.

Family events highlighted for Stone and Brown Blackwell transi-

227

tions to their roles as mature matriarchs. The first wedding among the next generation of Blackwell women, the marriage of Brown Blackwell's eldest daughter, Florence, to Elliott Mayhew in July 1882 brought great joy to the immediate family; among the wider network of Blackwell relatives, particularly those who had never themselves married, it caused some consternation. Many of them better appreciated the transition made by Stone's daughter the same year. After graduating from Boston University in 1881, Alice Stone Blackwell received her recognition when she undertook her first solo stint as editor of the *Woman's Journal* in September 1882, while her parents stumped for suffrage in Wisconsin and Nebraska. Although she would remain a member of her parents' household until their deaths, Alice Stone Blackwell now transformed the longstanding suffrage partnership into an equitable trio. Thus for both Stone and Brown Blackwell 1882 marked their newfound status as mothers of fully grown daughters.

Neither mother nor daughter seemed to question that Lucy Stone's only daughter would establish herself a public career closely linked to her mother's lifelong work. Alice Stone Blackwell worked closely, and deferentially, with her parents. Never while her parents lived did she differ publicly with them, although she did carve out her own particular area of competence and expertise. Like her parents, she spoke and stumped for suffrage and served as an officer in the various interlocking suffrage organizations. But she created a special role for herself in editing the "Woman's Column," a news sheet that summarized woman's rights developments covered in greater depth in the *Woman's Journal;* her column was distributed to newspapers and periodicals across the country for reprinting to spread the suffrage message.

As the daughter matured, her mother aged rapidly. Stone's advancing years were particularly noticeable in the context of her extended family network. Stone continued to sponsor the education and lengthy visits of her nieces, both Blackwell-born and adopted, and encouraged her own daughter to maintain close ties with her aunts and cousins, especially through summer trips to the families' retreats on Martha's Vineyard. Moreover, Stone still freely dispensed her advice on household management to her nieces, the daughters of her old friend—and to their mother. But in 1887 she admitted to Brown Blackwell, "I am an old woman."[1] Although the exchange of daughters among the kin network did not end until her death, Stone recognized her decreasing fitness for this self-appointed vocation and found her responsibilities with her husband's sisters' adopted children particularly wearying.

Seven years younger than Stone, Antoinette Brown Blackwell experienced the years in which the next generation came of age as a period of progressive rejuvenation. Relatively free from physical complaints, Brown Blackwell reveled in her new role as comrade and confidante for her niece and appreciated the developing autonomy of her daughters. Less troubled than Stone by the intricacies of the relationships among her Blackwell sisters-in-law and their adopted children, she struck a careful balance between sympathetic concern and salubrious distance. Also contributing to her sanguine outlook was the stable and remunerative employment of her husband, who finally settled as the auditor of the Mexican and Central and South American Telegraph Company. In addition, in 1883, the long series of moves that had absorbed so much energy over the previous twenty-five years concluded when her household settled in El Mora, a community on the outskirts of Elizabeth, New Jersey. Brown Blackwell remained rooted here for over a decade.

With her family now well provided for and her five daughters growing up, Brown Blackwell expanded her public contacts. Her increasing prominence in the AAW and her initiation into the American Association for the Advancement of Science (AAAS) in 1881 gave her new platforms from which to expound her developing ideas. She regularly presented papers to both groups, and their publication in addition to the appearance of *The Philosophy of Individuality* in 1893 increased her professional visibility. Much of her reputation, however, continued to rest on her role in opening the ministry to women. The public prominence resulting from this achievement made her extremely valuable in organizational work. During these years, she was particularly active in the AAW, and expanded her role in the AWSA through her endeavors for its New Jersey affiliate.

Despite recurrent illnesses, Stone retained her prominence as a central figure in the woman suffrage movement. In the 1880s she made frequent extended trips west with her husband to speak for woman suffrage at state conventions and in state campaigns. After 1889, however, her deteriorating health forced her to restrict her travels to brief excursions and she drastically curtailed most of her speaking engagements.

To the end of her life, Stone's primary political activities remained her various positions in the AWSA and its state and regional affiliates, and her editorship of its newspaper, the *Woman's Journal*. Both remained taxing and difficult work, particularly as Stone's arguments with collaborators ultimately gave way to alliances with old adversaries. In 1883, Stone and Henry Blackwell began sparring with their old friend and coeditor Thomas Wentworth Higginson over Massachusetts Democratic gubernatorial candidate Benjamin Butler. Higginson, a reformer, distrusted Butler, whose shady business dealings, shifting party allegiances, and opposition to temperance legislation all raised doubts about his political program. Stone and Henry Blackwell, on the other hand, backed Butler when the state Republican party abandoned its commitment to woman suffrage and the Democrats, under Butler's prodding, added it to their platform. The battle between the two sides, played out in the pages of the *Woman's Journal,* undermined the framework of cooperation the three had worked within for over a decade.[2]

The structure finally collapsed when Higginson and Stone took opposing sides in the 1884 presidential election, Higginson favoring reform Democrat Grover Cleveland, while Stone condemned Cleveland as a despoiler of female virtue after undenied reports surfaced that he had fathered an illegitimate son. At the end of the campaign Higginson resigned his post with the paper, although he continued to participate sporadically in the suffrage organization.[3]

Fortunately, most of Stone's political forays proved more successful. Her close attention to developments at the state level had already paid off in Massachusetts, where in 1879 women had gained the right to vote for members of their local school committees.[4] Throughout the 1880s, with her husband and daughter, she worked to extend municipal suffrage to women in her home state and encouraged AWSA affiliates in other states to pursue this strategy. Although she did not have success in her own backyard, Stone regarded the achievement of municipal suffrage in Kansas and of school suffrage in New York and Montana as vindications of her analysis.

Yet as the years passed, Stone also recognized the limits of her efforts and the efforts of the AWSA. Aware of her own aging, concerned for the future of the movement, and leary of burdening her daughter and heir apparent too heavily, she began to take seriously the possibility of the reunification of the woman suffrage movement. In 1887, after many years of intransigence and animosity, she finally consented to negotiate with the leaders of the rival NWSA on the conditions for establishing a new organization to join together the preexisting associations. Two decades of mutual hostility and mistrust were not easily overcome, however, particularly in light of Stone's growing concern for the way in which posterity would view her efforts.

In 1876, when Susan B. Anthony and Elizabeth Cady Stanton had requested her cooperation in their efforts to compile the *History of Woman Suffrage,* Stone had refused; her suspicion that the ongoing divisions would preclude objective reporting prompted her to announce her "ceaseless regret that any 'wing' of suffragists should attempt to write the history of the other."[5] Stone revived her quarrel with the leaders of the NWSA in 1882 when she printed in the *Woman's Journal* Thomas Wentworth Higginson's negative review of the first volume of Stanton and Anthony's suffrage history, and she heightened the ill feelings when she published her own attack on the second volume of the series in 1883, charging that "no one reading this book would get an accurate or adequate idea of the real history of the woman suffrage movement in this country from autumn of 1867 to 1871 and '72, its most critical and trying time."[6]

Stanton and Anthony retaliated by seeking the support of the influential Unitarian minister and former abolitionist William Henry Channing when they visited him at his London home during their European tour later in 1883. Their success at enlisting his sympathy with their position angered even Brown Blackwell, who had struggled to remain on good personal terms with her friend's political enemies. In 1885 Stone rejected the invitation for a social visit Stanton proferred through Brown Blackwell.[7] Anthony returned the rebuff when she traveled to Boston to claim funds bequeathed to Stone and Anthony by Eliza Eddy, an early supporter of the woman suffrage movement, but refused to respond to Stone's solicitous request for a reunion.

By 1887, however, Stone was ready to reconcile. She and her daughter, Alice Stone Blackwell, met with Anthony and her protégée Rachel Foster to negotiate conditions for the reunion. Despite the failure of Stone's proposal to have the leaders of both factions decline the presidency of the new organization, the merger was completed in 1890, with the first meeting of the National American Woman Suffrage Association (NAWSA), held in Washington, D.C., February 18-21. Stanton became president, Anthony vice president, and Stone, for whom an illness prevented her attendance, was appointed to chair the executive committee.

Stone believed the merger was an important element in the political legacy she would leave for future suffragists. Her growing desire to clarify her own role in the history of the woman's rights struggle was a crucial motive in other actions during this decade. Although usually modest about her accomplishments, Stone now demonstrated a desire for recognition of her life's work on behalf of woman's rights. Her friend and coworker Brown Blackwell expressed similar hopes. As public esteem for the woman suffrage cause rose, the two increasingly enjoyed the attention paid to them as pioneers. Three important occasions, the Oberlin Jubilee in 1883, the meeting of the International Council of Women in 1888, and the Columbian Exposition of 1893, all provided the old friends with reason to reflect together on their joint record as well as their individual achievements.

The Oberlin Jubilee celebrated the fiftieth anniversary of the College. Accompanied by Henry Blackwell, Stone and Brown Blackwell returned to their alma mater to accomplish in a few short days what they had been unable to achieve during their student years and thus to vindicate their old goals. More than three decades after her departure, Brown Blackwell finally received recognition as a graduate of the theological department of the school when her name was entered into the alumni records; however, the institution never awarded her a diploma for her studies.

Stone at last received the opportunity to present her own oration to a mixed audience in Oberlin. At the Jubilee Day exercises held on Independence Day, the only woman on the platform, she spoke on "Oberlin and Woman." She described how the faculty and the Ladies' Board of her own student days "shook its minatory finger at the daring girls who wanted the discipline of rhetorical exercises and discussions, and to read their own essays at Commencement." But, she concluded with satisfaction, "time has altered all this and settled it right."[8] Nonetheless, she could not restrain herself from admonishing "this younger Oberlin to take another and the next step in the great movement for the political equality of women . . . to affirm the principle of the consent of the governed in its application to women."[9] Together, the old friends looked back to the origins of their relationship and viewed with satisfaction their accomplishments; yet even at this festive celebration, they set new goals for themselves and for the institutions with which they worked.

Brown Blackwell and Stone joined together for reminiscence and recognition again in 1888, at a meeting sponsored by the NWSA to celebrate the fortieth anniversary of the Seneca Falls convention. In recognition of its pending merger with the AWSA, the NWSA expanded the meeting into a gathering it now styled the International Council of Women. Featuring a week of speakers from around the world, the conference held sessions on topics ranging from the industrial conditions of women workers to social purity movements. Both Brown Blackwell and Stone held honored places on the program that emphasized their roles as "firsts." Brown Blackwell did triple duty; she offered the invocation at the opening session, presented a major paper, "What Religious Truths Can Be Established by Science and Philosophy," and offered comments at the "Conference of the Pioneers." At this last event, a one-day ceremony recognizing the key figures in the antebellum woman's rights movement, Brown Blackwell staked her claim that the Oberlin debating society she and Stone had founded in 1846 was the first organized woman's club of the nineteenth-century club movement. Stone was a featured speaker at the meeting of the pioneers, an honor she shared with Elizabeth Cady Stanton. Stone used the occasion to air her view of the history of woman suffrage, underscoring the importance of her woman's rights speech before her brother's congregation in Gardner, Massachusetts, in 1847, one year before Stanton's Seneca Falls convention. And she reminded her listeners that from 1847 until her marriage to Henry Blackwell, she supported herself by lecturing on woman's rights.[10]

But the conference hardly proved the conciliatory event its sponsors desired. Brown Blackwell was angry that her talk on science and religion was poorly summarized and badly printed by the *Woman's Tribune,* the newspaper providing official coverage of the conference. Stone resented the account of the early years of the woman's rights movement offered by Stanton because it omitted any mention of Stone's role. In both cases, the concerns of Stone and Brown Blackwell for the accuracy of the documentation of their historical roles outweighed their pleasures at the event itself.

Stone and Brown Blackwell collaborated for the last time on events planned around the Columbian Exposition in Chicago. In 1892, the year before the fair officially opened, the General Federation of Women's Clubs celebrated its first biennial meeting in Chicago. Invited to address the gathering by the first president of the Federation, her sister-in-law Charlotte Emerson Brown, Brown Blackwell determined to use her appearance to reiterate her claim that the Oberlin debating society founded by the friends in their student days constituted the first organized woman's club in nineteenth-century America. Stone eagerly—if inaccurately—joined her in the project, supplying misinformation on their meeting place as well as other accurate anecdotes that Brown Blackwell edited for the occasion. The following May both Brown Blackwell and Stone spoke at the Congress of Representative Women, a gathering sponsored by the Women's Board of the exposition. Brown Blackwell commented at sessions on women's moral responsibilities and on dress reform. Stone, who had herself worn the bloomer costume, presented her "Reminiscences of Early Dress Reform," but, more important, spoke on "The Progress of

Fifty Years" at a session sponsored by the NAWSA. The address pointed out advances in woman's status in marriage, in women's education, and in women's organizations, all matters of great importance to Stone. Although not overtly autobiographical, Stone clearly structured this version of the history of woman's rights around familiar personal landmarks, thus giving her own achievements renewed prominence.[11]

Lucy Stone planned to return to the fair to address the Woman Suffrage Department of the World Congress on Governments in August, but her deteriorating health prevented the journey, so her husband and daughter replaced her on the program. Antoinette Brown Blackwell did return to Chicago in September for the Parliament of World Religions, to which she spoke on "Woman in the Pulpit," and she stayed to attend the meetings of the AAW. But her pleasure on this trip was overshadowed by the news she received of her friend's rapid decline. She responded by writing the last letter included in this volume. Two days later, she wrote to Henry and Alice Stone Blackwell to assure them of her belief in Stone's "conscious future," adding, "I should so much like to see her and talk over the many things in which we are both so much interested and for which we have both given the best of our lives."[12]

Lucy Stone died on October 18, 1893, at her home in Dorchester. According to her daughter some of her last audible words were, "Make the world better."

Perhaps because of a desire to keep her grief and emotions private, Brown Blackwell did not offer a public eulogy of her friend Lucy Stone until January 1894. When she did speak at a memorial service for Lucy Stone held in New Jersey, she paid tribute to Stone as "a pioneer . . . not a palterer who waited for the advance of the crowd . . . she went forward confidently, wrapped in . . . sustaining conviction, clad in it as with a warm garment which sheltered her." Brown Blackwell might have noted her own role in helping to fashion and maintain Stone's vestments. Instead she explained simply, "In the older days, to me she was a close friend; in the later days, she was both friend and sister."[13]

Brown Blackwell remained active in the struggle for woman's equality. She continued her work with the AAW and persevered in the campaign for woman suffrage. When well over eighty years of age, she rode with Lucy Stone's daughter, Alice Stone Blackwell, at her side, in an open carriage in the massive New York City suffrage parade of 1915, and she lived to cast her vote for president in 1920.

Brown Blackwell also maintained her interest in religion, metaphysics, and the ministry. In 1914 she published *The Making of the Universe,* followed the next year by *The Social Side of Mind and Action.*[14] She became active in organizing the Unitarian society of Elizabeth, New Jersey, where she was given the title Minister Emeritus.

Although she keenly felt the loss of her beloved friend and sister-in-law Lucy Stone, Antoinette Brown Blackwell still took an active role within the network of the Blackwell family. With her husband, Samuel C. Blackwell, she traveled to Europe in 1895 to see the relatives living abroad. She delighted in the expansion of her own branch of the clan. In 1897 her daughter Agnes became her second child to marry, and in 1901 Ethel too took a husband.

Antoinette Brown Blackwell's daughters were profoundly influenced by their mother and their Blackwell aunts in their career choices. Florence eventually became a lay preacher within the Methodist church; Agnes pursued art like her aunt Marian Blackwell. The decisions of Edith and Ethel to pursue careers in science, an area of ongoing interest for Brown Blackwell, provided a source of great pride for their mother; both ultimately became doctors like their aunts Elizabeth and Emily Blackwell. Brown Blackwell retained a special patience with Grace, the middle daughter, who had always been emotionally troubled, and she remained for her a loving and attentive mother.

Brown Blackwell continued to reach out to Henry Blackwell and to her niece Alice Stone Blackwell, with whom she developed a particular sympathy, for Alice was the only member of the next generation of Blackwells to pursue professionally the cause of woman's rights that had been so central to the lives of her mother and her aunts. When in her eighties, Antoinette Brown Blackwell spent many days with Alice reminiscing about the early days of the woman's rights movement, modestly recalling her own involvement but describing in great detail the key role Lucy Stone played in bringing about advances for women. Later Brown Blackwell dictated her own memoirs, remembering with clarity and affection her friendship with Stone and the support it offered her throughout her lifetime.

Brown Blackwell watched the passing of her generation with sadness. By the turn of the century, all of her Brown siblings were dead. Her fellow pioneers in the woman's rights movement, too, were passing away, with the death of Elizabeth Cady Stanton in 1902 and Susan B. Anthony in 1906. Samuel Blackwell died unexpectedly in 1901, although Henry Blackwell, Lucy Stone's husband, survived until 1909. In the following years, the rest of her Blackwell in-laws also passed away. Antoinette Louisa Brown Blackwell died in her sleep after a short illness on November 5, 1921. The path she and Lucy Stone had cleared together sustained each of them and bound them together in a special friendship. It also marked the trail upon which many still travel today.

NOTES

1. LS to ALBB, July 23, 1887, BFP-LC.
2. See *WJ*, Sept. 30 and Nov. 11, 1882; also Jan. 13, 1883.
3. See *WJ*, Nov. 3 and Dec. 27, 1884.
4. LS herself never exercised school suffrage, since local registrars would not accept her signature as "Lucy Stone" on the poll lists, and she refused to sign herself "Lucy Stone Blackwell." See ASB, *Lucy Stone,* pp. 173-77.
5. LS to Elizabeth Cady Stanton, Aug. 30, 1876, BFP-LC.
6. *WJ*, Sept. 23, 1882, and Mar. 10, 1883.
7. Elizabeth Cady Stanton to ALBB, Dec. 29, 1885, BFP-SL.
8. LS, "Oberlin and Woman," in *The Oberlin Jubilee, 1833-1883,* ed. W. G. Ballantine (Oberlin, Ohio: E. J. Goodrich, 1883), pp. 316-17.
9. Ibid., pp. 318-19.
10. See ALBB, "What Religious Truths Can Be Established by Science and Philosophy," *Report of the International Council of Women, Assembled by the National Woman Suffrage Association, Washington, D.C., U.S. of America, March 25 to April 1, 1888* (Washington, D.C.: National Woman Suffrage Association, 1888), pp. 407-17; Stone's remarks appear in ibid., pp. 331-35.
11. LS, "The Progress of Fifty Years," in *The Congress of Women Held in the Woman's Building, World's Columbian Exposition, Chicago, U.S.A., 1893,* 2 vols., ed. Mary Kavanaugh Oldham Eagle (Chicago: W. B. Conkey Co., 1894), 1:58-61.
12. ALBB to HBB and ASB, Sept. 30, 1893, BFP-SL.
13. *WJ*, Feb. 10, 1894.
14. *The Making of the Universe* (Boston: Gorham Press, 1914); *The Social Side of Mind and Action* (New York: Neale Publishing, 1915).

Dear Nettee

I will enclose a check for ten dollars which will cover the balance of the expense you incurred for the Louisville meeting,[1] that the Orange contribution towards a delegate, did not make up—you may send a receipt.

I want to give Florence something towards her outfit,[2] and propose 2 pr. Blankets, if they will be acceptable, and are not already provided—if they are let me know what other thing would be useful. Alice means to give the lamp. I suppose, in the hope that it will shed light on the domestic problems. It is a very grave business is it not Nettee dear. But every one speaks so well of Eliot, his good sense, his good feeling, and his helpful ways, that it lightens the anxious thoughts one must have at such a time. I suppose too that Edith's plans for the future must be a good deal in mind with some uncertainty about them.[3] But things have a way of settling themselves.

Harry proposes to give Flo. each year, the income of $500, thinking it better to do this, than to give the $500 outright—The little sum will come handy a good many times. He, and we, wish it were more. Did you know that the Suffragists have hope of a legacy. Mrs. Eddy, Francis Jackson's daughter left about fifty thousand dollars to be equally divided between Susan and me. But it is contested, and we are not sure how much we shall get, or whether we shall get anything.[4]

Love to all
L.S.

Robert Kedzie has just buried another son, 29 years old.[5] He went south to teach, and took a fever.

ALS-LC
Written on the stationery of the *WJ.*

1. The twelfth annual AWSA meeting was held in Louisville, Ky., October 25-26, 1881.

2. ALBB's eldest daughter, Florence, was engaged to marry Elliott Mayhew, a member of an established family on Martha's Vineyard and the owner of a general store on the island. LS discussed her contribution to the trousseau.

3. ALBB's second daughter, Edith, planned to become a physician like her aunts Elizabeth and Emily Blackwell, but she suffered from recurrent bouts of depression.

4. Eliza Eddy (1816-81), daughter of Boston abolitionist and suffragist Francis Jackson, left a substantial bequest to be shared by LS and Susan B. Anthony for use in the cause of woman's rights. Thirty years earlier,

when Eddy's father had willed to woman's rights a portion of his estate, the bequest was ruled invalid by the courts since the cause was not a legal charity. Eddy, however, had taken great care in drawing up the bequest, and even though a son-in-law attempted to challenge the legacy, her bequest stood. In 1885, the sum of $48,250 was split between Anthony and LS for use in the woman's rights cause.

5. Robert Kedzie (1853-82), son of LS's and ALBB's classmate of the same name, taught chemistry at Oberlin. He died February 13, 1882, of typhoid.

[Somerville May 5, 1882]¹

Dear Bostonians. You will have heard before this that S.C.B. is again going into business in N. York. To day will close the 2½ weeks since he began; he will continue this month and next at 200 per mo. as acting auditor of a South American & Mexican Telegraph Company.² The auditor died. They have sent to Mexico for another of the company to take his place; and meanwhile S. acts as interregnum. It has been hard to slip in, with present and some weeks past work on hand; and S. has given himself to the work without stint. Last Saturday he looked fagged, but I hope he will soon get accustomed to the duties and find it easier.

Ann is back again to my immense relief; but I am factotum still, indoors and out, hoping for a little more leisure when the house cleaning is over. Why cannot you all come to us in July? Probably the event will be on the first week, before it is very warm. You dont have a niece married often.³

ABB

ALS-LC

1. This date appears upon the letter, added in a later hand.
2. In 1880 SCB located a temporary position as an accountant with the Mexican and Central and South American Telegraph Company when the real estate business continued to be unprofitable. This employment became permanent and was the longest continuing position SCB ever held.
3. Florence Blackwell married Elliott Mayhew July 6, 1882, in Somerville.

Somerville Sept 3 1882

Dear Bostonians,

Safely home again after the Montreal refreshment.¹ We had really a very pleasant time, with a great deal both of good scenery and just

the people one likes best to meet; both the old friends and the new,
especially the latter. There were a good many Bostonians. Mrs. Cheney said she was to report for the Journal.[2]

But my paper on "Cross Heredity from sex to sex" was printed
in full by the Montreal Star. Ill send it to you, and if it seems fitted
for the Journal, as it is, will you perhaps publish it giving credit to
the Star. It will be good to get it started, as I mean to follow it up
with a much more detailed paper hereafter, probably offered first to
A.A.A.S. next year. You see they take you half fare and give you
unlimited excursions besides! "Cheap!" and "so goot." Deference and
snubbing get mingled a little, like sweetened acid!

Dear Alice, I half expect you only will be in Boston to receive this
as I see your respected parents are soon bound for the great West.[3]
Cant they stop off here? going or coming? And wont you sometime
write me just how it all seemed to you about Florence and the others
at M.V.[4] I should be so glad to see through your eyes — in confidence
or otherwise, as you say.

Where is Dr. E.B.? With love to all.

[Antoinette Brown Blackwell]

AL-LC

1. The annual meeting of the Association for the Advancement of Science
(AAAS) was held in Montreal, August 23-30, 1882.

2. Ednah Dow Littlehale Cheney (1824-1904), abolitionist, woman's rights
advocate, and writer, was active in the Massachusetts WSA, the NEWSA,
and the AAW. She worked to open medical education for women and
campaigned to extend municipal and school suffrage to Massachusetts
women.

3. LS and HBB attended the Wisconsin WSA convention held in Madison, Wis., September 7-9, 1882, and continued on to attend the AWSA
annual convention in Omaha, Neb., September 12-13, 1882.

4. Martha's Vineyard.

[Dorchester February? 1883]

Dear Nettee

You will have seen by the papers that Susan has sailed for Liverpool
&c.[1] She will of course see Mr. Channing, and tell her own story to
him.[2] You know she wrote him as he said a "depressed letter," and
he wrote to Sam. May, that he thought "desire of leadership, jealousy
and personal antagonism" was the cause of the opposition to Susan.
Now it *is* a small thing to be judged of any man's judgement — but

I hate to have so good a man as Mr. Channing think that such motives actuated me, in that old time. And I wish you would write to him as of your own motives, and give your view of it, and do it soon if at all. It is not *much* matter,—and if you are very busy why let it go.

We are very busy. Our question is up at the State House[3] &c. &c. Mrs. Tracy Cutler[4] has been with us for a week, and we are generally rushed.

> But with love to all
> Yours always
> Lucy Stone

ALS-LC

1. Susan B. Anthony traveled through Europe February-November 1883.
2. LS feared that Anthony would misrepresent the reasons for the split in the suffrage movement and the ongoing rivalry between the NWSA and the AWSA to her old friend William Henry Channing, who had lived in England since the end of the Civil War.
3. A bill to grant municipal suffrage to women was hotly debated in the Massachusetts state legislature February-March 1883.
4. A friend of LS's and ALBB's since Oberlin, Hannah Tracy Cutler was then touring New England in an effort to organize the Vermont WSA.

> Somerville April 12 1883

Dear Lucy

You shall hear as soon as I do, plus the time it takes for a letter to reach you, from Mr. Channing. The newspaper slip will not be lost; but I sent that on to him, asking for its return as it was "not mine."[1] It was better that Mr. C. should see the slip. It enforced what I had to say, which, of course, had to be done in my own way. It would have been better to have written you about it. But so many things crowded that I did not.

We all rejoice that Alice has gone to Cal. It will do her a world of good. If our money tree had only dropped its fruit into all the wells of debt that must be filled up, Edith should have a similar change. Meantime she is doing well on the whole. My brother and his wife have been here the last ten days. The children have acted charades, dumb crambo,[2] etc. Edith showing unusual ability in that line; yet except when roused up, she is mentally depressed and nervous. So she must go on resting. She clings to home.

We are getting the house ready to offer it furnished. Unless it rents, and we do not much expect it will; we shall not, for the present, leave Somerville.

Yes, I should like to join you and Henry in a lecturing trip at such time as you think best. A change would do me much good. I mean, in any case, to be at Oberlin if all is well.[3]

Our friends leave to day. I am so glad we are just coming to warm weather. It will help your throat almost certainly. But do be careful during the rest of the changable season.

We are all fairly well. Grace is at home now and in pretty good case physically though not very strong; in a certain pain that comes at odd times. She shows weakness still.

A.B.B.

ALS-SL

1. ALBB probably sent William Henry Channing a copy of LS's review in the *WJ*, March 10, 1883, of the second volume of the *History of Woman Suffrage* (Rochester, N.Y.: Susan B. Anthony, 1883), Elizabeth Cady Stanton, Susan B. Anthony, and Matilda Joslyn Gage, eds. In it LS attacked the book because it appeared while the battle for woman suffrage was still being waged, and, more important, because the editors were "not in a position to write an impartial history."

2. Dumb crambo is a rhyming pantomime game.

3. ALBB, HBB, and LS together attended the Oberlin Jubilee, held June 28–July 4, 1883, to celebrate the fiftieth anniversary of the founding of Oberlin College.

[Somerville] Tuesday A.M. March 17, '83[1]

Dear Lucy

I send you Mr. Channings reply without delay. Isnt it characteristic? He misunderstands my suggestion not that he should advise me— but that he should suggest to S.B.A to *let the dead past bury its dead;* since, *if* the burden of the Am. Society was laid to the charge of your ambition to rule, too persistently, I should be forced to state some of the true causes, in the interest of simple justice—

How much are you and H.B.B. committed to Gov. B., I wonder? One cannot entirely read between the lines of the Journal, though following the course of events never so interestedly. I have always wished we could stand nearer to principles and further off from policies, good or bad. Still there are many workers and many ways of working! Do you think our friends abroad exagerated your position towards the "slimy track" to influence Mr. Cs criticism![2] or was it only a conscientious wish toward wholesome "plainness" of speech. One leaf of the letter was never enclosed to me, haste probably causing its omission.

Please send the letter back before sunday, if convenient, that Sam may read it. You need have no fear that Mr. C. does not believe in you very thoroughly. I dare say he feels like giving us all a final solemn admonition; in the way of solemn duty.

Alices opening journey notes, was admirable.[3] She is spicy, cultivated, conscientious and broad. If all these good qualities stick to her through life, she will make a very high mark. So let it be! And the best of all is her girlish simplicity and self-unconsciousness.

Shall I put you in a stamp for return postage, or not? Will you hate the sight of one as I do when you enclose one to me? Dont ever do that again unless I am on the town in extreme poverty, especially when the matter written about interests us both equally. Love to Henry, and as soon as you know about *when* you will go to Ohio, let me know, please. Our Congress meets at Chicago in Oct. Cant you arrange an Am. Suffrage then in the West somewhere?[4] Earlier than the other might be best since all the speakers would be fresh.

                                                                    A.B.B.

ALS-SL

1. Internal evidence indicates that this letter was written in April, not March, of 1883.

2. William Henry Channing wrote to ALBB, April 5, 1883: "According to my conscience, [LS] has plunged heady and drawn others into as bottomless a bog in following the notorious B.B.'s [Benjamin Butler's] slimy serpent like track. She may strike my name from the book of her trust worthy compeers, if she chooses. But add that her noble self-sacrificing labours for thirty years will never be forgotten by this veteran of many a tough battle."

Benjamin Franklin Butler (1818-93), abolitionist, Civil War general, businessman, lawyer, and politician, was then running for governor of Massachusetts. A controversial figure, he supported woman suffrage, labor laws, and civil service reform, but he also opposed temperance legislation, and was tinged with hints of scandal from his days as military governor of Louisiana. In addition, he was a Democrat, which offended former abolitionists who wished to remain with the Republican party.

3. From April through July of 1883, the *WJ* published ASB's reports of her travels to California and back.

4. The eleventh Congress of Women met in Chicago, October 17-19,

1883; for reasons LS subsequently explained, the AWSA did not meet in the West but instead in Brooklyn, N.Y., October 9-10, 1883.

Pope's Hill—Dorchester
Apr. 18—1883

Dear Nettee

I enclose the letter of good Mr Channing. He does not know me, any better than he does the other two women who champion he is. How Mrs. Stanton must have laughed inside, after all his questioning about her views on Free Love. Poor simple hearted man! But I hate to have him misunderstand me all the same, for he *is* a good man— As to Ben Butler I never had any respect for him, and no line or word of mine ever implied any. I said over my own initials in the Journal, that "women could not vote for him"[1]—But it is not worth (under the circumstances) saying anything to Mr. Channing about it. If he thinks I go with Butler, it is only a feathers weight more, in the scale on the side where he thinks I belong—so let it go.

I will let you know about the Ohio meetings, when we know[2]— We want to have the Meeting of the American Society in Trenton or Newark (probably the latter) so that dear old Elizabeth Chace[3] who is the president, may preside. That will be near enough for her to go. We want to manage it so that the speakers to the Congress can take our meeting on the way—

We get a card every day from Alice who is enjoying the trip—

I have been shut up at home the last two weeks with a cold that has really made me ill. At this moment I am smarting with mustard, and I have flax seed tea and onion syrup, and oil of tar, and who knows what not, to take, but I trust the worst is over.

Harry is only pretty well. He works hard. He misses Alice, and the house seems empty without her. Why dont you go and return your brother's visit, take care of the children, and stay a week or ten days? It would give you an outing, & chance to see the Orange households[4] and the expense of getting there is not much—

Love to the daughters & to Sam.
L.S.

ALS-LC

1. On November 11, 1882, the *WJ* published an item, "Hoist with Their Own Petard," initialed by LS, stating that women "would not have voted

for Gen. Butler, because he stands for the liquor interest, and for principles which the women of Massachusetts will not support."

2. LS, ALBB, and HBB made suffrage speeches in Ohio while on the way to the Oberlin Jubilee.

3. Elizabeth Buffum Chace (1808-99), active in the antislavery and woman's rights movements, served as president of the Rhode Island WSA for many years and in 1883 was president of the AWSA.

4. Ellen Blackwell and George and Emma Lawrence Blackwell then lived in Orange, N.J., as did ALBB's brother William and his wife.

Somerville May 24 1883.

Dear Lucy

Yours is just received. Yes; I will be ready to do my best in the Ohio meetings. You may fully rely upon me.

Your throat trouble is aggravated, I suppose, by the long, cold, wet spring. That is now about over at any rate. So we will expect the health to mend speedily. But we are all extremely sorry for that tendency to an ailing throat. It is like Gracies, the least exposure brings hers to fresh grief; yet it is on the whole improving we think. Yours may also with steady care.

Ah well! I anticipate a jolly time at Oberlin on the whole. It ought to make us all young again. Please write when all arrangements are made. The week before the 20th I shall spend at Henrietta to visit, rest, and think a little in preparation for meetings.

Alice must be tired when she returns. Yet physical stress is sometimes just what is needed.

Edith does not dislike the study of medicine. She is in a morbid, tired state; but would enjoy beginning next week—with the feeling of good health. It is all nerves and the dismay of them. Sam had a good letter from H.B.B. on Sunday.

Love to all till we meet,
A.B. Blackwell

ALS-SL

[*Dorchester*] Monday Sept 24—1883

Dear Nettee

The enclosed ten dollars comes late, but better than never, for the meeting in Elyria Ohio.[1] It is sent by Miss Kelsay,[2] and I have acknowledged the receipt of it.

I shall expect to see you at Brooklyn but drop me a card please, to say you have the ten.

Alice is at home looking brown, and well—she had a pleasant time with Flo. and with renewing acquaintance with Grace & Agnes—and is ready for work.

> With love and loyalty
> Lucy Stone

Tuesday 25th

Alice has just received a letter from Edith, which caused me to open this, to say that since old Ann has gone, I wish Edith would take the house work all of it, except the washing. Just see what it has done for Flo. She is ever so much stronger, plumper and healthier since she has the active use of her muscles—Muscular activity is what *all* our girls need, and the best way to get it, is at home, with the daily house work—Grace and Agnes would help, and so would Ethel and they would all study better for the work. It will save the board of one person, and this, and the wages of Ann could be given to Edith—Now I have said my say, & you will accept it, as I mean it, all for good will—But, I am concerned for the girls who have not health, and who need something.

ALS-LC

1. ALBB, LS, and HBB spoke at a suffrage meeting in Elyria, Ohio, on June 27, 1883, on their way to the Oberlin Jubilee.

2. Dr. Kate I. Kelsey, an active suffragist, studied law and medicine in Cleveland and later moved to Wyoming.

Boston, Oct 31 1883

Dear Nettee.

I sent you yesterday by mail a pattern, cut for me by a woman who makes the combination undergarments.[1] They are rather too open, above the seam in the leg. But that can be remedied—They are easy to make from the underdrawers worn by men, and the shirt worn by women. Marian made them so, long ago—Edith has a good "knack" at fitting, and can make them a great deal cheaper than they can be bought—and they will be just as good—

I hope you are better. The Congress seems to have been very good.

We are in the thick of a political excitement[2]—and as usual we are crowded and overbusy—But pretty well, though Harry and Alice

are tired, and my throat rasps. Grace will find it good to inhale the
hot fumes of oil of pine a teaspoon in a bowl of boiling water. The
oil must be cut with alcohol, and when poured in the boiling water
she must breathe through a tunnel—put a cloth around the bowl to
hold it.

Alice has just gone to Providence to spend Halloween and may
be a day or two more.

I wish Ellen could be persuaded to send Paul[3] to Mrs. Anna C.
Fields' Orphan's home.[4]

Love to all
L.S.

ALS-LC
Written on the stationery of the *WJ*.

1. Dress reformers and woman's rights activists, including LS, advocated
the use of undergarments that combined tapered pants on the bottom with
a close-fitting bodice on top. These garments were said to be more comfortable and more hygienic than standard women's undergarments.
2. The gubernatorial election of 1883 pitted the controversial Democratic
incumbent Benjamin F. Butler against Republican nominee George D.
Robinson.
3. Paul Winthrop, the adopted son of Ellen Blackwell.
4. Anna C. Field was cofounder of the Brooklyn WSA.

Somerville Sept. 6 1883.[1]

Dear Lucy

Thank you and Alice both for all the trouble you have taken about
the combinations. It will save us both in expense and labor.

Thank you also for your suggestions about Ediths teaching. She
is teaching one little girl daily in German. Our children did study
with her, but they needed the stimulous of others and a fixed lesson.
So they returned to the German minister who lives in one of our
houses close by. Also Edith reads German books which her father
brings from the New York library. She has daily house, and up to
this time garden and lawn duties, as she has picked most of the
vegetables, and cut the large lawn with the lawn mower all summer.
She reads as much as her eyes will allow, and goes with me to a
"Thursday Evening Club" of gentlemen and ladies who write essays
on special topics, discuss these topics, and read brief bits of fine prose
or poetry, Edith taking her share so far very nicely. You see she has
occupation enough, though if she walked more or played lawn tennis

as Agnes is doing now, it would be better. We shall get another racket
or two so that the older girls can play when Agnes' club is not here.

But Edith is *not* well. All the doctors in the world could not
convince me that there is not some real difficulty which keep her
nervous, often depressed, and unable to use her mind. What it is I
dont know; and am sure a real interest will be the right medicine.
But it must take time.

Yes; they say the Congress was good. So it seems were your meetings! I have not left home and am busy with many duties and dull,
rather mentally yet there is more need of time than of brains for
real work.

We have a new Ann, a better cook but slow and not therefore
extremely efficient; yet a great improvement on the last, and a comfort.

The children are well, busy, happy, etc. Grace is about as usual,
but with trouble in the throat still, yet she busies herself with her
paintings.

Do you dread the winter. Do you still wish to leave home for
February and March or longer and if so do you want me to Edit for
you?[2] or have you made other arrangements? If you could decide in
advance, and care to have me, then let me know and I can then
arrange and go.

A.B.B.

Where did the Wis. Society meet? Why did they not go to Racine?[3]

ALS-SL

1. Internal evidence indicates this letter was misdated; ALBB probably
intended to give the month of November instead of September.

2. Concern for LS's increasingly troublesome health prompted ALBB to
tender this offer, but ALBB never replaced LS as editor of the *WJ*.

3. The meaning of this reference is unclear; the annual meeting of the
Wisconsin WSA was held in Racine in March 1883 and in Richland Center
in 1884.

Somerville Dec. 17, 1883

Dear Henry and Lucy,

We are seriously thinking of moving to Elmora[1] between this and
April. The decision is not really made; but will be next Sunday in
all probability; and as so many things culminate in that decision, I

decide to throw my weight solidly into the affirmative, and think that is likely to carry all other overriding opinions. There are trains every 15 minutes to half an hour, both morning and evening, so that I dont believe Sam would find the cars *very* much of a fetter; and as N.Y. seems not feasible at present, and property here can be left — though at a disadvantage — and as the girls *can* take lessons in N.Y. if they choose, we, on the whole, had better move. You will see that if you wish me to help you in Boston for a longer or shorter time, I must know when and how long in order to make all things here move on easily. As there is a range and furnace in Elmora and stoves here, we *could* move in winter. But you may have some one in view to Edit, for you, or may not leave Boston. That will suit me about as well; though it would be pleasant enough to spend a little time in Boston, either boarding there, or at your house. As for the paper, of course you would still be Editors and direct the policy entirely as you choose. If you could send me a line before Sunday saying what you think about it, please do so — if not, never mind.

We dont know whether any of the East Orangeites will be here during holidays or not. Our children are painting, knitting, etc. Alice is earnestly and cordially invited to spend a week or more with us holiday time to share in turkey, roast beef, and plumb pudding; and if either of you will come with her, so much the better. Sam will be at home xmas. All fairly well here and not more busy than usual.

Always with much love and with advance xmas greetings.

A.B.B.

ALS-LC

1. El Mora, N.J., is a suburb of Elizabeth.

[*El Mora, N.J., August 1884*][1]

Dear Lucy

I wonder whether my girls have been a bother to you!

It has doubtless been a pleasant change to them; but you should not be troubled! So just send *the Baby* back *as soon as you like.* She can be efficient! If you have any thing for her to do for a week or two longer, let her help you while I am away; though she can come home *as well as not* and be here with the girls.

I enclose you an A.A.W. circular lest you have not had one.

I am to stop with an own cousin of John Brights[2] in *Philadel.* and hope to have a pleasant as well as profitable time.[3] When you see just what I have been doing you will thank me in the interest of Women. It is marvelous how clear a case is made out of figures to prove; that while the sexes *as a whole,* are kept equal in numbers; that the small boys are in excess; and that women *at all* periods of life live longer than men; *especially in late life,* so that *the race owes a steady Increase in Longevity to Women.*

I already count up several hundred Millions, and there is no exception any where, *in any country.* (I have over a dozen) to this same law.

Always with love and gratitude.

Affectionately to you all,
Nette

Poor Sam is better. It was a bad boil and the foot is not yet *well.*

ALS-SL

1. Although a later hand dated this letter "[c. 1886?]," internal evidence places it in August 1884.

2. John Bright (1811-89) was an English reformer, orator, and member of Parliament. Although he had voted to extend the franchise to women under the influence of John Stuart Mill in 1869, he later reversed his position.

3. ALBB attended the meetings of the AAAS held in Philadelphia, August 1884, where she presented a paper entitled "The Comparative Longevity of the Sexes."

Elizabeth Jan. 6 1886.

Dear Lucy

Half a dozen times I have been on the point of writing you, when something prevented.

Thank you for remembering old times. I do wish we could meet occasionally! The other day I had a brief letter from Mrs. Stanton; she said she did wish I could get you to meet with her and Susan & me once more, to have it seem like the old days; before we all go forward "to work or rest." So should I like to be we four together, with all the remembrances not desirable buried; and judgement left where it belongs. She said nothing of all that. It was only a brief mention, incidentally.

Poor George and Emma, and poor little Laurie! But I trust he *is* improving. Incidentally it is nice to have them in Boston, isnt it?

Can you tell me the address of Mrs. Dunn; the woman who was intending to write our biographies. She has two photographs of mine.

We had pleasant holidays and are just settling down to work again. Love to Henry and Alice and George and Emma & the tinies, and especially to yourself, the oldest friend of them all to me.

Nette

ALS-SL

[*Dorchester*] At Home. Sunday Jan 10/86

Dear Nettee

I was glad to get a sight of your old familiar hand. We hear of you all, through your children now and then. But it would be good if we lived near enough to meet occasionally. Geo. is here today to help Harry [*with*] the Journal accts.

Laurie is getting stronger but his poor little back seems to curve just the same. He is to go into a jacket next week so that he can run around in the hope of securing a better appetite. Emma has a hard time. Even with all the help she gets.

As to meeting Mrs. Stanton it is out of the question with me. She sent a letter to Mr. Shattuck[1] of this city, which he read to a little group, of which I was one, in which she said I was "the biggest liar and hyprocrite she had ever seen"—After that, you will see that I cannot with any self respect meet her with a pretence of good fellowship. For yourself, of course, such a letter ~~to~~ about me need make no difference—Mrs. Stanton is as bright and as witty as ever and Susan just as egotistical.

When Susan came here to get her share of the Eddy fund, I invited her to come and spend the day with us. I gave her a time table, and told her I would meet her at any train, if she would let me know—Instead, she sent a hateful note, that made me feel the last plank between us had broken—I am too busy with the work that remains, to take time to mend broken cisterns.

We were glad of the letter of Grace lately received, and to see that she still goes on with her painting—Agnes too gives us family glimpses—

Alice is taking a little outing in Providence with Mrs. Elizabeth B. Chace, and with some of her old school mates. She is dreadfully brain tired and ought to have a years rest and change—

I saw by last evening's paper that the ladies Boarding House in Oberlin had burned up.[2] What a pity!

It is bitter cold here today, the first cold. The snow flies in wild wind drifts, like the old fashioned winter times.

Why could not your girls get some subscribers to the Woman's Journal in Elizabeth? We pay a dollar for every *NEW* yearly subscriber, and at the same rate for six and three months subscribers— Two or three people sometimes write to take it—Will they try. With love to all, and always with warm remembrance.

Ever aff
L.S.

ALS-LC

1. George Cheyne Shattuck (1813-93) was a Boston physician and educator.
2. The Ladies' Boarding Hall at Oberlin College was destroyed by fire on January 9, 1886.

Boston, Feb. 28 1886

My dear Nettee

How the old times come back with the name!

Ellen has written to me to see if I can help her to a place on a farm for little Paul—she says it is more and more undesirable to take him to the Vineyard, as he needs more occupation than she can give him—I have written to everybody I can think of—and shall bear the child in mind. If she has not written you, about him, will you not help her to find a place, i.e. bear it in mind—some of the Jersey farmers might be glad of him. Is there anybody in Somerville who would—I do not know what she *will* do with the child—

Harry is much too busy, with building houses, and he has a bad cold too—Little Laurie now runs about for half an hour each day— Geo. thinks him better. He is bright and playful, but he is a little skeleton & eats hardly enough for a sparrow—It does not seem as though he could pull through—*We* are always over work, but we pu[*sh*] on. Alice is very thin, she tries to do her part and ours too— Is it not a great deal to hard for Agnes to go at 8 and stay till six? I suppose you are writing profound things as usual. You must remember to send the Journal something as you are a contributing subscriber—The Washington Convention seems to have been very good indeed. It is a great comfort to feel that it helped rather than hindered.[1] We seem not to have much hope of success this year, anywhere. But all the same, the end is right. With love to Sam and Grace and all.

Yours always,
L. Stone

ALS-LC
Written on the stationery of the Massachusetts WSA.

1. The NWSA met in Washington, D.C., February 17-19, 1886. HBB and LS were at the time planning to lobby in Congress for equal suffrage in the territories. The NWSA voted to cooperate with the AWSA in this lobbying effort.

Elizabeth N.J. March 28 1886

Dear Lucy and Alice:

A year or two ago you suggested through some one that we might have some of your raspberries, the yellow ones. I have red and black. I should like a few yellow; and know that yours are good. We all like them, and have room for them.

Also, if you can, send us a few Lilies of the Valley, & oblige us.

It is a shame to trouble you busy as you are, both of you. I add Alices name because it may be that a little going into the garden and attending to the matter will give her a not undesirable change, so far as health and rest go. I fear it will seem a nuisance, all the same. Take that as an exercise of benevolence, Alice dear, please.

We are adding flowers and shrubs to our grounds this year and think it will be an improvement. I enclose postage stamps; but if it will be more convenient, send the bundle by express—in that case send direct to *S.C.B. 97 Wall st.*

Thank Harry for his letter, duly received. Also, Wise and Otherwise is duly gratified at the solicitation for exchange. Miss Higgins was greatly astonished at first, and all the girls entertained and delighted.

In my, "Mrs. S. versus Mrs. S." there is one word near the beginning—"if to these *gifts* we add yet one other grace," etc. the word gifts should be *acquirements*. "Thought and preparation" are hardly gifts. It would make no difference if it were not an article criticizing language. But if not too late will you get that word changed.[1]

All well. Aunt E. still here and not quite usually well. Edie will leave Dansville[2] on Wednesday but will probably spend a week with my sister.

With love
A.B.B.

ALS-SL

1. ALBB's article "Mrs. Stanton *versus* Mrs. Stanton" appeared in the *WJ*, April 3, 1886. Responding to Stanton's call for "thought and preparation" in writing, ALBB discussed neologisms referring to women and to the woman's rights movement. The sentence about which ALBB was concerned in her letter was finally printed as "An artist of the pen may rank immeasurably higher even than the artist of the pencil, if to these gifts, we add yet one other grace—harmony of composition." So the word was not changed.

2. The Dansville Water-Cure in upstate New York specialized in hydropathy. ALBB's daughter Edith spent a year there, 1885-86.

Dorchester July 23 1887.

Dear Nettee

I want to write you about 2 things. First, can you not go quite frequently to see Emma? She is almost absolutely without sympathy in Orange—Geo. does all he can, but there is a large side of her that he cannot share, and besides it is a woman she needs at this time—Books and baby things and house interests &c &c.[1] I asked you before, about this.

The next is about Ethel. I am very willing to try having her with us.[2] She is a very nice bright child and we all like her. I think she will be a great comfort to Harry's sociable side—But it is more of a doubt about me—I am an old woman. In one month I shall be 69—and what would have been no trouble to me once takes all my courage away now. I have to have quiet, or I cannot write—We have been so long accustomed to just our little trio that an addition of an active frolicsome inmate may upset me. I could not write, or *feel* peace, while Cornelia was here for a few days, for the added interruption and care.[3] She would get my ink and pen, and not return them. She left the piano open every time she used it—She got needle and thread and never put it in place again. I am too old to be running after such items—and I do not know how to take an ounce of added care with all that I have for the different suffrage societies, and the Journal and the house &c. Of course Edith will be Ethel's advisor & Ethel will be herself busy with books and she may fit in all nicely—

But I say all this now, so that in case it is too much for me, it may not be set down against Ethel, but to my old age, which cannot take added care. We could always get her a safe boarding place. But I hope we shall get on well—She will have to take an attick on the same floor with Alice. Can you furnish blankets for her. I have plenty of other bed covering—and we will assume and hope that we shall get on well. But I cannot afford to feel a worry all the time—such as I should not if I were young.

Did I write you about a plan of union I had thought of with Susan?[4]

It is this. The 2 National Societies to unite under the name of "the United Suffrage Associations" all other societies to be auxiliary to them. The American & National to be called branch societies, auxiliary, but as they are accustomed to work each by itself ~~together~~, let them continue their organizations for the cause sake as free lances— There would be one annual meeting at which all the societies would come by delegates thus taking away the feeling that there is opposition between suffragists—Probably it would be best to let Mrs. Stanton, Susan and I be honorary members, who never hold office—the *work* devolving on younger people—This is the essential idea in the rough. What do you say?

In regard to Ethel, assume that it will be all right—

aff,
L.S.

Edith will write you about her excursion to the White Mts. this week. She is very well and very useful.

All this is between you and me, in the frankness of old fellowship.[5]

ALS-LC
Written on the stationery of the Massachusetts WSA.

1. Emma Lawrence Blackwell bore her fourth child, George Kenyon Blackwell (1887-88), two months later on September 27. Her son George Lawrence Blackwell had died the previous July, so she was understandably anxious.

2. Ethel, the youngest child of ALBB and SCB, attended the Massachusetts Institute of Technology to prepare for her studies at the Women's Medical College of the New York Infirmary. She resided with LS and HBB while she attended classes.

3. Cornelia Howard, the adopted daughter of Ellen Blackwell, frequently visited LS and HBB when she was enrolled at nearby Wheaton Seminary.

4. In the summer of 1887 LS and ASB met with Susan B. Anthony and Rachel Foster to begin the process by which the AWSA and the NWSA

merged to form the National American Woman Suffrage Association (NAWSA) in 1890.

5. This sentence appears in the margin on the first page.

[*Dorchester Winter 1888*]

Dear Nettee—

I wish you lived nearer—Your two girls now go to school, & it was good for Edith to have some new stir.[1] It will do her good to go out every day—They are both well.

About Union with S.B.A. We did suggest Mrs Livermore for Prest. and also Mrs. Howe. But Susan said neither of them stood distinctively for Woman Suffrage—She so much wishes to be president herself! To bring her to the top at last would be such a vindication she cannot bear to forgo it. I withdraw in my whole soul from all of the set. She (Susan) said you were to be asked to offer prayer. But in a letter, Sam says you have written your *paper* for the International Council—Have you a paper?[2] I think we ought to puncture the bubble that the Seneca Falls meeting, was the *first* public demand for suffrage.[3] *You* can do that—Alice dreads these people even more than I do, but wants to have Union, to take the burden of work of the American from me, and to save it from coming on her, when I drop out.

But the whole phase *must* change, before long anyway. Some party will take it up—

I am more than half sick with a cold.

So I stop, only sending love as your two nice girls would if they were here.

aff.
Lucy Stone

ALS-LC

1. Edith Blackwell had attended M.I.T. before she was joined there by her youngest sister, Ethel.

2. As president of the NWSA, Anthony organized a celebration of the fortieth anniversary of the Seneca Falls Woman's Rights Convention. The gathering, known as the International Council of Women (ICW), met in Washington, D.C., March 25–April 1, 1888; ALBB offered the invocation and several prayers; in addition to the recollections she shared at the Conference of the Pioneers, she also presented a paper, "What Religious Truths Can Be Established by Science and Philosophy?" at the ICW Religious Symposium.

3. LS felt strongly that her 1847 address to her brother's church in Gardner on woman's rights should receive recognition. In addition, by October of 1848, when the Seneca Falls convention was held, LS was already speaking primarily on woman's rights and addressed abolitionist audiences only on weekends. Both LS and ALBB sought acknowledgment of their Oberlin debating society and ALBB's addresses to the community of Rochester, Mich., in the winter of 1846-47.

Elizabeth N.J. Feb. 10 1888

Dear Lucy

Thanks for all your continued kindness to those "nice girls." — As I understand it, you are to make the *long* speech on Pioneers day, and the rest of us ten minute speeches.[1] My paper, of 25 minutes, comes the next day, Sunday, and will be something else. Ten minutes speeches will be partly preordained and partly voluntary. So be on hand in that line if any thing needs another side!

I did immediately protest against the *not correct* statement about the first "public," etc. If you notice Susan's last little long slip, with names secured, she has changed that to 'organized' movement, which is true if understood in a public sense and with some qualifications. Nothing could be fittingly said publicly, it seems to me, about what Mrs. Stantons convention was *not;* but it is wholly in order to say what else was, and to fix dates. My ten minutes speech is to tell, in *writing* of our class discussion; of the first organized woman's rights or womans suffrage "Club" — "not public, but *very* private indeed;" which means, do you comprehend, our discussions at the old colored womans. One must meet Greeks with Greek fire; and that *was* a club, and was organized in the literal sense of that assertion; and was exactly as characteristic as their first meeting — though of course only a sentence is devoted to it. Then comes your graduation and the Jubilee; and some of Letice and my experiences. That fills ten minutes — For the rest, I believe a good deal in Susan. She has the strength to work and should work; but under the circumstances she has no *right* to ask to be first union President; and I shall tell *her* so and why. Of course she will be President soon; and probably ought to be. As a spinster, she has given All her time!

Yes; I profoundly wish we lived near together. We wanted Emma here; but probably she wont come. One so longs for any one to speak with without perpetual reserve and caution, and about things one really cares for.

I meet every week now with our El Mora women and it does us all good, and hearing their prattle or else teaching them something without their exactly realizing it, or reading together is social and refreshing;[2] but it *is* like meeting nice children very largely. Some of them are educated and intelligent on most subjects; and a Mrs. Pope, wife of the Electrician, who by the way will be in Washington, is enthusiastically intelligent & a yankee school teacher; but was and nominally is *a democrat,* but innately democratic.

Tell Edie we can*not* find her box—of course it *is* somewhere. They must buy what they need.

The girls are getting ready for a Valentine Party, and so extra busy; as of course we all are to a most troublesome extent. We shall miss the Absentees!

They must, one of them, say something each week, if only on a postal. Will Alice go to Washington? or Henry? I mean to take Agnes. It will do her good; and be a good opportunity. She is working hard!

Always cordially, with love to all.
Nette.

ALS-SL

1. The ICW set aside the morning session on Saturday, March 31, 1888, as the Conference of the Pioneers, at which LS gave an address on her career as a woman's rights speaker in the 1840s and 1850s. ALBB made a short speech at this session.
2. In 1886 ALBB helped to organize the El Mora Woman's Club.

Boston, Aug. 20 1888

Dear Nettee

We took it for granted that Ethel would come here to finish her time at "Tech." Of course she will miss Edith and will no doubt find our house a dull place. But it will be safe—

I am glad they are all having so good a time at the Vineyard.

We dont hear from them. They returned a batch of Alice' letters without adding a line—

They are all artists, (your chicks) and I am not sure, but they are more artists than doctors. But Ethel will do well at any thing—

Glad the debts are all paid, and we rejoice not only in Sam's $5,000 but in the tribute which the increase pays to his *super* excellence.

Sorry for the strain on Grace, but she will pick up, and be all right. I am glad the Woman's Tribune is to hear from you—They have a way of making lies appear the truth, and they need to be overhauled[1] —

They had an article in the Union Signal,[2] which announced Rev. Anna Shaw, as having formerly been a lecturer for the National W.S.A. & I hate liars, and lies and shams.[3] I wish you lived near neighbor to us—It would be good to *confer* about so many things!

Emily writes that it has been very quiet there this summer—Alice enjoys camping. The party seems to be rather exceptionally fine with good common sense, and brightness as well.[4] Do you and Sam get any holiday? I am writing in the city, and have endless interruptions—

aff—for the old times

L.S.

ALS-LC
Written on the stationery of the Massachusetts WSA.

1. Clara Colby (1846-1916) began publishing the *Woman's Tribune,* a suffrage paper reflecting the views of the NWSA, in Beatrice, Neb., in 1883. In 1888 she moved the paper to Washington, D.C., to cover the ICW. ALBB did not like the excerpted summary it published of her ICW paper in its April 3, 1888, edition.

2. The *Union Signal,* the official paper of the Woman's Christian Temperance Union (WCTU), was published in Evanston, Ill., 1875-1903.

3. Anna Howard Shaw (1841-1919), minister and physician, began suffrage work speaking for the AWSA, but was recruited by Anthony at the ICW to work for the rival NWSA. After the merger of the two organizations, she served as national lecturer, vice president, and, later, president of the NAWSA.

4. ASB vacationed at Lake Memphremagog, Quebec, Canada, at the summer camp of her friends, reformers Isabel Barrows and Samuel Barrows, editor of the Unitarian weekly the *Christian Register.*

[El Mora] Aug 23 1888

Dear Lucy

This morning Grace, my last home girl, started for Rochester; and as Sam is away too I begin to feel very much like a childless widow. Agnes and Ethel will probably return tomorrow; and S.C.B. this evening.

Is it of any use to sincerely thank you again or to express the "most sincerest" appreciation of your kindness in taking Ethel for another long term. Words are of little value and yet one must speak

if nothing more! The child will be starting off to Boston in a little
over four weeks. Time does fly too rapidly!

So you are 70![1] I never thought about it and if I had, should have
supposed the time was later in the year. Well, may you have at least
15 more happy returns with ever increasing happiness! And on some
one of these may I be there to see and wish you joy. Why not live
to 95? Let us both do it!

Did Henry see the curious hash of the Sun, making Henry R.
Blackwell the husband of A.B.B. the first woman minister; his chiv-
alry, and his Treasuership of Mexican Telegraph; and did you see
your picture; labeled "Lucy Stone, the First Woman Minister" in
some Magazine. I have seen neither but heard of both. Isn't it queer?
and absurd!

No Woman's Tribune came to me at all this week; it may have
gone astray or gone for yet another vacation. Mrs. Colby *may* not
have read my paper fairly when she wrote a cordial reply offering
to print "any thing whatever." We shall see.

We are having water pipes laid from the house into the grass-plat-
well and are in a very torn up condition—

Always cordially
Nette of old.

ALS-SL

1. On August 18, 1888, the *WJ* reported that LS was given a surprise
party at their offices to celebrate her seventieth birthday.

[El Mora August 1889]

Dear Lucy

Why dont we live within talking distance? To me it is generally a
task to write but a wonderful pleasure to talk. The embarassment of
riches is so great that in doubt where I should first begin I neglect
them all.

How do you like the autobiography:[1] It is spicy and readable at
any rate; but occasionally it says what one fancies it was not intended
to put altogether so clearly between the lines. But Mrs. Stanton is
bright, broad, and delightfully self-poised. I do like a woman who
can both know and speak her own mind and stand on her own feet.
With some quickening of conscience and a sense of concrete practical
justice she would be magnificent.

Where do you hold your next large meeting or is there to be no other until the Washington annual?[2] We wish something would bring you into this region and hold you here for at least a day or two.

It must be nearly time now for Alice to make her appearance at the Vineyard. Does she entirely give up the camping out or not? Even a week or two would be a gain.

Always lovingly
A.B.B.

ALS-SL

1. Stanton published her memoirs in the *Woman's Tribune,* April 1889–January 1890.

2. The last AWSA convention was held in Cincinnati, November 20-22, 1888; the first convention of the NAWSA met in Washington, D.C., February 18-21, 1890.

[*Dorchester*] Pope's Hill Sept. 18 [*1890*]

Dear Nettee

There *is* to be a 40th Anniversary Celebration but it is deferred till January when the state society holds its meeting.[1] We mean to make a great occasion of it as it was the first *National* W. Rights meeting and was the one *really* to stir the public thought—There *is* a report of the Seneca Falls meeting but I think it was made long after the meeting. You must come in in January with the gathering of the clans—

My heart is much better and I hope it is to get entirely well.

As to Cornelia—I did not feel as though I *could* have her. But she is a child badly born, badly brought up, with no habits of application or industry and nobody wants her. Emily was at her wits end to know what to do with her, and as here seemed a chance for her to learn a possible occupation, I consented to take her. We shall all try to make the best of it.

I expect Geo. and his family tomorrow.

Ellen & Grace are to be here on the 28th I believe—my niece Phebe Stone and her husband[2] will be here when Ethel arrives & I have now all the time a young German girl 15 years old the child of my old Servant Mary Lapp. I needed some one to take steps for me. She is a good child tho not strong.

We expect Harry Oct. 1st. He thinks we have no chance at all in S. Dakota. Susan visited the old state suffrage committee. Every one of them resigned. Then she took command which made ill feeling.

The prohibitionists have made bad work, and altogether, we have no case.[3] While in Mississippi we seem to have a chance—I feel very well now only I am stiff with rheumatism.

Love to you all
[*Lucy Stone*]

Ethel's corner will be ready for her. Alice hopes to take next week with Lucy Anthony (Susan's niece)[4] at the Cliff house.[5]

AL-LC

1. The fortieth anniversary of the first national Woman's Rights Convention occurred October 23-24, 1890, but was celebrated January 26-27, 1891, in conjunction with the annual meeting of the Massachusetts WSA.
2. LS's niece, Phebe Stone Beeman, and her husband, Reverend L.H. Beeman, a Methodist minister, were supporters of temperance and woman's rights. Phebe Stone Beeman was active in the WCTU and the AWSA.
3. HBB campaigned for passage of a woman suffrage referendum in South Dakota, August-September 1890. When it had achieved statehood the previous year, South Dakota had incorporated a prohibition on alcohol into its constitution, but anger at its passage alienated many from woman suffrage. The woman suffrage measure did not pass.
4. Lucy Anthony (1861-1944), the niece of Susan B. Anthony, was herself an active suffrage worker. In 1888 she began to serve as manager for Anna Howard Shaw. Anthony and Shaw had recently been at the Canadian camp where ASB had also vacationed.
5. Cliff House was the summer home of LS and HBB at Chilmark, Martha's Vineyard.

Elizabeth April 20 '92

Dear Lucy

Will you please put on your thinking cap and recollect *every thing* you can about our discussions in that little just out of village house at Oberlin. Just *who* besides ourselves took part, at least now and then! Helen Cook did. Lettice did not, much I think, but she was there once or twice was she not? and Rebecca French? Any one else? No one but you and I were really in earnest, I believe, but we were, and it was a real club though without officers or constitution. Some one the other day described a club over which C[urtices] daughter really presides, though still they are intirely informal, as we were.

I think we met, not at a colored house, but at the mother of that young man you befriended so much, I forget his name, but you will remember. Please think of *every thing* and remind me. We discussed ways & means of work what else? You never put your best foot forward, nor do I very often; but I go to Chicago on *purpose to immortalize* that primary woman's Club.[1] A little was done towards that at the Council. Now, in a brief speech, I mean to tell all there is to tell and not a bit more; but *it* was much more to the beginning of Clubs than that first Convention to its kind; and it shall not want an age witness historian in a modest way. Even Mrs. Brown does not know at all what I am to say; but it will come in part to the subject and at just the right place.

I wish you felt, as I do, that all of these Collateral issues are the best ways, in part, to help suffrage and women! Alice does. Good for Alice! I shall meet her! If you did feel as I do, you would, with a good conscience, send me 25 dollars from the Suffrage fund for expenses. I belong to so small a club they can hardly help pay the regular fees. But no matter; the earth is the Lords and we will all work in our own ways. Miss Green, Nenie More's[2] ~~daughter~~ niece, is here, and a dressmaker and my hands are three times full, but with cordial love.

Always, as ever,
the old Nette

Mrs Howe told me just how nice and dressed up Harry looked at the Lady Somerset reception[3] with his cut hair, but I liked the long curls better all the same.

ALS-SL
Written on the stationery of the AAW.

1. ALBB spoke to the first biennial meeting of the General Federation of Women's Clubs held in Chicago, May 11-13, 1892; her sister-in-law Charlotte Emerson Brown was president of the federation.
2. Nina Moore, daughter of Augustus Moore, Cincinnati friend of HBB and at one time HBB's partner in the agricultural book publishing venture, married Francis Tiffany October 16, 1889; she later wrote on American history.
3. Lady Isabella Somerset (1851-1921), temperance campaigner, was appointed president of the British Woman's Temperance Association in 1890 and later served as president of the World Woman's Christian Temperance Union. She made a triumphant American tour, 1891-92. In January 1892, Lady Somerset spoke at the annual meeting of the Massachusetts WSA in Boston.

Boston, May 5 1892

Dear Nette

I did reply to you at once with all I remembered after hunting up the triennial catalogue to refesh my memory of names. Sorry you did not get it.

It was at the house of a colored woman whom I was teaching to read. I think she was the mother of Langston.[1] His father was a white man who brought her with her children there to educate. But this is nothing. I asked her to return the favor of my teaching by letting me have the use of her parlor one P.M. a week. She asked if there would be any boys, and I said no, and then she let us have her little parlor. You and I and Lettice Smith, and Helen Cooke and I think Elizabeth Wakely[2] and perhaps Emmeline French. We discussed educational, political, moral & religious questions, and especially we learned to stand and speak, to put motions, how to treat amendments, &c. All this I wrote you before and perhaps more. But now I am for the cars with today and tomorrow crowded with committees and a convention. Tell Agnes Alices dress is a very plain princess for which bill has only just come hence with a bill of $62.40—!!

Alice is to go to Chicago[3]—If I think of anything more I will tell her.

[Lucy Stone]

AL-LC
Written on the stationery of the Massachusetts WSA.

1. John Mercer Langston (1829-97), OC 1849, OS 1853, was a black attorney, politician, and diplomat. This recollection appears to be in error, however, since Langston's father, a white planter, died when the child was quite young, and while Langston attended Oberlin, he was under the care of a guardian.
2. Elizabeth Wakeley (1820-1902), OC 1846, married classmate John Patchin the year she graduated. The two then taught at a school for blacks in Michigan.
3. ASB traveled to Chicago to report on the meeting of the General Federation of Women's Clubs.

[Chicago] Woman's Dormitory Sept. 28 '93.

Dear Lucy

I cannot tell you how sorry I am to hear that you are not getting better as I thought when I left home. Probably you must wait to find what Nature can do for you, but she is a wonderful physician! I hope, I do hope, that she can even make you, through all this, younger and stronger than ever. If there was any thing I could do to make you better or more comfortable, be sure I am more than ready to do it.

I am back here in these rough quarters, but on the whole I like the freedom of the place. One has no social duties; and yet a good deal of busy, stirring, social experience. It is a curious study of human nature. You had an unfortunate night here and cannot fully appreciate the good points which abound with curious incidents.

But the Parliament of Religions was a grand demonstration in favor of toleration and an underlying unity for all.[1] It was like a new Pentecost. I have no time to attempt to describe it; but you have many exchanges and will read all you care to see.—I had another meeting in the Woman's Building where we were together; and then the Women Ministers meetings and other things keep me extremely occupied. A.A.W. holds its anniversary—21st birthday on Aug 4th.[2] On the fifth I shall start for home after the morning business meeting.

By then you may be more comfortable. Alice must keep us posted as to how you are. It is so good that Emily can be with you; at any rate she will give the best, most sympathetic advice possible though she may be called back soon to N York duties or probably has gone home already. There are so many things I would like to talk over with you; one is, those bound volumes you have been getting up. I have wondered whether or not you had the matter reprinted or only gathered up from papers and reports. Oh dear, I hope you are only comfortably sick and are still full of hope and good cheer. Everything grows brighter!

Most lovingly your old friend & sister
[*Antoinette Brown Blackwell*]

AL-SL

1. LS had attended meetings on woman suffrage scheduled as part of the 1893 Columbian Exposition in Chicago in May and had planned to return in August, but she was too ill. ALBB attended the Congress of Religions held September 23-27, 1893, and presented a paper on "Woman and the Pulpit."
2. The AAW meetings took place October 4, 1893, not in August.

A Note on Sources

The most important sources on Lucy Stone, Antoinette Brown Blackwell, and their friendship are their own writings, which have been preserved in several different collections. The Library of Congress houses the Papers of the Blackwell Family, which include the bulk of the letters Stone addressed to Brown Blackwell as well as most of the extant papers of Lucy Stone. This collection is available on microfilm, and a register to the papers is available from the Manuscript Division of the Library of Congress. The Arthur and Elizabeth Schlesinger Library on the History of Women in America at Radcliffe College in Cambridge, Massachusetts, includes three relevant collections, the most important of which is the Blackwell Family Papers, A-77 (microfilm M-35), which contains the letters of Antoinette Brown Blackwell to Lucy Stone, and most of Brown Blackwell's other papers, including a partial typescript of her own memoirs edited and assembled by Mrs. Claude U. (Sarah) Gilson, as "Antoinette Brown Blackwell: The First Woman Minister." Another Schlesinger Library collection, the Blackwell Family Papers, A-145 (microfilm M-37), has some additional materials on Stone, Brown Blackwell, and their husbands, as well as other Blackwells, especially their sister-in-law Elizabeth Blackwell and her adopted daughter, Kitty Blackwell. In October 1983 the Schlesinger Library acquired approximately thirty cartons of additional Blackwell family materials. These materials had not been processed as of 1986; according to the library's archivist Eva Moseley, preliminary investigation revealed that these materials do not relate primarily to Stone, Brown Blackwell, or their immediate families, but rather to their nephews, sons of George Washington Blackwell.

Primary sources

Manuscripts

American Antiquarian Society
 Abigail Kelley Foster Papers
 Miscellaneous Manuscripts
Boston Public Library
 Antislavery Collection
Library of Congress
 Records of the National American Woman Suffrage Association
New York Public Library
 Horace Greeley Papers
Oberlin College Archives
 Alumni Records
 College Catalogs, 1843-50
 Faculty Records
 Former Student Files
 Ladies' Board Records
 Ladies' Literary Society Minute Books
 Necrology Files
 Official College Correspondence
 Robert Fletcher Papers
 Student Organizations
 Trustee Records
 Yearbooks

Newspapers and journals

Agitator
Anti-Slavery Bugle
Anti-Slavery Standard
Boston Evening Transcript
Liberator
New York Tribune
Oberlin Evangelist
Oberlin Review
Revolution

A Note on Sources 267

Woman's Journal
Woman's Tribune

Published primary materials

Ballantine, W. G., ed. *The Oberlin Jubilee, 1833-1883.* Oberlin, Ohio: E. J. Goodrich, 1883.

Blackwell, Antoinette Louisa Brown. *The Physical Basis for Immortality.* New York: G. P. Putnam's Sons, 1876.

———. *The Sexes throughout Nature.* New York: G. P. Putnam's Sons, 1875.

———. *Studies in General Science.* New York: G. P. Putnam's Sons, 1869.

Blassingame, John W., ed. *Frederick Douglass Papers.* 3 vols. New Haven: Yale, 1979-85.

DuBois, Ellen Carol, ed. *Elizabeth Cady Stanton, Susan B. Anthony: Correspondence, Writings, Speeches.* New York: Schocken Books, 1981.

Eagle, Mary Kavanaugh Oldham, ed. *The Congress of Women Held in the Woman's Building, World's Columbian Exposition, Chicago, U.S.A., 1893.* 2 vols. Chicago: W. B. Conkey Co., 1894.

Hunt, Harriot Kezia. *Glances and Glimpses: Or, Fifty Years Social, Including Twenty Years Professional Life.* 1856. Reprint. New York: Source Books Press, 1970.

Merrill, Walter M., and Louis Ruchames, eds. *The Letters of William Lloyd Garrison.* 6 vols. Cambridge, Mass.: Belknap Press of Harvard University Press, 1971-78.

Report of the International Council of Women, Assembled by the National Woman Suffrage Association, Washington, D.C., U.S. of America, March 25 to April 1, 1888. Washington, D.C.: National Woman Suffrage Association, 1888.

Reports of the Association for the Advancement of Women.

Sewall, May Wright, ed. *The World's Congress of Representative Women.* 2 vols. Chicago: Rand, McNally & Co., 1894.

Stanton, Elizabeth Cady. *Eighty Years and More: Reminiscences, 1815-1897.* New York: T. Fischer Unwin, 1898.

———. *Elizabeth Cady Stanton as Revealed in Her Letters, Diary and Reminiscences.* Edited by Theodore Stanton and Harriot Stanton Blatch. New York: Harper, 1922.

———, Susan B. Anthony, Matilda Joslyn Gage, et al. *History of Woman Suffrage.* Rochester: Susan B. Anthony, 1881-1902 (Vols.

268 *A Note on Sources*

1-4). New York: National American Woman Suffrage Association, 1922 (Vols. 5-6).

Testimonials to the Life and Character of the Late Francis Jackson. Boston: R. F. Wallcut, 1861.

Wheeler, Leslie, ed. *Loving Warriors: Selected Letters of Lucy Stone and Henry B. Blackwell, 1853 to 1893.* New York: Dial Press, 1981.

Secondary sources

Unpublished

Horn, Margo. "Family Ties: The Blackwells, a Study in the Dynamics of Family Life in Nineteenth-Century America." Ph.D. Dissertation, Tufts University, 1980.

Hubbard, Mrs. J. Geraldine H. "Garrison's Abolitionism vs. Oberlin Anti-slavery." Oberlin College Honors Thesis in History, 1929.

Merk, Lois Bannister. "Massachusetts and the Woman Suffrage Movement." Unpublished manuscript, 1961. Schlesinger Library microfilm M-19.

Reference works

James, Edward T., Janet Wilson James, and Paul S. Boyer, eds. *Notable American Women: A Biographical Dictionary.* 3 vols. Cambridge, Mass.: Harvard University Press, 1971.

Johnson, Allen, ed. *Dictionary of American Biography.* New York: Charles Scribner's Sons, 1956.

National Cyclopedia of American Biography. New York: James T. White and Co., 1898.

Our Famous Women. Hartford, Conn.: A. D. Worthington and Co., 1884.

Willard, Frances, and Mary A. Livermore, eds. *American Women: Fifteen Hundred Biographies.* 2 vols. New York: Mast, Crowell and Kirkpatrick, 1897.

Published books and articles

Baum, Dale. "Woman Suffrage and the 'Chinese Question': The Limits of Radical Republicanism in Massachusetts, 1865-1876." *New England Quarterly* 56 (1983): 60-77.

Bartlett, J. Gardner. *Gregory Stone Geneology: Ancestry and Des-*

cendants of Dea. Gregory Stone of Cambridge, Mass., 1320-1917.* Boston: Stone Family Association, 1918.

Bigglestone, William E. *Oberlin: From War to Jubilee, 1866-1883.* Oberlin, Ohio: Grady Publishing Co., 1983.

Blackwell, Alice Stone. *Lucy Stone: Pioneer of Woman's Rights.* Boston: Little Brown and Co., 1930. Reprint. New York: Krause Reprint Co., 1971.

Cazden, Elizabeth. *Antoinette Brown Blackwell: A Biography.* Old Westbury, N.Y.: Feminist Press, 1983.

Croly, Mrs. J. C. *The History of the Woman's Club Movement in America.* New York: Henry G. Allen and Co., 1898.

DuBois, Ellen Carol. *Feminism and Suffrage: The Emergence of an Independent Women's Movement in America, 1848-1869.* Ithaca: Cornell University Press, 1978.

Fletcher, Robert S. *A History of Oberlin College from Its Foundation through the Civil War.* 2 vols. Oberlin, Ohio: Oberlin College, 1943.

Flexner, Eleanor. *Century of Struggle: The Woman's Rights Movement in the United States.* Cambridge, Mass.: The Belknap Press of Harvard University Press, 1959.

Ginzberg, Lori D. "Women in an Evangelical Community: Oberlin 1833-1850." *Ohio History* 89 (1980): 78-88.

Hallowell, Anna Davis, ed. *James and Lucretia Mott: Life and Letters.* Boston: Houghton Mifflin and Co., 1884.

Harlow, Ralph Volney. *Gerrit Smith: Philanthropist and Reformer.* New York: Henry Holt and Co., 1939.

Harper, Ida Husted. *The Life and Work of Susan B. Anthony.* 3 vols. Indianapolis: Bowen-Merrill Co., 1898-99 (vols. 1-2). Indianapolis: Hollenbeck Press, 1908 (vol. 3).

Hays, Elinor Rice. *Morning Star: A Biography of Lucy Stone, 1818 to 1893.* New York: Harcourt, Brace and World, 1961.

————. *Those Extraordinary Blackwells: The Story of a Journey to a Better World.* New York: Harcourt, Brace and World, 1967.

Hersh, Blanche Glassman. *The Slavery of Sex: Feminist-Abolitionists in America.* Urbana: University of Illinois Press, 1978.

Kerr, Laura. *The Lady in the Pulpit.* New York: Woman's Press, 1951.

Leach, William. *True Love and Perfect Union: The Feminist Reform of Sex and Society.* New York: Basic Books, 1980.

McKivigan, John R. *The War against Proslavery Religion: Abolitionism and the Northern Churches, 1830-1865.* Ithaca: Cornell University Press, 1984.

McPherson, James M. *The Abolitionist Legacy: From Reconstruction to the NAACP.* Princeton, N.J.: Princeton University Press, 1975.

Melder, Keith E. *Beginnings of Sisterhood: The American Woman's Rights Movement, 1800-1850.* New York: Schocken Books, 1977.

Pease, Jane H., and William H. Pease. *They Who Would Be Free: Blacks' Search for Freedom, 1830-1861.* New York: Atheneum, 1974.

Phillips, Wilbur H. *Oberlin Colony: The Story of a Century.* Oberlin, Ohio: Oberlin Printing Co., 1933.

Robinson, Harriet Jane Hanson. *Massachusetts in the Woman Suffrage Movement: A General, Political, Legal and Legislative History from 1774 to 1851.* Boston: Roberts Brothers, 1881.

Rossi, Alice, ed. *The Feminist Papers: From Adams to deBeauvoir.* New York: Bantam Books, 1973.

Ruether, Rosemary R., and Rosemary S. Keller, eds. *Women and Religion in America, Vol. 1: The Nineteenth Century.* San Francisco: Harper and Row, 1982.

Suhl, Yuri. *Ernestine L. Rose and the Battle for Human Rights.* New York: Reynal and Co., 1959.

Index

Abolitionism, 5, 17, 97, 108, 110, 114, 129, 145, 157, 159-60, 164, 206; and religion, 6, 9, 37, 39; Antoinette Brown Blackwell and, 13, 24, 83, 101, 106-7, 109, 113, 128, 129, 163; divisions within, 9-10, 108, 111, 113, 122, 123, 125; Henry B. Blackwell and, 91-92, 145, 164; Lucy Stone and, 6, 8, 10, 12, 47, 72, 73, 87, 116, 117, 120, 145, 163, 167, 206; relation of, to woman's rights, 10, 12, 73, 122-23, 157

Adams, George Athearn, 74, 75, 101, 104

Adams, Mary Ann, 16, 18, 25, 26, 27, 29-30, 32, 173

Agitator, The, 167, 175, 176

Alcott, Bronson, 112, 113

Alofsen family, 182

American and Foreign Christian Union, 133

American Anti-Slavery Society (AASS), 10, 74, 132, 140, 146

American Association for the Advancement of Science, 229, 239, 249

American Equal Rights Association (AERA), 164-65, 166, 176, 177

American Female Guardian Society, 96-97, 98-99

American Woman Suffrage Association: Antoinette Brown Blackwell's participation in, 168, 175, 186, 187, 215, 218, 229; founding of, 166, 175, 176; Lucy Stone's leading role in, 171, 205-6, 229, 230; merger of, with National Woman Suffrage Association, 254-55, 258; national meetings of, 166, 175, 176, 187, 188, 190, 205, 206, 215, 216, 237, 239, 242, 243, 259-60; rivalry of, with National Woman Suffrage Association, 166, 172, 177, 258

Ames, Charles G., 189, 190, 206, 207, 209

Andover Theology, 101, 102

Andrews, Jane, 176, 214, 215, 217, 218, 219, 220

Anthony, Lucy, 261

Anthony, Susan B., 132, 153, 154, 158,

164, 174, 235, 237, 238, 256, 260;
and temperance movement, 128,
129, 131; as opponent of slavery,
159, 164; early friendship of, with
Lucy Stone, 135, 138, 140, 144, 145;
in National Woman Suffrage Association, 166, 176, 189, 190, 254, 255;
lecture tours of, with Antoinette
Brown Blackwell, 88, 128-29, 130-31,
155, 156-57; quarrels of Lucy Stone
with, 163, 165, 166, 175, 230-31,
239-40, 241, 249, 250, 255; views of,
on divorce laws, 90, 131
Anti-Slavery Bugle, 10
Anti-slavery movement. *See* Abolitionism
Association for the Advancement of
Women (AAW), 168, 176, 186-87,
197, 229, 234, 248, 264. *See also*
Congress of Women, annual
Atkins, Mary, 27, 29, 32, 43, 50, 173

Barnes, Almira Porter, 96, 97, 98
Barry, Kitty, 149, 150, 169, 185, 192,
193, 215, 223
Bartlett, Hannah, 175
Bartlett, Mary, 175
Bateham, Josephine Cushman. *See*
Penfield, Josephine
Bateham, Michael B., 30-31, 33
Beecher, Catharine, 168
Beecher, Henry Ward, 176, 177
Beeman, Phebe Stone, 260, 261
Bell, Jenny, 131
Bird, Francis, 179
Blachly, Sarah, 47, 48
Blackwell, Agnes, 94, 170, 181, 198,
210, 213-14, 216, 219, 235, 247, 257,
263; and Lucy Stone's family, 201,
202, 203, 204, 205, 208, 209, 222,
245, 250, 258, 263
Blackwell, Alice Stone, 92, 185, 189,
200-201, 205, 206, 219, 221, 234,
245-46, 251, 260, 261, 264; as partic-
ipant in equal rights movement, 170,
228, 230, 231, 234, 235, 255, 257,
262; as young child, 149, 150; close
ties of, to Antoinette Brown Blackwell's daughters, 151, 169, 185, 197-
98, 199, 205, 217, 222-23, 237, 245,
254, 263; education of, 170, 175,
176, 198, 199, 200, 221; health of,
191, 192, 252; in Antoinette Brown
Blackwell's household, 174, 178, 179,
222, 248; travels of, 171, 183, 193,
210, 212, 213, 215, 240, 242, 243,

244, 245, 246, 250, 258
Blackwell, Anna, 91, 215
Blackwell, Catherine Barry. *See* Barry,
Kitty
Blackwell, Edith, 94, 178, 210, 216,
217, 220, 221, 223, 240, 245, 246-47,
252-53; career of, 170, 235, 237; education of, 193, 194, 195, 196, 200,
201, 222-23, 244, 255; in Lucy
Stone's household, 180, 181, 182,
183, 253, 254, 255, 257
Blackwell, Elizabeth, 149, 150, 175,
192, 193; as pioneer woman doctor,
38, 40, 91, 112, 176, 235; visits by
relatives to, in London, 169, 189,
190, 191, 215
Blackwell, Ellen, 91, 144, 146, 169,
180, 190, 194, 244, 246, 251, 260
Blackwell, Emily, 40, 91, 179, 180, 182,
192, 201, 211, 218, 221, 235, 264;
visits of nieces to, 169, 219, 258
Blackwell, Emma Lawrence, 191, 216,
244, 250, 253, 256; children of, 217,
249, 254; marriage of, 182, 187, 188,
189, 190, 253
Blackwell, Ethel, 94, 167, 184, 189,
210, 222; and Lucy Stone's family,
204, 217, 253-54, 255, 258-59, 260;
career of, 170, 235, 257
Blackwell, Florence, 92, 147, 170, 184,
192, 196, 197, 204, 214-15, 217, 235;
and Alice Stone Blackwell, 185, 197-
98, 199, 237, 239, 245; and housekeeping, 198, 207, 210, 216; and
public speaking, 170, 202-3, 204,
209; as a young child, 148, 149, 151,
156; in Lucy Stone's household, 182-
83, 189, 196, 197-98, 199, 200, 212,
213, 220; romances and marriage of,
195, 197, 199, 228, 237, 238; travels
of, 191, 212, 213, 220-21; reading by,
185, 205; visits to relatives by, 191,
193, 216, 220
Blackwell, George Kenyon, 254
Blackwell, George Lawrence, 217, 218,
249, 250, 251, 254
Blackwell, George Washington, 181,
182, 183, 191, 192, 193, 206-7, 244,
250, 260; children of, 218, 249, 251;
marriage of, 182, 187, 188, 189, 190,
253
Blackwell, Grace, 94, 198, 207, 211-12,
217, 250, 252, 258; education of,
214, 215, 219, 220-21; emotional
problems of, 170, 219-20, 235, 257;
family visits by, 181, 210, 223, 245,

260; health problems of, 241, 244, 246, 247

Blackwell, Hannah Lane, 145, 146, 174, 182

Blackwell, Henry B., 87, 148, 150, 195, 209, 221, 235, 242, 244, 257, 259, 262; and Antoinette Brown Blackwell's family, 164, 169, 178, 191, 192, 193, 205, 207, 220, 234, 235, 237, 252, 253, 262; and other relatives, 181, 189, 193; as abolitionist, 91-92, 145, 164; as activist for woman suffrage, 153-54, 164-65, 166, 170, 195, 196, 229, 230, 239, 241, 250, 252, 260; courtship of, and marriage to, Lucy Stone, 90-91, 143, 150, 233; business career of, 93, 145, 146, 170-71, 192, 200, 201, 205, 206, 210, 218; financial position of, 150, 164; health problems of, 191, 193, 204, 212, 243, 245-46; travel to Europe by, 210, 212, 213, 215

Blackwell, Laurie. *See* Blackwell, George Lawrence

Blackwell, Mabel, 91, 93, 148, 149, 153

Blackwell, Marian, 170, 178, 182, 190, 192, 235, 245

Blackwell, Samuel Charles, 92, 148, 149, 159, 169, 189, 191, 195, 205, 215, 217, 235, 242, 244, 248, 252, 255; as woman's rights advocate, 92, 153, 191; business career of, 93, 145, 146, 170, 201, 206, 215-16, 220, 222, 229, 238, 257; financial position of, 152, 153, 154, 171, 229, 257; health problems of, 169, 193, 211, 213, 249; marriage of, to Antoinette Brown, 92, 146-47; time spent by, with Antoinette Brown Blackwell, 156, 158, 175-76, 185, 235, 248, 258

Blanchard, Harriet, 173, 174

Blondin, Charles. *See* Gravele, Emile

Bloomer, Amelia, 105, 130, 131

Bloomers, 122, 125, 126, 131, 136; worn by Lucy Stone, 90, 126, 127, 136, 138, 233

Bradley, Dan, 47

Bright, John, 248, 249

Brokaw, David, 31, 33

Brooke, Samuel, 45, 74, 82, 112

Brooks, Sophronia, 52

Brown, Abby Morse (mother of Antoinette Brown Blackwell), 39, 44, 45, 57, 63, 69, 121

Brown, Addison, 49, 80, 109, 115, 155

Brown, Agnes, 156

Brown, Augusta, 23, 35, 39; as student at Oberlin College, 12, 38; death of, 114, 118; health problems of, 23, 32-33, 44, 45, 51, 59, 61, 66, 69, 80, 110, 116

Brown, Charlotte Emerson, 220, 233, 262

Brown, Ella, 23, 62, 142, 143, 145; as student at Oberlin College, 12, 38, 39, 67, 69, 70, 71, 74, 79, 132, 139, 141

Brown, Joseph (father of Antoinette Brown Blackwell), 31, 38-39, 57, 63, 107, 115

Brown, Mary Messinger, 95, 96, 104

Brown, Rebecca, 7, 23, 24, 80, 141, 142, 190

Brown, William B., 7, 34, 37, 53, 79, 82, 104, 115-16, 155, 156, 199-200, 220, 244; as a minister, 35, 36, 38, 53, 96

Buckpitt family, 214, 215

Buffum, James Needham, 101, 102

Burke, Emily Pillsbury, 68, 71

Burleigh, Charles, 57, 60

Burritt, Elihu, 70, 71, 114

Butler, Benjamin, 230, 241, 242, 243-44, 246

Carey, Samuel Fenton, 144, 145

Centennial Exposition, 186, 187

Chace, Elizabeth Buffum, 243, 244, 250

Channing, William Henry, 145, 146, 176, 231, 239-40, 241, 242, 243

Cheney, Ednah Dow Littlehale, 239

Cholera, 13, 56, 59, 61, 121

Churchill, Elizabeth K., 187-88, 209, 210

Civil War, 94, 163, 164

Clarke, James Freeman, 206, 207

Cleveland, Grover, 230

Cochran, Helen Finney, 47-48

Cochran, William, 47-48

Coe, Annie, 183

Coe, Emma Robinson, 109, 111, 115, 121, 122, 125

Coffin, Cynthia Curtiss, 80, 81

Colby, Clara, 258, 259

Columbian Exposition, 232, 233, 264

Compromise of 1850, 106-7

Congregationalism, 6; Antoinette Brown Blackwell and, 7, 9, 88, 168; Oberlin College and, 7, 8, 9, 10

Congress of Religions, 264

Congress of Representative Women, 233

Congress of Women, annual, 186, 197, 204, 205, 217, 219, 222, 242, 243, 245
Cook, Helen, 17, 18, 46, 68, 73, 74, 110, 111, 261, 263
Cowles, Helen, 70, 71
Cox, Jacob Dolson, 47, 48, 173
Creighton, Samuel T., 19, 20, 22
Croly, Jane Cunningham, 188
Cushman, Josephine Penfield. *See* Penfield, Josephine
Cushman, Richards, 28, 29, 44, 46, 56, 60
Cutler, Hannah Tracy, 81, 240

Dall, Caroline Wells Healy, 124, 126, 158
Dana, Charles, 88
Darwin, Charles, 168
Davis, Pauline Kellogg Wright, 120, 122, 124, 126, 127, 128, 131, 137, 144
Day, William Howard, 68, 71, 74
DeForest, Jane O., 188
Diseases, 13-14, 39; at Oberlin College, 23-24, 44, 49. *See also* Cholera; Typhoid fever
Divorce question, the, 90-91, 131
Douglas, Stephen A., 108, 111
Douglass, Frederick, 37, 39, 108, 110, 111, 113, 123
Dress reform, 233, 245, 246. *See also* Bloomers

Eastman, Mary F., 185, 187
Eddy, Eliza, 231, 237-38
Ellis, Sarah Stickney, 38, 39
Emerson, Ralph Waldo, 57, 58, 60, 72, 99, 112

Fairchild, Edward Henry, 17-18
Fairchild, Harriet Eliza, 17, 18, 29, 46, 79-80, 173
Fairchild, James Harris, 32, 33, 139, 173
Fairfield, Sarah, 32, 33
Farnsworth, Charlotte, 24, 25
Female Guardian Society, 88
Field, Anna C., 246
Finney, Charles Grandison, 9, 26, 29, 38, 42-43, 67, 69, 107, 121, 122, 128, 137
Finney, Elizabeth Ford Atkinson, 51, 52
Follen, Charles, 57, 60
Foote, Charles C., 28, 29, 106

Ford, Anna Dyer, 103-4
Ford, Lewis, 103, 104
Foster, Abby Kelley, 10, 12, 13, 48-49, 52, 70, 82, 89, 109, 115, 126, 165
Foster, Rachel, 231, 254
Foster, Stephen, 10, 39, 52, 89, 109, 111, 137
Fourteenth Amendment, 165
Fowler, Lydia Folger, 129-30, 137
Free Church, 151, 153
Free Soil party, 10
French, Rebecca Emeline, 20, 22, 32, 33, 261, 263
Frothingham, Octavius Brooks, 184, 185
Fugitive Slave Law, 106-7
Fuller, Lucy Dale, 115, 117, 122
Fuller, Margaret, 147, 148

Gage, Frances Dana Barker, 157, 158, 159
Garrett, Elizabeth, 175, 176
Garrison, William Lloyd, 6, 9, 10, 73, 101, 102, 111, 122, 167, 175, 207
Gates, Clarinda, 50-51, 52
General Federation of Women's Clubs, 176, 188, 220, 233, 262
Gladden, Washington, 208
Goodell, Maria, 23-24, 25
Goodell, William, 23-24, 25
Graham, Sylvester, 185
Graham diet, 8, 185
Grant, Ulysses S., 170, 179
Gravele, Emile, 156, 159
Gray, Angeline Skinner, 74, 75
Gray, Robert, 74, 75
Greeley, Horace, 88, 89, 108, 111, 132, 143, 179
Grimké, Angelina, 6, 17, 18, 122, 212
Grimké, Sarah, 6, 17, 18, 122, 212

Hall, Heman Bassett, 52
Hallowell, Sarah C., 191
Harper, Frances Ellen Watkins, 197
Harris, Edward P., 15, 16, 18
Harris, Elizabeth Gillet, 15-16, 18
Hay, William, 155, 156
Hayes, Rutherford B., 193, 194
Henry, Edward, 28, 29
Henry, William. *See* McHenry, Jerry
Higginson, Thomas Wentworth, 150, 153, 167, 175, 206, 230, 231
Hill, Anna, 52, 67, 70, 74
Hill, Hamilton, 48, 52, 67, 70, 74, 80
History of Woman Suffrage (Anthony and Stanton), 231

Hodge, Mary Merrill, 74, 75, 80
Holley, Sallie, 10, 32, 33, 82, 106, 107, 115, 116
Holmes, Lettice Smith, 20, 22, 32, 44, 46, 74, 95, 109, 256, 261, 263; as theology student, 12, 22, 42, 43-44, 71
Holmes, Thomas, 22, 46, 52, 71, 74, 95
Hooper, Mary, 178
Hooper, Nell, 204
Hope Chapel, 152, 153, 154, 155
Hopedale community, 112, 113
Hopkins, Mary Sumner, 67, 71
Hopper, Anna Mott, 158, 159
Howard, Cornelia, 180, 253, 254, 260
Howe, Julia Ward, 166, 167, 175, 176, 188, 255, 262
Hudson, Timothy, 80, 81, 102, 108, 118, 122
Hughson, Simeon, 26, 29
Hunt, Harriot Kezia, 112, 124, 126

Ingersoll, Luman Church, 17, 18, 122
Ingraham, Harriet C., 74, 75
Ingraham, Sarah R., 38, 39
International Council of Women, 232, 255, 257
Irving, Washington, 117
Island Neighbors, The (Brown Blackwell), 167

Jackson, Francis, 153, 237-38
Jacobs, John S., 37, 39
Jones, Jane Elizabeth Hitchcock, 73, 74, 157, 158

Kedzie, Robert, 18, 28, 29, 45, 46, 79-80, 221, 237, 238
Keep, John, 102
Kelsey, Dr. Kate I., 244, 245
Kendall, Sewall, 70, 71
Kinney, Lester, 26, 29

Lane Theological Seminary, 9, 18
Larison, William, 26, 29
Lawrence, Anna, 183
Lawrence, Emma, 144, 145-46
Lawrence, Henry, 5, 146, 183
Lawrence, Sarah Stone, 5, 57, 145-46, 183, 220
Legal Rights, Liabilities and Duties of Women, The (Mansfield), 56, 60
Legend of Sleepy Hollow, The (Irving), 117
Lesdernier, Emily, 112, 113

Lewis, Graceanna, 204, 206
Liberator, The, 12, 52, 57, 68, 71, 72, 102, 124, 126, 127, 134, 139
Liberty party, 108, 111
Little Women (Alcott), 208
Livermore, Mary Ashton Rice, 167, 172, 175, 176, 187, 188, 195, 255
Livingstone, Charles, 74, 75
Lloyd, Mercy, 25, 26, 46, 47
Lovell, Louisa Jane, 20, 22, 30-31, 33
Lyon, Mary, 6

McCullom, Alexander, 145
McGrawville Central College. *See* New York Central College
McHenry, Jerry, 129, 135, 136
Magill, Edward H., 193, 194
Mahan, Asa, 9, 10, 11, 18, 31, 33, 66, 71, 79, 96, 107
Maine Law, 128, 129
Maine Sugar Beet Company, 201, 215, 217
Making of the Universe, The (Brown Blackwell), 235
Mansfield, Edward Deering, 56, 60
Marriage, views of, 144; by Antoinette Brown Blackwell, 13, 31, 46, 65, 80, 90-91, 92, 131; by Lucy Stone, 13, 56-57, 73, 90, 91, 92, 131
Marriage question, the, 144
Massachusetts Anti-Slavery Society (MASS), 12
Massachusetts Woman Suffrage Association, 195, 196, 209
May, Abigail Williams, 195-96
May, Samuel J., 115, 120, 121, 129, 134, 195, 239
Mayhew, Elliott, 228, 237, 238
Mayo, Amory Dwight, 155, 156
Merrill, Addison, 74, 75
Minturn, Samuel, 212, 213
Mitchell, Maria, 168, 204
Monroe, James, 52, 173
Moore, Nina, 262
Morgan, John, 9, 34, 35, 37, 43, 44, 66, 173, 208
Morgan, John Paul, 208
Mott, James, 71, 142, 159
Mott, Lucretia, 10, 14, 73, 77, 137, 142, 158, 159, 177
Mott, Lydia, 128, 129, 143
Mt. Holyoke Female Seminary, 6
Mowatt, Anna Cora Ogden, 112, 113
Moyers, Peter, 16, 18, 21, 25, 31-32, 33
Murray, James Ormsbee, 189, 190

National American Woman Suffrage Association (NAWSA), 231, 234, 255, 260

National Anti-Slavery Standard, 145, 146

National Woman Suffrage Association (NWSA), 185, 190, 232, 252; Antoinette Brown Blackwell and, 168, 184; founding of, 166, 172; merger of, with American Woman Suffrage Association, 232, 254-55, 258; rivalry of, with American Woman Suffrage Association, 166, 172, 177, 189, 230, 231, 258

New England Anti-Slavery Society, 139, 140

New England Woman Suffrage Association (NEWSA), 166, 175, 206-7

New England Women's Club, 183, 184, 192, 206

New York Central College, 74-75, 118, 119

New York Tribune, 89, 132, 139, 143, 145, 178, 184

New York Woman's State Temperance Society, 113-14, 118-19, 130, 131, 134, 135

North State, The, 123

Oberlin College, 7, 9-10, 121, 123; Antoinette Brown Blackwell's sisters at, 12, 27, 35, 38, 44, 69, 71, 74, 79, 132, 139, 141; debating society at, 11, 233, 256, 261-62; illnesses at, 13-14, 23-24, 41, 44, 49; Ladies' Board of, 10-11, 12, 26, 27, 29, 38, 41
— and Antoinette Brown Blackwell, 5, 7-8, 10, 11, 24; in Theology Department, 12-13, 26-28, 29-35, 40-44, 45, 47, 50-51, 62-63, 66, 69, 70, 77-78, 79-80, 81-82; treatment as a woman at, 11, 12, 26-28, 29-30, 41, 42-44, 51, 61, 77-78, 232; visits to, 117, 120, 122, 132, 244
— and Lucy Stone, 5, 6-7, 8-9, 10, 11, 19-20, 191; attitude toward, 48, 56, 57, 68, 72, 77, 173, 232, 250
— and status of women at, 5, 8, 10-11, 29, 74, 98, 121, 123, 139-40, 232; in Theology Department, 11, 12, 26-28, 29-30, 41, 42-44, 51, 61, 63, 77-78, 112-13, 232

Oberlin Collegiate Institute. *See* Oberlin College

Oberlin Female Moral Reform Society, 10

Oberlin Jubilee, 232-33, 241, 244

Parker, Theodore, 57, 60, 100, 112, 153, 154-55, 190

Parliament of World Religions, 234

Parsons, Anna Q. T., 139, 140

Peace movement, 80, 81, 114

Peck, Henry E., 34, 35, 139

Pellet, Alonzo, 74, 75

Pellet, Sarah, 28-29, 30, 44, 47, 52, 53, 56, 80, 99, 122, 125; advocacy of women's equality by, 121, 123-24; as lecturer on temperance and women's rights, 29, 125, 142; as friend of Antoinette Brown Blackwell, 26, 30, 103; correspondence of, with Lucy Stone, 32, 36, 40, 45, 48, 70, 73-74, 82; friendship of, with Lucy Stone, 28, 53, 57, 59, 60, 61, 64, 117; outlook of, on life, 27, 30, 99, 117

Pelton, Brewster, 108, 110

Penfield, Charles, 20, 22, 173

Penfield, Jane, 24, 25, 41

Penfield, Josephine, 20, 22, 29, 30, 44, 46, 56, 60, 81

Pennsylvania Anti-Slavery Society, 125

Phillips, Wendell, 57, 60, 113, 120, 152, 153, 154, 157, 158

Philosophy of Individuality, The (Brown Blackwell), 229

Phonography, 20, 22

Physical Basis of Immortality, The (Brown Blackwell), 167, 190, 191, 216, 217

Pierpont, John, 138

Pillsbury, Parker, 81, 82-83, 157

Putnam, Caroline, 10

Quakers, 73

Radical Republicans, 165

Rawson, Martha, 50, 52, 80, 173, 193, 194

Reid, Agnes, 210, 211, 214-15

Religion, Antoinette Brown Blackwell and: as pastor, 88, 89-90, 137, 142; desire to become a minister, 7, 9, 33-35, 88, 206, 208 (*see also* Oberlin College, Antoinette Brown Blackwell at); ordination, 88, 107, 118, 120; preaching, 66, 67, 79, 93, 101, 103, 116-17, 143, 150, 154; theological views, 7, 9, 33-35, 36-37, 49-50, 78, 94, 97, 101, 120

Religion, Lucy Stone's rejection of or-

ganized, 6, 8-9, 37, 49, 53-56, 63, 120, 138
Remond, Charles Lenox, 37, 39, 113
Republican party, 165, 166, 178, 230
Revolution, The, 165, 174
Rochester Academy, 11, 14, 15-16, 20-22, 25, 31-32, 46
Rochester Anti-Slavery Convention, 113, 115
Rose, Ernestine Louise Siismondi Potowski, 98, 99, 125, 128, 129, 140, 141, 142, 156-57

Safford, Jacob, 17, 18
Santo Domingo, 181, 182, 192
Schutze, Leonore Congden, 193, 194
Servants: in Antoinette Brown Blackwell's household, 148, 151, 180, 181, 207, 209, 211, 238, 245, 247; in Lucy Stone's household, 260
Sexes throughout Nature, The (Brown Blackwell), 167-68, 184
Shattuck, George Cheyne, 250, 251
Shaw, Anna Howard, 258
Shorey, J. L., 190, 191
Sigourney, Lydia, 38, 39
Skinner, Edwin Smith, 74, 75, 104
Slavery. *See* Abolitionism
Smith, Elizabeth Oakes Prince, 124, 125, 126, 127, 128, 129
Smith, Gerrit, 75, 108, 111-12, 122, 123-24, 125, 129
Smith, James McCune, 145, 146
Smith, Lettice. *See* Holmes, Lettice Smith
Smith, Stephen, 125, 126
Social Side of Mind and Action, The (Brown Blackwell), 235
Somerset, Lady Isabella, 262
Sorosis, 188
Southworth, Louisa, 196, 197
Spencer, 168
Spiritualism, 151, 153, 154
Stanton, Elizabeth Cady, 71, 120, 122-23, 127, 155, 174, 233, 235, 249, 253, 256, 259; and National Woman's Suffrage Association, 166, 176, 177; as opponent of slavery, 122-23, 159, 164; quarrels of Lucy Stone with, 163, 165, 166, 175, 177, 230-31, 233, 243, 249, 250; views of, on divorce laws, 90, 131
Stone, Francis, 5, 57, 191
Stone, Frank, 5
Stone, Hannah, 5, 57, 191
Stone, Luther, 5, 81, 82

Stone, Phebe Cutler, 82
Stone, Phebe Williams Robinson, 124, 126
Stone, Rhoda, 6
Stone, William Bowman, 5, 11-12, 53, 60, 124
Streeter, Sereno Wright, 33-34, 35, 37-38, 39
Strong, Lucina, 40, 45
Studies in General Science (Brown Blackwell), 94, 167, 174
Sunderland, Rev. Byron, 125, 126, 128

Tappan, Arthur, 9
Tappan, Lewis, 9
Tefft, James, 12, 22, 40, 42, 45, 74
Temperance movement: and Antoinette Brown Blackwell, 82, 89, 100-101, 113-14, 118-19, 128, 129, 134, 135; women in, 89, 90, 113-14, 128, 129, 130, 131, 132, 134, 145
Theological Literary Society (Oberlin College), 30, 43, 45, 79
Thompson, George, 95, 96, 101, 102
Thoreau, Henry David, 111-13
Tilton, Theodore, 175, 176, 177
Tracy, Hannah, 25, 26
Train, George Francis, 165, 174
Truth, Sojourner, 99-100
Typhoid fever, 13, 82, 116

Uncle Tom's Cabin (Stowe), 112, 113
Union Signal, The, 258
Unitarianism, 212; Antoinette Brown Blackwell and, 168-69, 206, 209, 210, 234; Lucy Stone and, 9
Upham, Thomas Cogswell, 100

Wadsworth, Elijah M., 44, 45-46
Wadsworth, Thomas Arthur, 122, 123, 128
Wakeley, Elizabeth, 263
Walker, Captain Jonathan, 37, 39
Washburn, William, 178, 179
Watson, Ada, 214
Webster, Daniel, 38, 39, 68, 71
Weed, Edward, 97, 99
Weed, Zeruiah Porter, 96-97, 98-99
Weld, Angelina Grimké. *See* Grimké, Angelina
Weld, Theodore Dwight, 211, 212
Wellington, Oliver H., 137
Whipple, Edwin Percy, 117, 150
Whipple, Henry, 79, 80, 102
Wilkinson, John, 125, 126-27
Wilson, Elizabeth, 69, 73

Winthrop, Paul, 180, 211, 212, 246, 251
Woman suffrage, 35; efforts to achieve, in Colorado, 192, 195, 196; efforts to achieve, in Massachusetts, 173-74, 178, 179, 240; efforts to achieve, in South Dakota, 260, 261; Lucy Stone's emphasis on, 87, 163, 164; Republican party and, 165, 178, 179. *See also* American Woman Suffrage Association; National Woman Suffrage Association
Woman's Journal, 26, 150, 182, 184, 196-97, 207, 227, 230, 231, 248, 250, 251; Alice Stone Blackwell and, 169, 228, 229; Antoinette Brown Blackwell as reader of, 186, 190, 192, 241; Antoinette Brown Blackwell as writer for, 168, 192, 208, 222, 239, 251; financial problems of, 178-79, 182, 200; origins of, 167, 175, 176
Woman's National Loyal League (WNLL), 164
Woman's rights: Antoinette Brown Blackwell as lecturer on, 51, 101, 107, 109, 128-29, 132, 155, 164, 244; Antoinette Brown Blackwell's early advocacy of, 20-21, 32, 33-35, 38, 51, 233, 256; conventions held in support of, 87 (*see also* Congress of Women, annual; Woman's Rights Conventions); divisions within the movement for, 114-15, 124, 127, 144 (*see also* American Woman Suffrage Association; National Woman Suffrage Association; Anthony, Susan

B.; Stanton, Elizabeth Cady); Lucy Stone as leading activist for, 87-88, 134, 139 (*see also* American Woman Suffrage Association; *Woman's Journal*); Lucy Stone as lecturer on, 109, 120, 124-25, 175, 244; Lucy Stone's early advocacy of, 12, 13, 46, 47, 62; narrowed focus of, in late nineteenth century, 163, 166; opposition to, 5, 17-18, 38, 42-43 (*see also* Oberlin College, status of women at); relation of, to anti-slavery movement, 10, 12, 73, 122-23, 157; religion and, 33-35, 38, 88, 89, 98, 120. *See also* Woman suffrage.
Woman's Rights Conventions: in 1848 (Seneca Falls), 123, 253; in 1850 (Worcester, Mass.), 13, 72-73, 78-79, 80, 87, 88, 95, 217, 218; in 1851 (Worcester, Mass.), 106, 107, 109; in 1852 (Syracuse, N.Y.), 120, 122, 124, 126; in 1853 (Cleveland), 135, 136; in 1854 (Philadelphia), 141, 142, 144; in 1858 (New York), 93; in 1859 (New York), 151, 153; in 1860 (New York), 91; in 1861 (canceled), 164
Woman's Rights Fund, 152-53, 154, 155, 156, 158
Woman's Tribune, 233, 257-58, 259
Wright, Frances, 35
Wright, Susan Allen, 32, 33, 173

Youmans, Edward Livingston, 183, 184-85